THE SIX SIGMA FIELDBOOK

THE SIX SIGMA FIELDBOOK

HOW DUPONT SUCCESSFULLY IMPLEMENTED THE SIX SIGMA BREAKTHROUGH MANAGEMENT STRATEGY

MIKEL HARRY, PH.D., AND DON R. LINSENMANN

CURRENCY

DOUBLEDAY

NEW YORK   LONDON   TORONTO   SYDNEY   AUCKLAND

AUTHORS' NOTE

This book covers the deployment of Six Sigma at DuPont from 1998 to 2004. Some of the people and businesses referenced herein are no longer a part of DuPont.

The following are registered trademarks and when referenced in the book are to be interpreted as such: DuPont® as DuPont, Cyrel® as Cyrel, Teflon® as Teflon, Lycra® as Lycra, Kevlar® as Kevlar, Stainmaster® as Stainmaster, Elvanol® as Elvanol, Lannate® as Lannate, Corian® as Corian, Nomex® as Nomex, Adipure® as Adipure, Zodiaq® as Zodiaq.

A CURRENCY BOOK
PUBLISHED BY DOUBLEDAY

Published in the United States by Doubleday, an imprint of The Doubleday Broadway Publishing Group, a division of Random House, Inc., New York.
www.currencybooks.com
CURRENCY is a trademark of Random House, Inc., and DOUBLEDAY is a registered trademark of Random House, Inc.

Book design by Chris Welch

Cataloging-in-Publication Data is on file with the Library of Congress
ISBN 0-385-50466-7

PRINTED IN THE UNITED STATES OF AMERICA

SPECIAL SALES
Currency Books are available at special discounts for bulk purchases for sales promotions or premiums. Special editions, including personalized covers, excerpts of existing books, and corporate imprints, can be created in large quantities for special needs. For more information, write to Special Markets, Currency Books, specialmarkets@randomhouse.com.

1 3 5 7 9 10 8 6 4 2

This book is dedicated to my loving wife, best friend, and endearing supporter, Wafa. As a motivating force, her tireless encouragement will always be deeply appreciated. This author would also like to acknowledge Robert (Bob) Galvin and the late Bill Smith. Their unique contributions to the field of Six Sigma are forever present.

Mikel J. Harry, Ph.D.

To Carol and Kimmy, the loves of my life, for all of their unwavering support.

Don R. Linsenmann

ACKNOWLEDGMENTS

Six Sigma is all about people. The statistics, tools, methodologies, data, and processes all need people to bring them to life. So is the case with this book.

For the Six Sigma content, I (Don) want to acknowledge and thank Mikel Harry for being my Six Sigma mentor and guru.

A special acknowledgment goes to Chad Holliday and his leadership team, for the courage to lead DuPont in our Six Sigma journey.

To the DuPont Six Sigma Champions, especially those mentioned in this book, thank you for constantly pushing.

And thank you to the DuPont business leaders who readily accepted change and to the DuPont Master Black Belts, Black Belts, and Green Belts for making it all happen.

Thanks to Jeff Immelt, Chairman and CEO of GE, for sharing his experiences with the DuPont leadership and staying connected with our progress, and to the Six Sigma Academy as our early consultants getting us started on the right trajectory. And thank you to our customers, especially those referenced in the book, for their business and support

For the process of pulling together this book, the following professionals guided me and I acknowledge their contributions: Chuck Martin for assembling, writing, editing, and orchestrating the content of the book. Neil DeCarlo for his early work capturing the ramblings of both Mikel and me and making sense of it. Jennifer Smith, my executive admin, for constantly keeping it all together and communicating with all of the above. To Justin Carisio and Julie Mazza for reviewing the text and their valuable inputs.

While publishing a book is NOT a Six Sigma process, these people enabled the "output." Thank you.

CONTENTS

INTRODUCTION

In the late 1990s, DuPont found itself undergoing a seismic shift as the knowledge economy became a driving force in the marketplace. Company leaders knew they had to reinvent DuPont's identity and corporate strategy.

The 200-year-old DuPont Corporation had come to a crossroads. In short, the oldest industrial company in the Fortune 500 had to decide nothing less than what it wanted to be for the next hundred years.

DuPont was established in 1802 essentially as an explosives company. In the 1900s, it transformed itself into a chemicals, materials, and energy company, and by the mid-'90s, it was becoming clear that another major transformation was necessary. It was as if DuPont had reached a performance ceiling, given the industry it was in, its history, strategy, and size, and the marketplace in which it operated. Its chemicals and materials businesses were no longer seen as the growth engine of the company, even though they boasted some of the world's best-known creations, including nylon, Teflon, Lycra, Kevlar, and Stainmaster.

The company handed the task of a corporate overhaul to Chad Holliday, who had worked his way up through the ranks to become CEO in 1998.

On analyzing DuPont's future, Holliday and his management team raised such "ultimate destiny" questions as:

- Was the era of manufactured chemicals coming to an end? The industry was experiencing a downward trend in value with decreasing margins.
- Were new trends in the economy and environmental protection constricting the company's ability to grow?
- Was it time for DuPont to reinvent itself and align itself with the emerging knowledge economy?

DuPont had invested billions in new plants and equipment, but those investments were not yielding enough profits to the corporation. Holliday and his team needed to reassess where DuPont was headed.

DuPont's due diligence began with an assessment of the company's vision and mission. What Holliday came to realize was that it was time for DuPont to reconfigure its strategy and its business model to fit the new mold in which it operated. In a transition that was even more significant than its move from explosives to chemicals at the beginning of the twentieth century, DuPont had to re-create itself in order to sustain its legacy as one of America's strongest and longest-standing corporations.

But Holliday believed the company's future would have more to do with business intangibles than with making and selling chemicals. Going forward, DuPont needed to focus on science-based solutions for customers under the banner of "One DuPont." He and his team intended to reorganize around customers rather than around products. DuPont was taking essentially the same steps Lou Gerstner had taken when he took over the reins of an ailing IBM. However, in contrast to IBM, DuPont was embracing those changes while business was still strong, if not growing.

To assert its new place in the world, DuPont developed a new mission: to achieve sustainable growth and increase shareholder value through integrated science and knowledge-intensive products and businesses.

Each of the company's objectives required a break with the past. In integrated science, DuPont had to move from being a chemicals company to being one based on many sciences, including biotechnology and biomaterials. In knowledge-intensive products and businesses, DuPont had to shift from a material- and labor-based value proposition to one based on intellectual capital. Put simply, it had to move from making things to providing solutions.

DuPont's business consists of five major market segments: Agriculture and Nutrition (with annual revenues of $5.5 billion), Coatings and Color ($5.5 billion), Performance Materials ($5.4 billion), Safety and Protection ($4.1 billion), and Electronics and Communications ($2.9 billion). The company's major markets are businesses in the automotive, electronics, agriculture, construction, and aerospace industries.

To support its new strategy, Holliday knew DuPont would also need to change its corporate image. This had last happened in 1935, when DuPont reinvented itself from "the powder people" to "peacetime manufacturer." At that time, the company's new ad campaign promoted DuPont's role in improving daily life with the slogan "Better Things for Better Living . . . Through Chemistry." In 1999, DuPont decided to make another shift, from being a chemicals company to a company that brings "the miracles of science" to its customers.

To achieve its goal of sustainable growth and increased shareholder value through productivity gains, the company decided to embrace Six Sigma.

DuPont hoped to drastically cut costs using this approach, aiming to reduce its operating costs by 15 to 25 percent of its annual revenue. And that was only a starting point. It also set out to use the Six Sigma breakthrough management strategy to take the company to new levels beyond cost reduction.

DUPONT'S CULTURE

Having endured—successfully—for more than 200 years, DuPont was not a company that readily embraced radical, massive, or rapid change. Its employees have an average of twenty-four years of service and an average age of forty-seven. The intense transformation that Six Sigma typically causes didn't necessarily seem like a good cultural fit. Because of the longevity of its employee base, DuPont employees typically watch out for each other. Past experiences and relationships count a great deal. DuPont maintains a "gentlemanly" atmosphere where everyone's opinion is genuinely respected and taken into account, even if there is disagreement. Meetings typically last an hour and tend to start and end on time.

The culture at DuPont seems to be embodied in its physical presence as well. It is headquartered in downtown Wilmington, Delaware, in a thirteen-story structure that also houses the DuPont Hotel. The corporate offices begin on the ninth floor, where the ceilings are low and ornate marble lines the hallways. DuPont has well over 100 separate buildings scattered throughout Delaware, ranging from campus-like office space to a 400-acre "experimental station" complex, where scientists and engineers invent and develop future products. This is the facility where nylon and DuPont's other great brands have been created. The company also has a country club and several golf courses, where employees can use payroll deductions to relax.

Given its history and culture, the traditionally run DuPont did not at first glance appear to be a likely candidate to take on a radical transformation such as Six Sigma. Over time, however, key executives at DuPont came to see what Six Sigma had done for Allied Signal, GE, American Express, Abbott, and many other companies. And they decided Six Sigma could take DuPont to a new level and transform the company and everything it did.

As a multinational corporation that has $27 billion in revenue, DuPont has eighteen major businesses, operations in seventy countries, and more than 60,000 employees. Unlike other management initiatives, the goal of Six Sigma is to change the way a corporation gets work done, rather than just tweak the existing system. Persuading DuPont's 60,000 employees in 135 manufacturing and production facilities and seventy-five research labs throughout the world to change the way they worked would be, to put it mildly, no small feat.

PREVIOUS FAILED PROGRAMS

One of the greatest challenges DuPont faced in introducing and implementing Six Sigma was a general feeling among the managers and employees that Six Sigma was yet another improvement program that ultimately would fall by the wayside.

- In the late '80s, DuPont initiated an experiential learning program. This program took a team-building approach. Managers maneuvered through obstacle courses and underwent other physical challenges. The executives at DuPont loved the time spent in the sessions, and the program helped to build strong bonds among team members. However, over time the teams changed, management changed, and the bonds weakened. The program faded away.
- In the early '90s, the Fibers business, a major segment of DuPont, competed to try to win the Malcolm Baldrige National Quality Award. Fibers was really a collection of businesses centered around such products as nylon, polyester, and Lycra, which are used in apparel. Nylon fiber is also used in tire manufacturing and carpeting. Also in the fibers group was Kevlar and Nomex, which are used in the aircraft industry and in many other industrial applications, and Tyvek and Sontara, which are used in nonwoven products. A Baldrige leader was appointed, people were assigned to lead up all seven performance areas that were evaluated for the award, and the company began to benchmark its performance and identify its weaknesses. Programs were implemented to close the gaps, and regular management reviews were conducted. But then DuPont lost, and the whole thing was over.
- The DuPont Continuous Improvement Program, another DuPont initiative, grew out of the Baldrige Award competition, with the company attempting to sustain its gains in improvement by using

the same metrics as the Malcolm Baldrige National Quality Award. The initiative hung around for a while, but eventually the reviews became more and more infrequent until the program ultimately faded away.

While each of these programs was good in its own way, none connected the quality of DuPont's businesses with bottom-line results. Six Sigma would be different because it would directly affect the company's profitability. But the memory of the failed initiatives stuck with many of DuPont's executives and managers as they came face-to-face with Six Sigma.

Holliday's own view of these past programs was that the Continuous Improvement Program based on the Malcolm Baldrige criteria had lacked the scope and depth to make a real impact. In terms of scale, the Baldrige approach at DuPont was limited to only certain groups, areas, and functions within the company. The "examination criteria" were too prescriptive and limiting. And the individual projects associated with continuous improvement failed to yield significant results.

Holliday recalls the time, during the height of its continuous improvement thrust, when quality guru Dr. Joseph Juran consulted with executives. Juran made a presentation stressing the importance of a project-by-project improvement approach. One proud DuPont executive stood up and said, "That's just what we are doing. We have thirty projects under way." Juran stingingly replied that the company should have *3,000* projects under way. No one could foresee at the time that Six Sigma would lead DuPont to have more than *9,000* projects in the works.

At the time, Holliday thought the suggestion of taking on 3,000 projects was impossible, though it did give him a perspective on what it would take to move a corporation the size of DuPont forward. Holliday realized that whatever DuPont had done with its quality program in the past was not what it should have done. There wasn't an obvious way to morph the Baldrige experience into something more powerful and pervasive.

HOLLIDAY INVESTIGATES SIX SIGMA

For Holliday and DuPont, there didn't seem to be a viable road map for leveraging quality-improvement projects so that they benefited DuPont's business performance. Like so many other corporations at the time, the verdict seemed to be that quality improvement was good for customers and good for solving certain problems, but it wasn't pervasive enough to move the business in the right direction. This led DuPont to shift its focus from quality initiatives to improving business fundamentals.

Among his other many tasks and responsibilities, Holliday had been very involved in DuPont's businesses in Asia, where he had established a strong network of peers and colleagues. In 1998, as he was working with the Japanese company Toshiba, the subject of Six Sigma came up. The Six Sigma concept of measuring defects was created in the early 1980s as a way to develop a universal quality metric that would apply regardless of the complexity of a product process or service. Ultimately, the higher the sigma level, the fewer number of defects there are per unit or service. Processes at a Six Sigma level of quality are virtually defect free—by definition, such a process has only 3.4 defects per million opportunities. Companies typically operate at four sigma, or 6,210 defects per million opportunities. Operating at near the Six Sigma level, DuPont could dramatically cut its process defects and save dramatically on operating costs. Holliday was struck by the project-by-project approach espoused by Toshiba leaders and the executives of other Japanese companies. It was a strong reminder of what Juran had told DuPont leaders about the power of numbers. Holliday was also impressed by the fact that Six Sigma had been embraced throughout all levels of the companies.

To Holliday, the key was the idea that many improvement projects could add up to a major change. An industrial engineer by background, Holliday was used to thinking in terms of how things got done and how to do them better. He returned to the United States intent on investigating Six Sigma's comprehensive approach to quality improvement. Holliday had a clear view of the direction he wanted to take DuPont in its third century. A quiet, team-building leader who generally speaks softly, with only a slight hint of his Tennessee roots, Holliday was highly regarded by the rank and file at the company. But no matter how much employees liked him, he knew DuPont was not the kind of company that could be transformed overnight—its culture and habits were too ingrained. He believed, though, that the power of Six Sigma might be able eventually to bring about such a cultural transformation.

Those who knew about Six Sigma pointed Holliday to AlliedSignal CEO Larry Bossidy, whose company had gotten dramatic results from Six Sigma at a time when the company's future looked bleak. So Holliday sat down with Bossidy in 1998 to discuss Six Sigma. Bossidy impressed the DuPont CEO with the extent to which AlliedSignal had deployed and implemented Six Sigma projects. Bossidy walked Holliday through specific project examples, giving him the firsthand knowledge of someone who had been through Six Sigma and understood what was going on.

Holliday also met with General Electric's then-CEO Jack Welch, whose company had successfully adopted Six Sigma as well, carving billions of dollars from its operating expense base and dramatically improving its bottom line. While Bossidy had conveyed the particulars involved in Six Sigma, Welch confirmed the legitimacy of those particulars as well as the business results they yielded at GE. Holliday decided that if Six Sigma worked for AlliedSignal and GE, it might work for DuPont.

The first and foremost responsibility of senior management was to carefully assess the extent to which DuPont was ready to undertake Six Sigma. If the executives relied on intuition alone, they might have assumed that assessing readiness would depend on such issues as establishing goals, developing leadership, and installing systems.

In fact, assessing readiness is a critical, irreplaceable first step in a corporation's Six Sigma journey. How well this task is performed correlates directly with the likelihood that a corporation will successfully install, deploy, implement, and realize benefits from Six Sigma. Holliday turned to then-COO Dennis Reilly to lead the effort to answer these questions. While Holliday would remain at the helm of Six Sigma, Reilly would handle the "nitty-gritty" of setting Six Sigma in motion.

During its assessment, DuPont quickly learned that its overriding first question should be whether the business was ready for outright transformation. Six Sigma is not a quality initiative that can be implemented incrementally, even though some have tried to position it that way. At heart, DuPont discovered, Six Sigma is a management tool for surgically transforming a corporate culture in a quantum manner. And DuPont found that it requires an extraordinary degree of commitment and courage.

IT'S ALL IN THE TIMING

When DuPont decided to implement Six Sigma, the company had already been doing some deep soul-searching. It was in the midst of adapting to emerging economic, technological, and business trends that were reshaping how companies survive and make money. The engine of global economic growth was shifting from information to knowledge, as it had shifted from services to information decades before, and from industry to services decades before that. The company's flat earnings signaled that it was time to usher the company into a new age.

As part of its readiness assessment, DuPont had to look at whether the company had the knowledge and experience to effectively take on Six Sigma. Management needed to decide if they had the type and number of people needed to become Champions, Black Belts, and Green Belts. It didn't take long to figure out that DuPont was lacking both, as is typical for every company at the edge of Six Sigma commitment. DuPont realized that Six Sigma calls for a corporation's historical performance trend to be disturbed. In any given company, the performance can be on a trend. The trend may be up, down, or flat. The introduction of Six Sigma will disturb this trend by focusing people on improving work and lifting the trend. The degree of the lift is a function of the depth of the deployment. In most companies, the capability and capacity for doing so lies dormant. An outside catalyst is needed to bring it to the surface, develop it, and put it in motion. For DuPont, that catalyst needed to be a Six Sigma consultant.

One of the key criteria for selecting a Six Sigma consultant is to choose one who fosters self-sufficiency within the corporation as quickly as possible. Du Pont wanted a consultancy firm that would get in, help transform the company, and get out.

Reilly had already learned from Larry Bossidy and Jack Welch that Six Sigma done right was a massive, targeted, rapid-fire, and highly coordinated initiative. Given that, DuPont would need a large and experienced consulting firm with the necessary firepower to prepare the initial wave of executive, Champion, and Black Belt pioneers. But they also wanted one that would foster self-sufficiency within the corporation as quickly as possible—a consultancy firm that would get in, help transform the company, and get out.

There were not many Six Sigma providers who had the reputation and could work on the scale DuPont would need. Reilly's list of candidates was relatively short. As the firm that had worked with AlliedSignal and General Electric, the Six Sigma Academy was at the top of the list. So in late 1998 Reilly met with Mikel Harry and Rich Schroeder, the Academy's two cofounders. Following their meeting, Reilly decided that the Academy's philosophy, approach, capability, and capacity would meet DuPont's needs. Harry and Schroeder were not interested in establishing a long-term, ongoing consulting relationship with DuPont. They were there to do what they had done for others before: transfer the knowledge necessary to set the company's people and performance on a new and improved path and then get out of the way and allow DuPont to get on with the business of deploying Six Sigma in their own way.

While Reilly examined potential Six Sigma providers, Chad Holliday conducted his own due diligence. He asked Bossidy how AlliedSignal picked Black Belts and how they kept them motivated. He inquired about how projects were overseen and how the Champions who oversee projects were supervised. He scrutinized Six Sigma methodology until he felt comfortable that the strategy would succeed at DuPont.

He came to realize that Six Sigma is a highly disciplined methodology, seamlessly integrated into the culture and business fabric of a corporation. If it were anything but, Bossidy and Welch would not have espoused it so strongly. It became clear to Holliday that the scientific and methodical nature of Six Sigma was a perfect match for DuPont. As a technology company, DuPont's people and systems would take to Six Sigma like ducks to water—or so Holliday and his team hoped.

FUNDING SIX SIGMA

Before DuPont could commit itself to Six Sigma, the company had to address how much it would cost. There was a capital element involved in building and sustaining Six Sigma capability. Among the costs DuPont anticipated:

- Six Sigma fees for outside consultants
- Acquiring and installing information systems
- Employing full-time Champions and Black Belts
- Lost productivity as people went offline for training
- Spending for the execution of thousands of projects

These costs could add up to $20 million, DuPont calculated. But it was obvious to Holliday that the benefits of Six Sigma far outweighed the investment—particularly if DuPont did it right the first time. Through Mikel Harry and Rich Schroeder, they'd learned of companies that had had to abandon their initiatives because of inadequate management support, misaligned training curricula, or a slow deployment. But they confirmed with Larry Bossidy, Jack Welch, and other CEOs who had instigated Six Sigma that, done right, Six Sigma would make their investment look minuscule compared with the return.

By late 1998, the only key decision remaining for DuPont's executives was whether to launch Six Sigma on a corporation-wide scale or run a pilot first before asking each of DuPont's businesses to immerse themselves in the methodology. They understood the need to commit to Six Sigma if the process was to have the desired effect. The corporation already believed that Six Sigma could improve productivity as well as contribute to its other strategic goals, at least in concept. But they wanted to sample the training process on a small scale before moving forward. So DuPont's top brass decided to send a small team from one of the company's businesses, Specialty Chemicals, to Scottsdale for a session with Harry and Schroeder.

In 1998, Reilly boarded a corporate jet with Jeff Coe, the head of Specialty Chemicals, and Gary Lewis, the executive in charge of the division's human resources and productivity functions, as well as the leadership team for Specialty Chemicals, and other key corporate executives. Together, they formed the core of what would become DuPont's Six Sigma pilot. They were going to see if all they had heard about the Six Sigma Academy was in fact true.

Lewis's key concern about Six Sigma was the fact that DuPont is a relationship-based company centered around networks rather than hierarchical control. "We get things done through matrix and influence management," says Lewis, "but there are a lot of good and bad aspects of that."

As Lewis knew, his company had a deep and broad network of "strong independents." DuPont does very well in short-term crisis management, initiating targeted projects in response to pressing business needs or objectives. If a mountain needs leveling or a valley has to be filled, DuPont's world-renowned emergency response team can save the day.

But the company is not skilled at taking on long-term, centralized initiatives such as the continuous improvement program they had tried earlier. With these types of projects, the leaders of DuPont's fifty worldwide locations tend to split themselves into three groups: A third says, "Let's make this happen"; a third acts like a good soldier and says, "I'll do it"; and the final third says, "Go pound sand, because I don't see how this fits into my operation."

DuPont was not the type of company that would do things just because they were supposed to be done, which is why various initiatives had never reached critical mass in the past. But if the project carries a real imperative, and if that imperative can be accomplished quickly, then the DuPont management structure tends to fall into place behind it.

DuPont managers generally have a short attention span. Harry and Schroeder would not have much time to capture the attention of the DuPont group in Scottsdale. Over the next thirty-six hours the founders of Six Sigma would have to frame a view of what Six Sigma could be at DuPont—and, more specifically, what it could be in the Specialty Chemicals business.

Harry and Schroeder first conducted an executive training session, which would later be replicated for each business. At this session, the DuPont executives learned the scope and approach for deployment. What Mikel Harry and Rich Schroeder told the DuPont executives was that Six Sigma is executed by training and deploying Champions and Belts for each project. The Process Owner is the person or manager responsible for the specific process on which a Six Sigma project is focused on improving. The Project Champion helps create the support structure for that improvement. His or her chief role is to clear any barriers that get in the way of the project. Being a Champion is a full-time position. Process Owners also take on some Six Sigma responsibilities in addition to their existing job. At a higher level, an SBU (Strategic Business Unit) Champion provides strategy, consultation, guidance, and support to the Project Champion. Finally, DuPont created a Top-Line Growth Champion, whose role is to identify opportunities and promote and facilitate Six Sigma projects targeted to improve revenue for the business.

At the execution level, Six Sigma is driven by Master Black Belts, Black Belts, and Green Belts. The role of the Master Black Belt is to work with the Project Champion and mentor individual Black Belts. The Master Black Belts also train others on Six Sigma methodology and help SBU and Project Champions identify new projects. Black Belts are responsible for leading teams to work on specific projects throughout the organization. Projects led by Black Belts usually are based on savings of $175,000 or more. For example, a Black Belt might head up a project to improve a given step in the manufacturing process or analyze the sales effectiveness of a given group of salespeople. Being a Black Belt is a full-time role within the company. Green Belts support the implementation and application of Six Sigma tools by participating in project teams. Unlike Black Belts, Green Belts retain their normal jobs and add Six Sigma responsibilities that fall within the natural scope of their work. Green Belt projects typically focus on customer satisfaction, a key business strategy, or other issues with smaller financial payback than those of Black Belts.

A simplified view of the Six Sigma structure:

- Senior Champions lead key changes at the corporate level.
- Champions lead operational changes required to support the corporate goals, such as HR policies to reward and recognize Black Belts or financial guidelines to be created to validate projects. Anything needed to allow the Belts to succeed in terms of infrastructure would be put in place.
- Black Belts lead process changes required to support the operational goals. For example, an operational goal would be to improve the capacity of a given plant. The Black Belts could work on hundreds of projects focusing on uptime, throughput, waste, and product quality.

In all, DuPont's Specialty Chemicals would have four full-time Project Champions: two focused on manufacturing processes and two focused on the transactional (nonmanufacturing) aspects of the business. One of the two process Champions selected was the former plant manager of the Chambers Works site in New Jersey, which made industrial chemicals and at the time was one of DuPont's largest sites. The other was a respected business engineering manager who managed capital investment. On the nonmanufacturing side, one of the two Champions was a top business director taken from one of the critical business segments inside of Specialty Chemicals, chosen to give heightened status to the assignments and show the organization the importance of the Six Sigma effort. The other transactional Champion was the sourcing director for all of Specialty Chemicals.

After the training sessions at the academy, many were still skeptical—none more so than Lewis, whom Coe asked to take on the role of lead Champion for the Six Sigma pilot in Specialty Chemicals. "For me, it was a very tough sell," says Lewis, who is now director of labor relations at DuPont. Though Six Sigma logically seemed to be perfect for DuPont at the time, Lewis didn't fully believe that Six Sigma could truly work and yield the kind of results it claimed, either at DuPont as a whole or at Specialty Chemicals.

While Lewis thought Six Sigma was a good initiative, he didn't necessarily believe it was broad enough to justify his direct involvement. He saw Six Sigma as a subset of the larger productivity improvement thrust at DuPont, something that smacked of the quality programs he had been involved with in the past, which were overwhelmingly focused on reducing defects in manufacturing areas. To Lewis, this was limiting because it did not address the idea of defect elimination in transactional, or non-manufacturing, processes such as sales and marketing. It did not cover the full spectrum of the supply chain—buy, make, sell, deliver; it covered only the buy and make phases.

"Other than safety, in my twenty-five years at DuPont, no effort had ever been launched centrally and been sustainable," says Lewis. "The track records to sustain these kinds of programs have been dismal failures."

Coe and Lewis knew each other well, having worked together in different capacities for years. On the jet ride back, the two men stood at the back of DuPont's spacious Gulfstream V, in the path to the plane's only restroom, and talked about Six Sigma and DuPont's past quality programs, as well as the role Lewis could play and the destiny of Specialty Chemicals.

"It was a tense, tense argument," says Lewis. "People would come halfway down the aisle and just turn around. I don't think anyone went to the bathroom the entire flight. It took the entire flight to convince me to take on the role of a Six Sigma Champion," Lewis added.

In the end, Lewis realized that Six Sigma was not as narrowly focused as he originally thought. It was a holistic initiative for eliminating both manufacturing and nonmanufacturing defects, one that could cover the gamut of performance improvement throughout the entire supply chain, not just productivity in manufacturing. By the end of the flight, Coe and Lewis had created a road map, outlining the steps they would use to start it up. Says Lewis:

> We took it as a leap of faith that we would be able to do the transactional selling and delivering work. There's a lot more to Six Sigma than statistics. It's fundamentally about how you think about work. It's a fundamental approach to work because of the data. The other things [we had tried] really were just programs and they usually withered away.
>
> On that airplane ride from Phoenix to Philadelphia, we mapped it out. We staffed up for this like we never did before, and we put the absolutely best people on it. The early champions were impeccable, and it was a significant cultural event.
>
> There were people who got it and were lining up. Then there were those who said all the right words but really thought, "I have more important things to work on." It takes them longer. It's how your feet walk, not what your words say. We wanted to take the basic knowledge about our products and extend that knowledge into the marketplace.
>
> For Specialty Chemicals, we quickly made an incredible amount of personnel changes and announced more than 100 organizational changes, and we did it in one fell swoop. We had 105 full-time people in Six Sigma in the first month or two. It was all driven by the leadership and quickly supported by the entire organization. This model was then duplicated throughout the corporation when the overall launch began. Every goal we set, we exceeded, in terms of numbers of projects and dollars validated.

Lewis concluded, "The people were the best. Six Sigma has changed how I approach work redesign. I wish I had it fifteen or twenty years ago."

Upon his return to Delaware, Lewis worked to build consensus and buy-in on Six Sigma, attempting to convince his colleagues that it was the right thing to do.

Conversations throughout the business unit were spirited and brought out different viewpoints—much as Lewis's own discussion at the back of the plane on the way home from Scottsdale had done. The concerns were mostly around why a corporate process was needed to help improve the business. People were proud of their business and felt that they were the world experts and did not need help. The discussion revolved around the fact that Six Sigma was not another *what* for them to do, but a *how* to help them improve their business.

But the real conversation began after the leadership team agreed to commit to Six Sigma and was faced with deciding exactly how much money it would target to save. In typical DuPont fashion, the team of four asked their leader, Coe, to leave the room while they debated among themselves about what the right number should be.

THE FIRST $80 MILLION SAVED

In the end, the team decided that Specialty Chemicals would commit to saving $25 million by the end of 1999 and $80 million by the end of 2000 through its Six Sigma initiative. These numbers represented an annualized run rate of additional income the business would realize as a direct result of completed Six Sigma projects. The annualized run rate is the amount of hard dollars that would hit the income statement in a one-year time frame. If a project saved $20,000 a month, it would be validated as an annual run rate of $240,000. At DuPont, only project savings that demonstrated ongoing, month-after-month savings would count as valid payback on Six Sigma training and project execution. For the Specialty Chemicals business, with about $1.5 billion in revenue, the $80 million goal was sizable, representing about 5 percent of revenue.

During the meetings in Arizona, the leadership team had been told that most corporations have a "cost of poor quality" on the order of 20 percent of revenue. DuPont's executives, like those in most corporations, had been amazed. How could companies succeed with that much waste?

Specialty Chemicals had seen enough about the promise and potential of Six Sigma to act boldly. The business set its sights high and committed the resources and people necessary to give itself a fair shot at achieving its goal. Specialty Chemicals redeployed about 4 percent of its workforce, or about eighty of their 2,000 people, to Six Sigma–related activities and projects. Specialty Chemicals became the first DuPont business to embark on the arduous Six Sigma journey toward dramatically improved success.

Before selecting projects or training Black Belts, the managers of Specialty Chemicals spent time with companies that had implemented Six Sigma, such as Asea Brown Boveri, to ask what they had done and learned as they deployed and implemented Six Sigma. The lessons they learned were many, but a few stood out above the rest.

1. Specialty Chemicals and DuPont would need to focus equally on both manufacturing and service opportunities. Other companies had made the mistake of pigeonholing Six Sigma as a manufacturing-based initiative.

2. Specialty Chemicals would need to develop its own project-tracking software so that it could track the details of project implementation, as well as graph how those projects aggregately contributed to the unit's higher-level aims.

3. The business unit would need to institute a reliable system for validating project savings. Results had to be tight, so that no one could doubt the credibility of Six Sigma or the project Black Belts, or the legitimacy of their savings to the bottom line.

4. The business would need to reward its Champions, Black Belts, and Master Black Belts with special incentives and stock options for their work (which we will discuss later).

Beginning in the first quarter of 1999, Specialty Chemicals selected its initial Six Sigma projects. These included process and transactional projects focusing on things such as yield improvements, inventory reduction, the quality of accounts receivable and payable, capacity, order fulfillment, and energy projects. Many energy projects were executed, for example, reducing natural gas needs by having more efficient heating processes in the manufacture of chemicals. The unit established a rigorous and methodical HR process to figure out how many people were needed for these projects and to select the individuals to be trained. They established a system evaluating the execution of each project, including periodic project reviews by the Champions involved, using the Six Sigma Academy model. By the end of the second quarter of 1999, the first wave of about forty Black Belts had been trained and the projects initiated.

At Specialty Chemicals, Coe, Lewis, and the others established a set of metrics for managing Six Sigma at the business level. The leadership team reviewed these metrics at least once a month formally and much more often informally. The business metrics included not only the validation of the initial savings in dollars but also a review of how the final numbers were tracking. During a project, the Black Belt lays out what he or she thinks might be the savings goal. The finance person checks it, saying that if the problem is solved it will be worth a certain amount. This is initial validation. After the project is complete and has been running for, say, six months, the finance person comes back and says how much it has delivered, usually more than initial validation. This after-the-fact process is the final validation. DuPont tracked the financial returns of these projects, which initially were in the hundreds but eventually grew to the thousands, versus the run rate milestones it had established from an overall business perspective. The run rate goal on a project was $175,000, and the average final validation on each project was $300,000. The people metrics were followed carefully as well, such as how many Black Belts were certified, promoted, and compensated (certification takes about eighteen months to two years). The current total of those certified comes to more than 1,500. Many Black Belts were promoted to roles of higher responsibility.

Initial results allowed Lewis and the others to quickly determine that Six Sigma was well worth its cost, even before the final results came in from the first wave of Black Belt training. Furthermore, it was clear that the results were evident in the service area as well as the more traditional manufacturing area. Independent finance experts were validating the dollar savings, and the impact to the bottom line was evident. The entire supply chain of Specialty Chemicals was becoming more efficient and more integrated. By the end of 1999, the business had realized a total savings of $35 million, $10 million more than its original target. At the end of 2000, its total was $100 million in savings, $20 million beyond the expectations and goals of those who had set it in motion twenty-one months earlier.

The success of the projects was obvious to top management early on. For example, one manufacturing project focused on minimizing the use of natural gas to generate power at a plant. The plant used four boilers that were designed to use either natural gas or "off-gas," a cheaper manufacturing by-product that generated more energy. One key objective for the facility was to optimize the use of off-gas and minimize the use of natural gas. After applying the Breakthrough Strategy, the team reduced natural gas consumption significantly. The Six Sigma Breakthrough Strategy, by using mathematical measurements, systematically reduces defects that occur in processes used to produce a product or service. The Strategy uses a series of steps that define how well processes and services are delivered. It shows companies how to improve their processes, reduce costs, and maintain the gains they achieve. The total annual savings: $190,000 to $280,000, based on the fluctuating price of natural gas.

Another early Specialty Chemicals Black Belt project focused on eliminating defects in the requisition process for site materials. The company found that it could save on procurement by using a tighter process. It was headed by Katy Stone, one of DuPont's first fifteen certified Black Belts (and now global strategic sourcing manager for Agriculture and Nutrition). As a Black Belt, Stone led the team through the five phases of DMAIC. In addition, she did analysis of the data, presented the solution to management, and then led implementation. The project goals were to eliminate rework, improve cycle time, and improve spending controls. Cycle time is the elapsed time from when the company went out for bids, decided on vendors, and then received the materials. Critical factors included training and upgrading information system workflow consistent with changes in the requisition process. Specific improvements included automated order processing, reduced fixed processing costs due to proper vendor setups, and reduced transactions due to pooled purchases. Total annual savings: more than $300,000 in annual pretax operating income.

We will describe the Six Sigma Breakthrough Strategy in detail in Chapter 1.

The pilot program at Specialty Chemicals was a resounding success. It showed Chad Holliday and his executive team that Six Sigma could work throughout DuPont. The systems and practices Specialty Chemicals built and installed would serve as standards for the rest of the corporation. They set a strong precedent for pulling key, visible performers within the company out of their traditional roles and having them spearhead the company's Six Sigma efforts. Specialty Chemicals also built a robust system for evaluating the performance of Black Belts and Master Black Belts, and for rewarding them for their contributions.

Although the Specialty Chemicals experiment was a microcosm of what was to come in DuPont, each business unit would develop its own unique Six Sigma signature.

Two years later, in 2001, at a Wall Street analysts meeting, Holliday would speak of DuPont's new strategic focus: "Science is the cornerstone of our ability to build and sustain a richer mix of businesses. We are focusing on market needs for electronics and high-performance materials, while we invest in new technology platforms such as plant science and biomaterials. At the same time, we are pursuing a 'knowledge intensity' business model, which leverages the value of our market knowledge, our brands, our technology, and know-how. This is being accomplished while also using Six Sigma to enhance productivity, build marketplace competitiveness, and grow revenues."

At that meeting, DuPont COO Richard Goodmanson discussed the company's management strategies and business targets, including capital allocations and technology resources. Goodmanson described the company's portfolio in terms of growth targets, focusing particularly on those businesses where growth was most challenging. For example, nylon and polyester were mature products in terms of their product life cycle. They were given growth goals that aligned with the growth of the country's general gross domestic product (GDP). Other businesses that introduced new technologies, such as DuPont's Displays and Electronic Technologies, were given double-digit growth goals. As a result, the overall portfolio was constructed to grow its earnings 10 percent a year, but each unit had realistic, differentiated goals. Goodmanson emphasized that integrating science, knowledge, and Six Sigma could help DuPont meet its business goals, and he described the rigorous management process DuPont had put in place to monitor progress toward achieving those goals.

From a strategic vision perspective, the litmus test for Six Sigma readiness is a visible commitment to breakthrough change, and DuPont was clearly ready. The company's new mission was ambitious enough to signify a distinct break from the past, and in this sense it was aligned and integrated with the nature of Six Sigma. DuPont's mission of sustainable growth was defined as increasing and meeting the financial goals of the company while reducing its "footprint on the environment." Financially, that meant growing its revenues and earnings per share 6 percent a year, as well as returning return on invested capital (ROIC) to the high teens. This simply meant targeting revenue growth at 6 percent each and every year.

While Six Sigma is a strategic initiative in and of itself, it is also a vehicle for realizing other strategic initiatives. Six Sigma was to be the "how" to accomplish DuPont's other two strategic initiatives—achieving sustainable growth and increasing shareholder value through integrated science and knowledge-intensive products and businesses. Using Six Sigma's approaches on thousands of projects, DuPont aimed to offer improved knowledge and technology to its customers. For example, a Six Sigma project in DuPont's automotive and paint business used Six Sigma to understand the voice of the customer when developing a new clear coat paint for a new truck model. Going through the steps, the group developed a new product to meet customer needs for a quick-dry and scratch-resistant paint.

It is more than coincidence that DuPont was reformulating its corporate mission at the same time it was getting ready to deploy Six Sigma. DuPont had determined that, in undertaking Six Sigma, there would be only one viable directional thrust for the company: quantum, quantifiable, and accountable change.

DuPont's CEO, Chad Holliday, understood that as much as vision is a prerequisite for a successful Six Sigma deployment, strong leadership is vital. In the sandy-haired Jeff Coe, he had a very strong business leader who always focused on results, and in Gary Lewis, he had a strong Six Sigma advocate who was a respected and outspoken leader. But now Holliday needed a strong corporate advocate to lead the deployment of Six Sigma into DuPont's seventeen other businesses.

Six Sigma is a strategy that relies on leverage to accomplish its aims. In this sense, not every employee in the smallest functions of a sizable corporation will be involved in Six Sigma. However, virtually everyone's job will be changed in some way as a result of Six Sigma, starting from the top down. While relatively few lead, the changes they bring about affect the lives, jobs, and destinies of many.

At heart is leaders who make Six Sigma successful, not Six Sigma that makes leaders successful. The top executives at DuPont had exposed some of their strongest leaders to Six Sigma when DuPont Specialty Chemicals executives initially met with Harry and Schroeder. In the wake of their meeting, Specialty Chemicals implemented Six Sigma with religious fervor, and banked $100 million to DuPont within the first two years. They did this by following the strategy outlined by the Six Sigma Academy in setting up the structures, projects, training, and systems. This book tracks that strategy. The steps are:

- Set a clear strategic target.
- Have the leaders lead.
- Pick great people.

- Select impactful projects.
- Follow the steps of DMAIC.
- Put in tracking systems.
- Celebrate the successes.
- Communicate, communicate, communicate.

Chad Holliday and Dennis Reilly asked me, Don Linsenmann, to take the job leading Six Sigma at DuPont. I had been at DuPont for eighteen years, since the company had acquired the highly entrepreneurial materials division of Exxon Enterprises in 1984. As the division's business director, I had built a career on taking calculated risks in new markets. It is what excites me.

My first assignment at DuPont had been to help develop the newly acquired division, a high-tech composite materials business. That business made components of carbon fiber, the material used in golf club shafts. We made medical products such as X-ray tables, aerospace products such as satellite structures, and industrial products such as paper machinery rollers.

After a few years in this role, I had a conversation with DuPont vice president Mike Bowman, my boss at the time. He felt I had grown out of my role in the composites business and told me DuPont management wanted me to try something different and new—to become the global director of industrial nylon, a product used mostly as reinforcing material in tires.

With the goal of expanding the Nylon business from being U.S.-based to having a global focus, I accepted the job. We built plants in Indonesia, upgraded facilities in Argentina, and completed joint ventures in Turkey and other countries. It was a high-intensity environment where I got to work closely with a team of talented professionals with whom I became good friends.

Our team improved Nylon's net income from $40 million a year to $80 million a year by injecting an entrepreneurial spirit into an old-school business. It was the kind of task I loved: a vague and unstructured assignment that represented something new for the company. I tend to gravitate to the lunatic fringe of business, where the rules are more often absent rather than just difficult to figure out.

After Nylon, I worked in a number of business leadership roles culminating in a position in Europe running DuPont's Lycra operations. But I realized that I didn't like working in more bureaucratic and political environments, and it seemed the higher up I went, the more this was the case.

At Lycra, in 1994, I was more involved in the maintenance aspects of DuPont than in aspects of invention. This is not to say that we didn't create new markets. The first wholly owned DuPont subsidiary we started, Initiativs Inc., was a company that designed, sourced, and manufactured women's apparel, mostly in Mexico. The second was an e-business helping the garment industry change the way it developed garments using digital means.

These subsidiaries were much smaller companies than I was used to, like small colonies operating outside the royal grounds of DuPont. I loved running them because I could do so in accordance with my own beliefs in the value of team building and the importance of cultural transformation. I believe a diverse group of folks together can accomplish so much more than individual performers. Building trust is central to building teamwork. Trust in the business environment means there is a very open and sharing approach to one's ideas and concepts. Putting this more informal trust-building culture in place is what I like to do. I was able to do whatever I had to do in the interest of starting new companies, growing those that already existed, and shutting down businesses that were not performing up to par—all without worrying too much about fitting into the larger entity called DuPont.

So when Chad Holliday asked me if I would consider running Six Sigma and, in doing so, move from the lunatic fringe to the middle of the core, my initial reaction was one of curious hesitancy. Then I had an epiphany. Maybe at the core, I could make changes that would better DuPont, change its culture, make it more nimble moving forward. Maybe I could create an entrepreneurial adventure in which Six Sigma would be the product and DuPont would be the market.

As soon as I figured this out, I became preoccupied with the question "What is Six Sigma?" I knew that AlliedSignal and GE had implemented Six Sigma to enormous and well-publicized success, but my knowledge beyond this was zero. Now I was being asked to lead a corporation-wide Six Sigma charge that was expected to save the company billions of dollars.

Was Six Sigma a quality program? Was it a flavor of the month? It looked and smelled to me like Total Quality and Malcolm Baldrige, both of which ended up in DuPont's recycle bin of failed change initiatives. I had seen new change programs come and go at a rate of about one a year, none of which had stuck.

What if Six Sigma was no different from other change programs? Was this an opportunity to advance my career, or was it an invitation to become the fall guy if Six Sigma failed? Such were the doubts that accompanied me as I made my transition from business leader to corporate Six Sigma Champion. What I ultimately learned was that the biggest difference between the other programs we had tried and Six Sigma was that Six Sigma was about the quality of our business, not about the business of quality. Most of the other quality initiatives were more focused on crossing the t's and dotting the i's of the company's compliance templates, while Six Sigma was really focused on profits and cash.

I didn't worship the DuPont structure, I didn't fly with the flock, and I didn't mind shaking up the status quo. As it turned out, these were the very characteristics Harry and Schroeder had advised Holliday to look for in a senior Champion. I knew I would be working closely with Holliday and the senior leadership team and that I would be squarely in the center of the storm of the Six Sigma strategy. If things went well, I would be a hero of sorts. But if things did not go well, as had been the case with the other corporate initiatives, I ran the risk of becoming the object of some pretty powerful finger-pointing.

My litmus test was the same as it had always been: Was Six Sigma something in which I could personally and passionately believe? I told Reilly I would seriously consider taking the job only after having interrogated Mikel Harry and Rich Schroeder about the viability of their program. I understood that the two top men at DuPont were convinced about Six Sigma, so it was now just a matter of finding out about Six Sigma for myself.

I set up a meeting with Mikel and Richard at their Academy in Scottsdale, hoping to return to Delaware with a more informed opinion about Six Sigma.

One fact I did know was that I didn't have a lot of time to make up my mind. Holliday had put me on the spot, saying, "We will do Six Sigma, and we want you to lead it." There wasn't a lot of ambiguity around the "We will do Six Sigma" part of Holliday's statement. The only question left was whether or not I would lead it.

Before leaving for Arizona, I spent time with Coe, the leader of Specialty Chemicals, and Lewis, its Six Sigma Champion. Both shared their enthusiasm and early success with Six Sigma in a way that made me wonder if they were talking about a quality program or a business initiative. Coe and Lewis spoke in terms of "filling unused capacity" or "creating additional capacity" or "saving $800,000" on a certain Black Belt project. These were the words of businesspeople, not quality program people.

The key to me was to determine if I would personally and passionately own Six Sigma or just own it in name for the greater good of DuPont. I had to be absolutely convinced that Six Sigma was not like any other corporate initiative. If I could say this, objectively and unequivocally, then the next critical task would be to understand Six Sigma as broadly and as deeply as possible.

In Scottsdale, I came to understand that the big ideas underpinning Six Sigma are driven by its relationship to a business. Mikel Harry and Rich Schroeder explained to me that Six Sigma success is a function of leadership, enablers, and ideas. When I began to understand the full import of ideas such as determinism, measurement, leverage, and transformation— and really saw how they interact to create business breakthrough—I began to understand why Six Sigma was much more than a quality program. Leverage in this context means that applying a small bit of force

(Black Belts) focused on a fulcrum (Six Sigma) can move large organizations (DuPont) if the lever is long enough. Think of a seesaw with one end a disproportionate distance from the fulcrum and imagine the multiplication effect of exerting a small force on that end. Thinking about Six Sigma this way encourages you to find the long lever so you can get the most out of your efforts. While I still didn't understand any of its details, I had learned enough about Six Sigma to know it contained the ingredients of a breakthrough. *Determinism*, for example, is absolutely key to Six Sigma belief. According to Six Sigma, you must accept that outputs, or effects, are determined by the inputs, or causes. For example, sales revenue growth, an output, is a result of the inputs such as price, market share, new technology, and sales-force effectiveness. In mathematical terms, this idea is represented by the equation $Y = f(X) + e$ with the outputs (Y) being the dependent variables, while the inputs (X) are the independent variables (allowing error, or e). If someone starts with this belief, he or she can be confident that the many projects launched to keep the X's in control ultimately deliver the required result, the Y's. The value of measurement is another foundation of Six Sigma. Measurement means understanding the capability of your measuring device to pick up the real differences in what you are measuring. For example, you don't use a yardstick to measure fractions of an inch. Many companies ignore the accuracy and repeatability of their measuring systems. Six Sigma forces the management to properly measure the data.

Similarly, *leveraging* ideas from one unit to another and *transforming* the way work gets done are pillars upon which a Six Sigma deployment is built. Leveraging ideas is the knowledge management of Six Sigma. In other words, using what is learned from one project can make it faster and easier to replicate that project elsewhere.

As the Senior Champion, I would not really be in charge of anyone or have anyone report to me. I would report directly to Holliday. All the Six Sigma leaders under me would report to their respective business units at their various levels. I would be an influence rather than a manager. As a rule, I was comfortable with such "influence management," because it freed me from the bureaucratic aspects of supervision. In the end, I decided to take the job.

The way to get all the DuPont businesses properly set on course was to have each of their leadership teams travel to Scottsdale to learn for themselves about Six Sigma's effectiveness as a business tool. I intended it as a rapid deployment approach, whereby we would leverage the Six Sigma Academy's knowledge to get each business set on the right course, one right after the other, in a matter of about six months. I would then rely on the combination of corporate enablers and local leadership to optimize the overall impact of Six Sigma within DuPont.

MAKING SIX SIGMA OFFICIAL

The corporate officers at DuPont get together twice a year in an extended leadership team meeting to discuss directional, strategic, and business issues impacting the company. At our January 1999 session, Six Sigma was on the agenda.

Before formally engaging in DuPont's goal-setting process, Holliday thought it important to let his top people know the company would be aggressively pursuing Six Sigma as a strategic edge. Holliday wanted to make it clear that they would very soon take on Six Sigma across the entire company.

The audience was aware that Specialty Chemicals was implementing Six Sigma, but they did not expect a corporation-wide announcement. After presentations by Coe and his team along with Dennis Reilly on the relevance of Six Sigma to all of DuPont's businesses, Holliday announced that DuPont was going to become a Six Sigma company: "We're going to begin our journey to Six Sigma, and this is absolutely essential for the success of DuPont to meet our strategies." Since Specialty Chemicals was really a portfolio of businesses, with twenty individual business units and a multiplant environment, much like the rest of DuPont, Holliday believed that what was good for Specialty Chemicals would be good for the entire company.

Holliday laid out the basic definition of Six Sigma, along with Six Sigma's baseline rules and other information that would help DuPont's business leaders come to grips with how they would drive Six Sigma in their respective organizations. Finally, Holliday introduced me to DuPont's leaders, calling me "the one who will lead us on our Six Sigma journey." That moment marked the beginning of the breakthrough transformation throughout DuPont.

Looking around the room, it was obvious that while some leaders were enthusiastic, others were noncommittal, and some just rolled their eyes. The savvy DuPonters had known that something was up, since Holliday had me sitting at his table. Some executives got up and said this was just what DuPont needed. Most, however, were silent. One leader claimed that it would be great for other DuPont businesses but that his was already at Five Sigma.

At the end of his remarks, Holliday communicated to everyone at the meeting that Six Sigma was not optional, and that the DuPont leaders should see me for details. Several came up to me at the break, congratulated me on my new job, and said, "Sign me up." Others said, "Congratulations," and that was it. A couple said, "Sign me up for last," probably thinking that Six Sigma would not be around by the time it was their turn. Interestingly, the early adopters at that meeting ended up being some of the best deployments with the best results in the company.

Over the next year, Six Sigma helped us to identify more than $1 billion in direct benefit to DuPont, a combination of money saved and earned. In five years, that number would exceed $2.3 billion. DuPont moved Six Sigma beyond just cost savings and created the concept of top-line growth (TLG). Rather than focusing on decreasing or eliminating costs by eliminating defects, the TLG focus would be on growing revenue, a nontraditional use for Six Sigma.

Although we concentrated on cost reduction initially, we observed that many Six Sigma projects were having a positive effect on customers. Looking closely at the data, we saw that one business, Crop Protection Chemicals, was registering great results in the areas of sales and marketing. Further examination revealed that while other businesses were focusing on increasing capacity, Crop already had plenty of capacity; their issue was to grow revenue. The Champion from Crop, Don Wirth, worked with his team and then leveraged what they'd learned with the other Champions and divisions. Based on this early work, we decided to form the top-line growth network to focus specifically on growing the top line for DuPont. Wirth worked inside his business, bringing sales and marketing to the table. He spent time with the team as they expanded the thinking of the process to apply to growth. Then some members were confident enough to try some experiments. He did this on some products in Canada and saw the return. They shared results openly with other Champions from the other businesses. This is a good case of leveraging, as the others took that little bit of information and applied it to their businesses. A top line growth (TLG) network was formed by picking seasoned marketing and sales professionals to pull together what had been learned, create a tool kit, and act as the center of gravity for growing revenue throughout DuPont. The group set out to make growth a key component of DuPont's Six Sigma journey.

In 2001, the concept of TLG did not exist, but by the beginning of 2004, DuPont had completed more than 2,500 TLG projects, increasing revenue by $1.5 billion.

By the beginning of 2004, DuPont had completed 6,147 Black Belt projects and had 9,406 more in the pipeline. In the following chapters, I'll show you how we did it.

## CHAPTER 1

BUY-IN AT THE ENTERPRISE LEVEL

DuPont's initial company-wide Six Sigma thrust was focused on productivity enhancement. Its goal was to realize $1 billion in annualized hard savings during the first eighteen months of full-scale implementation, in the period from mid-1999 to December 2000. Also, DuPont was targeting an additional $600 million in savings in year three and another $800 million in year four. Even for a company of DuPont's size and revenue, the numbers reflected the boldness of the company's goals, as well their high expectations for Six Sigma in achieving them.

While these targets were not yet set when DuPont was preparing for Six Sigma, CEO Chad Holliday and other key officers knew that their goals would be very ambitious. Six Sigma requires that a company set and achieve goals that are well beyond what a corporation has reached in the past. Those goals are ultimately met through the aggregate savings of individual projects.

As a general rule, in a Six Sigma initiative the average Black Belt project returns about $300,000 in cost savings, and the average Black Belt completes three or four projects per year. Given a first-generation Six Sigma goal of $1 billion in savings, DuPont would have to initiate, drive, support, and manage well over 3,000 projects.

Holliday understood the enormous size of his company's commitment. DuPont's Six Sigma goals would have to be cascaded down throughout the company and deployed in full alignment with its strategic intent. He knew that only by setting serious goals at every level would they provide the sense of urgency necessary to pull together the personnel, structures, systems, methods, technologies, and tools required to get the most out of Six Sigma. The operative principle is much the same when a Black Belt determines a project savings target, then defines the critical variables that will impact that outcome. In Six Sigma language, this process is called *identification.*

The system used in Six Sigma caused DuPont to look at problems and solutions in a totally different way than in the past. With Six Sigma, executives would be required to determine the Y, or result they wanted. They then would determine what critical steps were needed to achieve those results—the X's. At the corporate level, the configuration of identified Y-X–correlated goals would become the key measure by which DuPont's executive management would drive and monitor progress. Following the concept of $Y = f(X) + e$, DuPont set the critical X's for each year. These were the essential tasks to be done that would lead to success, which we detail later in this book.

At the operations level in the eighteen strategic business units, the Y-X goals would be central to how the DuPont business units drove and monitored their respective Six Sigma journeys while directly supporting the company's corporate goal of $1 billion in cost savings. At the process level, Six Sigma goals were formulated based on how specific Black Belt projects would support each division's operational goals.

Over time, the language of Y and X became part of the DuPont lexicon, to the extent that even in casual meetings having nothing to do with Six Sigma, it became common for one DuPont employee to ask another what Y they were looking for, or to suggest a critical X factor or two as part of a solution to an issue. This was reinforced in official meetings when the CFO stated in presentations, "Here is the big Y."

THE ECONOMICS OF SIX SIGMA AT DUPONT

The first step in establishing Six Sigma goals at a company is setting a high-level financial target. The figure targeted should fall between 15 and 25 percent of a corporation's revenue. This reflects the common cost of poor quality that can be extracted from the cost of operations in the form of bottom-line profit. The basic idea is that poor quality adds 20 to 25 percent to a company's operation cost. Setting an overall goal at, say, 20 percent shows the scope of the program over many years, as this figure could be in the billions of dollars. Matching financial goals to timelines is the next level. Setting the $1 billion in 18 months was aggressive for DuPont. Any nonquantifiable benefits realized through Six Sigma, and even quantifiable cost avoidances, are not part of this benchmark. (A good example of cost avoidance might be someone trying to claim savings by buying Fords as company cars rather than Mercedes-Benzes. While you could show savings on paper, it never could be validated on the income statement because the expense of the Mercedes-Benzes was never there to begin with.)

The driving idea behind Six Sigma is to set goals that are overtly ambitious and daring. Only through proper design, initialization, installation, deployment, and implementation of Six Sigma can a company expect to meet or exceed these ambitious financial targets.

The questions DuPont's executives asked as the company engaged in the goal-setting process were:

- What is the right corporation-wide goal?
- How do we break the goal down among our eighteen business units so that it is manageable and realizable?

The company knew the success stories of companies such as AlliedSignal and GE, which set and achieved ambitious Six Sigma targets. DuPont had not yet decided what its magic number should be. Moreover, its executives didn't even know how the company should go about arriving at that goal.

In early 1999, DuPont's top management team headed off to Scottsdale to meet for two days of intensive training with Mikel Harry and Rich Schroeder, including CEO Chad Holliday, as well as the company's chief operating officer, chief financial officer, chief technical officer, chief legal officer, head of human resources, head of strategic planning, and the leaders of each of DuPont's eighteen major businesses. At the time, those eighteen businesses were Nylon, Polyester, Lycra, Crop Protection, Chemicals, Pioneer Seed, Performance Coatings, Titanium Technologies, Packaging and Industrial Polymers, Engineering Polymers, Imaging Technologies, Electronic Technologies, Kevlar, Nomex, Advanced Fiber Systems, Specialty Chemicals, Safety Resources, and Nonwovens and Surfaces.

At the two-day retreat, Harry and Schroeder performed a sort of baptism by fire for those who would lead the Six Sigma thrust for the company. The first part of the session was focused on guiding DuPont's executives through the process of establishing DuPont's corporate Six Sigma goals.

Schroeder asked the head of one of the business units to articulate one of his current goals for his business.

"To grow year-on-year productivity by 4 percent," he replied.

"Good," Schroeder said. "That's a very good goal. It's very specific, it's quantifiable, and it has a time commitment to it." Then he asked how the business unit was doing in achieving that goal.

"Well, we were a little flat last year," the leader, a senior vice president, said. The businesses are run by vice presidents/general managers, who today at DuPont report to senior vice presidents, who lead a platform of businesses.

"Okay," Schroeder said. "How about the year before?"

"A little flat or even a little negative."

"Okay. So I gather that you have a great goal, and you've given that goal to your people again this year. So what makes you think you will be able to meet it this year? What are you going to do differently that gives your people the tools, the methodology, the knowledge, and the motivation they will need to meet this goal?"

The business leader remained silent.

Then Schroeder asked another business unit head what his unit's goal was, and went through the routine again. The reply was the same.

Next, he asked DuPont's chief technical officer what one of his goals was.

"To derive 5 percent of DuPont's revenue from new product development," the chief technical officer replied.

"An excellent goal," said Schroeder. "It's quantitative, you can measure it, and it is bound to time. How did you do in meeting that goal last year?"

"We did about 1 percent—not very well," said the chief technical officer.

"Well, what about the year before?" asked Schroeder.

"Again, maybe 2 percent."

"How about the year before that?" Schroeder continued.

"We didn't have that measure in place then."

Next Schroeder asked the technical officer about progress toward his goal in the current year.

"We have a lot of projects in the pipeline," he said.

"Define a lot," Schroeder asked.

"Well, many," came the reply.

"What percentage of revenue will they account for? Do you think you will meet your goal this year?"

The chief technical officer was not 100 percent sure. His goal was highly dependent on "market acceptance."

"What are you going to give your organization that's different with regard to tools, methodology, and the necessary courage to meet this goal when it has never been met?"

The chief technical officer lapsed into silence.

It was a painful process for DuPont's senior people as Schroeder and Harry exposed, questioned, and confronted the manager's effectiveness in setting and achieving their goals. Clearly, their efforts weren't working. Something different was needed at DuPont. Even if their aims were valid, they needed different tools to reach them. Harry and Schroeder told the executives that DuPont needed specific Six Sigma goals to make sure the company properly applied its resources to achieve the goals it set out.

Over the next two days, Harry and Schroeder laid out what DuPont could expect from Six Sigma and what they should consider in establishing the company's goals.

Schroeder asked the group what they thought DuPont's total cost of poor quality was. The executives went back and forth around whether it was 10 percent of DuPont's revenues or 12 percent or even 15 percent. What Schroeder said next shocked them all: "I'm telling you right now, it's somewhere between 20 and 30 percent. For a $25 billion company, let's be conservative and say you have a $6 billion cost of poor quality sitting inside your company waiting to be extracted." Schroeder defined the cost of poor quality as the amount of waste, defects, and extra cost at DuPont, divided by its revenue. This $6 billion cost, said Schroeder, was the overall opportunity DuPont could realize over a multiyear time frame.

At this point, a heated debate arose about whether some of the DuPont businesses could legitimately carve such a large percentage out of their operating expenses. It was difficult enough to accept that DuPont had $6 billion of wasted efficiency hiding in its operations, money that was being taken directly from the company's bottom line. But it was even more difficult for some of the business heads to believe that their organizations were operating so far short of where they could be running. "My business is a leader in its industry. I simply don't believe our cost of poor quality is as high as you say," said one DuPont executive.

Schroeder smiled. "It's probably higher," he responded. He had heard too many stories to count from high-powered executives about why their businesses were different and why they should set more modest goals. Schroeder understood that many of the past behaviors and assumptions of these highly successful, experienced, and educated people would soon be severely challenged. Harry and Schroeder's critique of DuPont's businesses eroded a lifetime of assumptions of the 200-year-old corporation in the space of hours.

Having shaken up DuPont's executives that very first day, Harry suggested everyone go out to his ranch to do a little roping. The executives looked around at each other in disbelief. All DuPont's top executives were there, spending an incredible amount of time, money, and energy on a very critical initiative. What were Harry and Schroeder up to?

Later that afternoon, the fifteen DuPont executives stood around the roping ring watching Schroeder and Harry rope cattle. As the ropes flew and cattle charged about madly, throwing clouds of dust into everyone's eyes and mouths, half of the DuPont leaders positioned themselves inside the roping ring, making themselves part of the action, while the other half remained outside, determined to protect life and limb. It seemed to demonstrate who were more inclined to embrace risk and who were inclined to shun it. Harry and Schroeder obviously enjoyed roping and giving the executives a chance to connect with their interests. It also gave the executives an opportunity to reflect on what lay before them in a non-business, out-of-the-box environment.

The executives had been told they would have to commit to a corporate Six Sigma goal the next day. At dinner that night, the group explored the questions they felt their decision rested upon:

- Was Six Sigma truly different from other transformation initiatives?
- How much of what Harry and Schroeder had told them was true and how much was fiction?
- If they tried Six Sigma and failed, what would be the damage resulting from their failure? Would they encounter even more resistance from their people when they tried to implement a different initiative?

But many on the corporate leadership team couldn't help thinking of how profoundly transforming it would be if DuPont found a way to save $6 billion over the next five years. If Six Sigma truly was the methodology to help them achieve their goal, then this small, select group of leaders was on the verge of doing something great for their company and for themselves. One thing was apparent as DuPont's top brass sat around the dinner table: Six Sigma is unusually aggressive and, as a result, doesn't tend to elicit many neutral reactions. Six Sigma tends to force intellectual and emotional polarization. After several hours of discussion, the DuPont executives decided to go forward with the Six Sigma initiative.

When the group reconvened the next day, Harry explained that a first-year 4 percent reduction in the cost of poor quality, totaling roughly $1 billion, would be a good benchmark for DuPont to pursue. While such a benchmark was aggressive, it was based on an established Six Sigma formula—that the average Black Belt nets roughly $1 million in cost savings benefits per year. Schroeder explained that another way of determining the right first-year Six Sigma target was to take 1 to 1.5 percent of the total number of employees, in DuPont's case about 80,000 at the time, and train them as Black Belts. Given that, he expected DuPont would need to install approximately 1,000 Black Belts throughout its businesses.

Schroeder said that DuPont leadership would have to accomplish a few key supporting goals as a leadership team to make Six Sigma successful. The Six Sigma Academy would provide the technology, the curriculum, the consultants, and the process for helping to install Six Sigma at DuPont. The DuPont executive team's job would be to:

- Tie a significant portion of each corporate leader's variable compensation to achieving the corporate Six Sigma financial target.
- Identify and train Six Sigma Champions for each of its eighteen businesses.
- Set aggressive business-level Six Sigma financial targets for each business unit.
- Install a budgeting and financial system to track Six Sigma project benefits.
- Institute a Six Sigma management review system.

These became known as the five X's of Six Sigma at DuPont.

On the surface, none of these tasks sounded terribly difficult except tying executive compensation to Six Sigma success. Until Schroeder broached this, everyone in the room was pretty much on board with implementing Six Sigma. But when they realized that part of their compensation would be tied to achieving their Six Sigma goals, some executives began to backpedal furiously. Attaching executive pay to performance was not new at DuPont, but now the Six Sigma method of performance improvement, along with setting the overriding goals to be achieved, was being prescribed by the corporation. Everyone would have to follow the corporation's Six Sigma goals and tie a portion of their finances to its destiny. They were uncomfortable committing a percentage of their variable compensation to achieving aggressive Six Sigma goals, based on a few stories and a couple of days with Harry and Schroeder.

This issue threw the team off balance and introduced doubts about the billion-dollar goal. Should it be smaller? Should they slow down Six Sigma deployment or follow the pilot program for a longer period of time? How much of their compensation should we place at risk? Schroeder and Harry left the room as the executives debated.

When Harry and Schroeder returned, they asked the DuPont team for its conclusions and decisions. Schroeder in particular wanted a decision, consistent with his experience in corporate cultures that were much more dictatorial than DuPont's. It was a defining moment, as Holliday's leadership style and the consensual nature of DuPont's executive culture revealed itself. Because Holliday knew they did not have a consensus in the room, he suggested that the team go back to corporate headquarters in Delaware to make a decision within ten days. He told Harry and Schroeder that he needed more time with his leadership team to make the proper commitment. As it turned out, they would make that commitment.

COMPENSATION

Although the compensation system would change over time, at the beginning of the Six Sigma implementation, the Champions were eligible for a Six Sigma incentive that could double their variable compensation in a year. Typically, this could represent as much as 40 percent of their total compensation. In the second year of implementing, to get wider impact, Six Sigma results were tied to the creation of a variable compensation pool for each business. In that year, whether a person was part of the Six Sigma initiative or not, that business's pot of variable compensation money was impacted by that unit's success in achieving its Six Sigma goals. Typically, the amount in the variable compensation pool equaled 20 percent of one's variable compensation, though it could reach 40 percent in any given unit. The average payout from the variable compensation pool ended up being 25 percent of one's total variable compensation.

A typical vice president of a medium-sized business unit at DuPont had an annual compensation of $360,000, including salary and variable compensation. One-third of his or her total compensation was variable, based on performance, and 20 percent of that was tied to achieving Six Sigma goals. So if Six Sigma failed at that business, that vice president would risk losing $24,000. The corporate average Six Sigma impact was $30,500.

Ultimately, Six Sigma compensation became more focused on individual achievement. Each person was given a set of critical operating tasks (COTs), and compensation was linked to achieving those tasks. Typical COTs might be to select, assign, and train sixty Black Belts by the third quarter or validate $30 million in benefits that year. These are objectives that are specific, timely, and measurable. Typically, one of five COTs was Six Sigma–related. In other words, each person's paycheck was impacted by his or her specific Six Sigma results. The Black Belts and Master Black Belts also received stock options and, in most cases, a percentage of the cost savings benefit from a project.

During the initial Six Sigma implementation process, DuPont also developed a special system for the Six Sigma Champions to receive variable compensation and stock options directly from the line leaders of their individual business units (remember, the heads of the business units were their bosses). The variable pay was based on how well the Champions did inside their businesses in initiating Six Sigma and meeting financial targets. This was in addition to the variable compensation pool set up within each business unit, discussed earlier. As an example, Mary Ruth Johnson had a primary role as a Champion in the Polyester business but also led the corporate Champions communication subteam. She worked with the Champions and DuPont's communications experts to lay the groundwork to communicate the company's success stories to all employees, building value for Six Sigma. In general, the Champions had to work in their roles for at least one year before becoming eligible for this special compensation.

When a business unit head paid out variable compensation and stock options to a deployment Champion, the actual amount would depend on the Champion's involvement with Six Sigma teams and subteams, how much he or she shared knowledge with other Six Sigma Champions in other business units (in order to help spread Six Sigma knowledge across the corporation), and how well he or she embodied the spirit and methodology of Six Sigma deployment. An energetic, involved individual who was a great team player could theoretically double his or her variable compensation, and some nearly did. Stock options could be increased as well, by up to 50 percent.

The compensation system succeeded in focusing the Champions' attention. Each would have to sacrifice to succeed in his or her commitment to Six Sigma. But the compensation package made them feel they were valued within the corporation.

As noted, this special compensation plan DuPont created was a one-time offer to deployment Champions. After the initial push to get Six Sigma off the ground, deployment Champions would be compensated like everyone else who was directly involved in Six Sigma: 20 percent of their variable compensation was attached to the achievement of their Six Sigma goals.

My job as DuPont's corporation-wide Six Sigma Champion would have been impossible without the strong backing and influence of the corporate executives and the business-unit heads. The policy of financial reward was essential in deploying Six Sigma at DuPont because it made Six Sigma an economic value proposition for everyone. Miss the $1 billion corporate first-year target and no one would get any of the money apportioned as a reward for achieving DuPont's Six Sigma goal.

DuPont began its Six Sigma training in mid-1999. Even with a compressed schedule, we figured it would take six months to fully install Six Sigma in each of DuPont's eighteen businesses. Given that, we planned on achieving the $1 billion savings run rate by year end 2000. While training was taking place, Chad Holliday worked with each of his business leaders in extracting specific commitments and handling their individual concerns, most of which related to compensation. Because the executives were required to place some personal skin in the game, they delved more deeply into the promise and the risk of Six Sigma. Some executives, more than others, believed that Six Sigma was the solution to DuPont's problems. Tying a portion of pay to the success of Six Sigma led these executives to be even more optimistic and committed. With their own compensation tied to Six Sigma's success, they were convinced that DuPont was serious.

Holliday had already started selecting Champions from each of the eighteen businesses. Deploying and implementing Six Sigma in a global corporation would take a small army of change agents: eighteen strategic business unit (SBU), or deployment, Champions, four of whom would also be functional Champions, and all of whom would report to their respective business leaders. Later, Legal, HR, and regional Champions would be added. The original group was twenty-three, comprising eighteen strategic business units, four business functions (Finance, IT, Global Services, and R&D), and me, Don Linsenmann. These project Champions would oversee the Black Belts in Six Sigma implementation, providing guidance to their respective business units and functions.

These eighteen Champions became the linchpins between corporate Six Sigma policy and its local application within DuPont's businesses.

They would facilitate the smooth and effective installation and implementation of Six Sigma by:

1. Reporting directly to their business unit heads, and indirectly to the Senior Champion, me, Don Linsenmann
2. Supporting their respective business unit heads and their executive leadership teams in all aspects of Six Sigma installation, deployment, and implementation
3. Serving as strong Six Sigma spokespeople within their business units
4. Coaching and developing the deployment Champions or Project Champions within their respective businesses
5. Providing leadership to any and all people involved in Six Sigma in their business

The basic task of the eighteen high-level SBU Champions at DuPont was to lead the Six Sigma effort within their business units to realize quantum change in the organization. Many of them had deployment Champions reporting to them to cover various geographic or business areas. These deployment Champions ensure the consistency and uniformity of corporate Six Sigma aims while driving Six Sigma through the various line operations within their respective businesses. The DuPont Champions had to be diplomats, ambassadors, politicians, motivators, guides, and coaches all at once.

Dennis Broughton, for example, who worked in Nylon Intermediates, had been at the Victoria plant in Texas as its manager for several years. Being a manager at a major plant at DuPont was almost like being mayor of a small city. Broughton was adept at dealing with conflict and creating a shared vision for his plant. And it was because of his skills and experience that he was selected as a Champion. Don Wirth, who came from the Crop Protection business unit, had been implementing a complex IT system in Asia Pacific. Wirth's project skills made him another good choice for the role of Champion.

All of the high-level Champions DuPont selected were senior employees in terms of their experience and position within the organization. They were highly respected change agents who understood the significance of interactions between people, processes, and systems. Mike Edenfield, for example, who was chosen as the Champion for DuPont Titanium Technologies, was a well-known and outspoken plant manager. He had a reputation for being up-front, open, and successful in delivering results.

High-level Champions such as Edenfield were typically drawn from outside the ranks of the quality engineers. DuPont wanted business leaders, not just experienced professionals. Certified quality engineers remain in their roles for many years; Black Belts and Champions, on the other hand, transition into business leadership roles after completing a two-year tour of duty. Realizing that business needs are always changing, DuPont sees Black Belts as remaining in their role from eighteen to thirty months, but the target is twenty-four months. DuPont made sure it selected only the best-qualified individuals to become deployment Champions; each had considerable experience in successfully running major operations. When they were selected as Champions, they answered directly to their respective vice presidents in charge of the business units rather than to a senior manager who in turn reported to a vice president.

Functional Champions, too, reported directly to the business unit VP. The functional Champions are located within the business unit rather than the corporate structure. This type of system makes DuPont's Six Sigma drive decentralized and highly focused on the needs and capabilities of each individual business unit. The four were in addition to the business Champions (Finance, IT, Global Services, and R&D), who function globally.

Those who became deployment Champions at DuPont were usually promoted after their tour of duty as a company Champion. Of the original twenty-three, four are still at it today, three have retired, and fourteen of the remaining sixteen were promoted. For example, Gary Lewis from Specialty Chemicals, who led the first group through the Six Sigma training, was promoted to lead DuPont's Labor Relations Group in Human Resources. Mike Edenfield, from DuPont Titanium Technologies, was promoted to run the company's SAP deployment. Keith Holliday (no relation to CEO Chad Holliday), the Champion from Engineering Polymers, was promoted to lead the company's Supply Chain efforts.

At DuPont, however, deployment Champions who were promoted were replaced with other full-time development Champions. The business leaders saw such a value in having a single-point accountability on Six Sigma that they replaced Champions in the same role. These "new" Champions were in more of a mode of building on the deployments created by their predecessors.

CORPORATE TRAINING BEGINS

Let me take a step back here and look more closely at the process of selecting and training the eighteen deployment Champions and four function Champions. Shortly after the corporation fully committed itself to Six Sigma, I informed each of the eighteen business vice presidents that in selecting their deployment Champions, they should choose one of their very best people. But the VPs gave me a lot of pushback regarding my request. Most executives feared that if they took their best manager away from a key plant, it would not continue to run effectively. The Six Sigma Academy warned us of such resistance—that business leaders would balk at giving up their best people. But Schroeder said that the candidates whom their bosses were most reluctant to give up were the best choices to become Champions.

The corporate senior vice president of human resources was a tremendous help during the deployment Champion selection process. DuPont already had a system in place that tracked future "stars"—people who had been in the most challenging jobs over the years and who had done well. When one of the business leaders recommended a Champion, it was easy for me to run the person's name by the human resources VP for his input.

In some cases, the human resources VP confirmed that the selected person was a strong candidate, based on the HR corporate personnel database. In some cases, the head of human resources didn't know enough about the individual selected or didn't have that person on his "promotability" radar screen. When this happened, he would contact the head of the business unit to explore the person's background and qualifications. In other cases, the head of HR had information that suggested the candidate was not ideally suited for the job. In such cases he rejected the proposed candidate and, when necessary, reclarified the requirements of the Champion job for the business unit head.

One could see which business units would embark on the Six Sigma journey the most eagerly by how quickly they designated an appropriate Champion. Some businesses selected highly respected and qualified deployment Champions in the short time available. I immediately publicized their choices, in order to encourage the other businesses to choose someone of similar caliber. Not all selections, however, went without a hitch.

One case entailed a business that wanted to send four Champions rather than one, because the business leader felt he didn't yet know enough about Six Sigma and wanted to have four people, each covering a different aspect of the business, fly out to find out about it and report back with their impressions. This was totally unacceptable to me and to our executive team. DuPont had already formed its impression of Six Sigma and was now moving headlong into full commitment.

In another case, Dave Andrews, who is now CIO and director of DuPont Canada, was chosen from the IT business to be their deployment Champion, and was told a week before the training that he would be required to go to Scottsdale. Unfortunately, Andrews had long before scheduled a ski vacation in France with family and friends. He wanted the job but asked if he could come out later. He was told that he had to be there—there would be no exceptions. With the apologies of his boss, Dave went off to Scottsdale, while his wife and their friends went skiing in the Alps without him.

"If you wanted the job, this is what you had to do," says Andrews. "It was non-negotiable. But it was also an opportunity to get in on the ground floor. I didn't realize how significant it was at the time."

Andrews's dilemma became an early water-cooler story about DuPont that signified how serious DuPont was about Six Sigma. The company didn't typically ask people, especially a thirty-five-year DuPont veteran, to change vacation plans at the last minute.

Andrews and the other seventeen deployment Champions and four functional Champions would serve in their new roles on a full-time basis and jump at least one notch up on the organizational ladder. The Champions would now sit at the same table with the head of their respective businesses, and other such business-level executives as the chief financial officer, VP of manufacturing, VP of technology, VP for Europe, for Asia, for human resources, and so on.

Integrating the new deployment Champions into the business leadership teams allowed DuPont to lend tangible credence to Six Sigma while honoring the people who were making significant career moves based on its promises. The deployment Champions were plugged directly into the power structures of their respective businesses, positioning them to influence their superiors as much as their superiors were in a position to influence them.

The night before their weeklong formal training began in Scottsdale, the group watched a short video of CEO Chad Holliday sharing his thoughts and personal commitment to Six Sigma. The video got their attention—afterward, many of them expressed how critical they believed it was for DuPont to succeed with Six Sigma.

Most of the Champions did not yet know each other, but with all of them together for a week, we would maximize the value of that time. We realized that this was DuPont's twenty-two best and brightest, a team with enormous potential, and one whose members needed to work together and respect one another.

To help break the ice, one of the first things we did was play the diversity game. This is a technique used to classify different people according to four different "thinking styles" delineated by brain researcher Ned Hermann. The Champions began the diversity game by passing around various color-coded cards on which were written such characteristics as *creative, controlling, meticulous, passionate, detailed, visionary, skeptical, inquisitive,* and so on. The characteristics were grouped into four clusters corresponding to Hermann's four thinking styles, and all the characteristics within each cluster were written on cards of the same color. The idea was to keep the cards that best described yourself, and trade the other cards with people. In the end, each person was left holding a set of cards that generally described himself or herself, and the predominant color of the cards indicated that person's thinking style.

Hermann suggests that those left with mostly red cards are prone to social thinking, which is to say they are more personable, passionate, emotional, and kinesthetic, and less cerebral. Those with mostly blue cards are primarily analytical in their thinking, which means they are drawn to and comfortable with measurements, facts, logic, and technical problem solving. The yellows are more future-oriented, which makes them holistic in their thinking, comfortable with their intuition, big-picture-focused, and inclined to integrate and synthesize. Finally, the greens are administratively inclined implementers who are detail-oriented and whose actions are carefully planned, organized, and prioritized.

The Champions connected with each other as they traded words, opinions, laughs, and color-coded cards. Each could see their peers and themselves falling into the Hermann categories of socially inclined, technically astute, managerially savvy, or positively visionary. Although no one likes to be pigeonholed, after the diversity game, everyone had a better sense of who their peers were and how they could play off each other's strengths and buttress their weaknesses. It was a powerful experience that helped to cement the group into a coherent and coordinated force.

RISK TO PERSONAL CAREERS

The other major discussion the group of twenty-two had was about how everyone in the room was taking a huge career risk. More than a few of the newly appointed Champions felt apprehensive. They had been taken from jobs at which they excelled and were thrust into the risky role of corporate change agent. In some cases, certain Champions had already been replaced by other people. For example, Dennis Broughton, the

Champion of the Nylon business unit, had been taken from his job as manager of a large plant and replaced the next day by someone else. There was nothing for him to go back to—a scary position to be in. Still, says Broughton, "I had come to a point of believing that we needed a new approach and I was out of ideas." For Broughton and the others, it was a no-look-back, warp-speed journey from the black-and-white into the gray. If the definition of a leader is someone who excels under ambiguous and uncertain circumstances, then Broughton and his peers would have their opportunity to lead.

They accepted the challenge, but not without mulling over what was in it for them. Here was a group of high-level, accomplished managers and executives who were leaving responsible positions with healthy stock options and variable compensation. If Six Sigma failed and became the next defunct program of the month, they felt they would be out in the cold. Yet their new job was alluring because they would have the opportunity to move into more influential positions after their tenures as Champions.

Ron Rawlins, one of the more outspoken Champions, suggested that each deployment Champion get 50,000 stock options if he or she met the Six Sigma goals. While the other Champions laughed at Rawlins's suggestion, they recognized that he had the right idea, even if the number was excessively high.

The next day Mikel Harry showed up and started demonstrating Six Sigma concepts and principles via computer simulation. Harry described the process steps of Six Sigma: Define, Measure, Analyze, Improve, and Control (DMAIC), which is the foundation of the Breakthrough Strategy. Next he defined Design for Six Sigma (DFSS), the methodology for creating new products, processes, and systems. While the traditional DMAIC strategy fixes broken processes, DFSS designs new processes and products to be effective from conception. The real power of DFSS is that it starts with what has been called the voice of the customer (VOC). By quantifying the specific needs of the customer, the process analyzes the necessary attributes to be designed into the product or process to deliver the maximum performance the customer has requested. A key part of DFSS is simulation: projecting how the product or process will operate before investing in plant or equipment. The result is robust products, services, and processes that do not need traditional DMAIC improvements.

At the sessions, Harry explained the design of experiment simulations, calculated various "sigma scores," and shared many concepts related to the big ideas underpinning Six Sigma. The simulations he ran were computer analyses that showed the output of a complicated process. He would construct a design problem in his computer and walk the Champions through the simulation process based on statistical modeling. The DuPont Champions watched thousands of possible outputs flash before their eyes, and then saw how the average outcome was used as a prediction, such as a simulation of production capability showing units produced based on a particular combination of production inputs. The power of the DFSS tool quickly became evident to everyone in the room. It was an epiphany of sorts for the skeptical Champions, as they began to understand how the big ideas of Six Sigma connect with the idea of leadership to create the force of breakthrough.

Schroeder talked about his background at AlliedSignal, where he had worked for CEO Larry Bossidy. "I had the job that Don [Linsenmann] now has," he said. He explained that Bossidy had been confronted by two options: to shut down the company and sell it for parts or transform it into a world-class operational powerhouse. Bossidy had brought Schroeder in to do the latter.

The next three days of training focused mostly on the leadership and structural aspects of Six Sigma deployment. There was a unit on change leadership that revolved around developing vision, empowering change agents, mobilizing commitment, installing support systems, auditing change, and controlling the change process. This is an adaptation of the change acceleration process originally developed by GE. Chad Holliday had set the vision for DuPont beginning its journey to Six Sigma. We were the empowered change agents as we defined our roles as Champions.

Mobilizing commitment is the entire process of getting Black Belts in the program. Our subteams were focused on installing the support systems, such as IT, HR, and Finance. We would use our IT systems to track progress and audit results. Finally, we would use the data to see what was under control and where the Champions needed to intervene. In that early meeting, we were mostly focused on mobilizing commitment, as that was our job. But over time we would come to feel ownership of all of the phases.

We spent time on setting up the governance structure of Six Sigma at DuPont. The structure of Six Sigma needed to be superimposed on DuPont's structure. Aligning the tasks to the structure enabled each person to go home knowing what needed to be done. Several Six Sigma Academy consultants worked with the Champions on this. Many discussions focused on leading the change rather than the details of the tools or methodologies. This turned out to be a powerful start that gave us a high trajectory.

At the end of the week, DuPont's twenty-two deployment Champions had begun to see how and why Six Sigma might be different. They started to see how Six Sigma would connect to their business and drive down operating costs, and they came to understand that the projects they undertook must have a dollar benefit. They realized that Six Sigma was not just about quality, but also about the quality of their businesses. They saw that their role in the change process was a big one, and that the scope of the change was their entire business, not just individual processes or products within it. The Champions also came away with an inkling of how Six Sigma was going to change how work got done at DuPont. Though their original week of training did not emphasize culture change, it would become more of the focus of their Six Sigma discussions as their deployments matured.

We also decided that the leaders of all the businesses should go through essentially the same program as the twenty-two leaders who'd already been to Scottsdale, and we established a schedule in which training took place one business unit at a time. On average, there were approximately fifteen executives for each of the eighteen businesses, depending on business size. They would expose themselves to the power of Six Sigma, agree to a financial goal, and go back home to name Project Champions and Black Belts and pick projects.

The executives' time with Harry and Schroeder set the stage for how enthusiastically each of the leaders would get on board and set his or her Six Sigma goals. Harry and Schroeder did this well, and high goals were set as a result of the process. Nylon, one of the biggest businesses, left the session with a commitment to create 180 Black Belts and create $180 million in benefits, which we detail later in the book.

I had started out by attending all of the business-unit sessions, which had gone well, and had planned on attending all of them. It was a great way for me to get to know all of our businesses and meet many of our leaders. But the fourth or fifth time we were scheduled for one of these business-unit executive sessions, I was asked to remain in Wilmington for another meeting. Following the session I couldn't attend, I got an angry phone call from the general manager of the Packaging and Industrial Polymers business unit. He had flown his entire team of fifteen to Arizona but did not see Mikel Harry or Rich Schroeder, who had sent in the B team instead. The DuPont leader felt shortchanged. The division finished its session with a financial goal that was less than I would have expected from the size of their business. But reflecting on it, maybe it was appropriate since they didn't gain the same level of motivation.

In the wake of this, I spoke with both Harry and Schroeder and emphasized the critical role that they had to play in motivating the business-unit executive teams and setting high financial goals for each business. Using their own Six Sigma language, I told them that they themselves were CTQs (critical-to-quality characteristics) and that they must attend each of the scheduled executive sessions.

This seemed to work, and the next five or six sessions went smoothly. Then I received a call from Rich Schroeder a couple of days before a scheduled session. He told me he was not in Arizona and would be unable to attend. After some probing, I discovered he was at a session for

another client that was being held in the Caribbean, and that flight schedules would not allow him to make it back to the ranch. Furious, I decided
to send our company plane to the Caribbean and fly Rich into Phoenix,
to get in his half-day session with the leaders of our business unit, then
back to the island.

I felt a bit nervous about commandeering the plane, but I knew the
greater benefit would come from Schroeder's involvement. Realizing our
resolve, Schroeder agreed; we had no further missteps throughout the
training.

DUPONT SIX SIGMA AT THE PROJECT LEVEL: RESEARCH AND DEVELOPMENT

While DuPont aligned its top executives and business units behind Six Sigma, the huge financial returns to the company ultimately came from thousands of smaller projects in every area of the company. It was at the project level that workers and customers could see the impact of DuPont Six Sigma in their day-to-day work and world. What follows is one example of a typical DuPont project, the kind that occurred in almost all areas of the organization.

Ph.D. chemist Nyla Dookeran came to DuPont in 1997, after having been a team leader for a nuclear energy quality-control lab at General Electric. Her initial job at DuPont was as an analytical chemist for the Crop Protection business. Then she became a Black Belt in DuPont's Central Research and Development (CR&D) group.

CR&D is a 1,500-person organization that is the foundation of DuPont's science efforts. It has been responsible for most of DuPont's major product breakthroughs, including the creation of nylon, Lycra, Kevlar, and Teflon. CR&D provides both scientific services to the corporation on specific projects or for specific clients as well as long-term research. Dookeran worked in the Corporate Center for Analytical Sciences (CCAS), one part of CR&D that provides cutting-edge capability, applied problem solving, and rapid-response services to assist other businesses.

Trying to implement Six Sigma in a research environment isn't easy, since most of the processes and prototypes there are nonrecurring (unlike, for example, a manufacturing plant). Many in the DuPont group believed Six Sigma didn't have a place in their laboratories. In spite of this, most Black Belts within CR&D were able to find good projects and work through the roadblocks.

Says Dookeran of one project she worked on, "The person running the unit said they would buy me lunch if I would just go away. Undertaking the project took a lot of goodwill and an understanding of their concerns. It's a sell on what value you can bring to their process."

The leaders of CR&D were primarily focused on increasing researchers' productivity. For example, they focused on improving the fabrication and testing of lithium polymer battery samples, reducing defects in the fabrication of photovoltaic cells, streamlining CR&D personal computer procurement and chemical inventory management, and improving capital project management.

To determine where to focus, a vice president and five directors brainstormed about what the researchers were doing and what was coming up in the job. For CR&D, its customers were other divisions inside DuPont. The big buzz at the time was researcher productivity, the desire to get research out the door faster.

Dookeran next spoke with the CCAS customers—the directors of the business units in biochemicals, chemicals, material science, and engineering. The directors specifically identified the hot programs, including the lithium battery, photovoltaic cell, and Versipol catalyst programs. During the following weeks, Dookeran spoke with the ten managers in each of those groups to get more clarity on what it was they wanted from each program. She also conducted a customer survey. The questions included:

- How often do you submit samples to the lab?
- List your most important criteria in the delivery of this service. Please rank in order of greatest importance to you.
- What is your desired turnaround time?
- State the benefits to your division if we were able to achieve your criteria.

The survey showed that customers wanted their lab work done with accuracy and precision, and they wanted the results delivered as quickly as possible. Some respondents complained that the analysis work done by CCAS took far too long and, as a result, they were starting to use outside labs. The shorter the time the analytical work took, the faster DuPont could get new products to market.

Dookeran decided that her first Six Sigma project would be to reduce the amount of time it took to analyze the composition and quantities of various metals. Metals analysis was selected partly because of the complaints from the fuel cell department, which needed metals analysis more quickly. "This guy was really agitated because he wanted his results faster," says Dookeran. "He was the squeakiest wheel, essentially, in the fuel cells program, which was a high-profile program. We were looking to develop better catalyst material that would convert methanol to hydrogen and oxygen, thereby producing energy."

A fuel cell is an energy-conversion device that converts fuel and air directly into electrical power. Fuel cells offer the promise of high efficiency and low emissions when compared to conventional technologies. If pure hydrogen is used as a fuel, the only products are heat, electricity, and water. Unlike a battery, a fuel cell does not store energy. It converts energy from one form to another. Fuel cells are used for a variety of applications, ranging from laptop computers and cell phones to tractors and weather stations.

The performance of fuel cells is related to the amount of energy produced. Different compositions of elements (platinum and ruthenium, for example) are produced and used to coat membranes. Next, the ability of this coated membrane to generate energy efficiently is tested. The metals analysis results reveal which combination of materials produce the best results.

Another CCAS customer was Konstantinos Kourtakis, a CR&D scientist working on a new fuel cell design. Kourtakis needed to measure the quantities of platinum and ruthenium used on carbon catalyst electrodes, in membranes in his fuel cells, and in catalyst powders. Kourtakis would correlate this data with fuel cell performance to make them more efficient.

The problem was that Kourtakis wanted his samples analyzed in two days, and the average time it was taking to analyze his metals was nine days. Kourtakis had calculated that decreasing testing turnaround by seven days for each of his fifty experiments would take a year off his fuel cell development time, with economic and market implications. And a reduction in metal testing cycle time would benefit many other new product development programs as well.

One of Dookeran's first actions was to shadow all the team members and key process steps involved in the metals analysis process. Since the lab had five technicians, Dookeran spent time with each of them.

The metals analysis lab comprises two large labs located on the same floor in the same building. One is referred to as the prep lab, and the second is the analysis lab. When a customer has a sample, he or she drops it off in the prep lab, along with paperwork such as material safety data sheets. It is weighed, converted to a liquid, then taken over to the analysis lab, where the metal's elemental composition is quantified and a repair generated for the customer.

"I looked at every single thing they did," says Dookeran. "On different days, I tracked each person. I became part of the team, even though some of the technicians did not want me there. Then I did a process flow diagram. The entire process took about a month. This is how you know exactly how the process works and where the opportunities are."

When Dookeran examined the activities in each of these parts of the process, she came up virtually empty-handed: There didn't seem to be much opportunity to strip time out of weighing, liquefying, or analyzing samples.

However, Dookeran did find that the technicians had divvied up the job functions, so that only two of the five in the group handled the mixing of the chemicals. Dookeran also discovered that samples would sit idle in between steps in the process for large periods of time. At the start of the process, one person would write in the logbook that the sample was received. Then the sample would go into another room and wait. "They would leave it and then another technician would come along and add a chemical, put it on a hot plate or whatever, and then label it and take it to another room," Dookeran explained. "All the technicians knew the samples were just sitting there, but that was the way it was." One time, the team found, the chemicals sat waiting even while one of the workers went on vacation. It was still there when the worker returned.

The log clearly showed that 70 percent of the total metals analysis cycle time was consumed by samples sitting in the queue waiting to be analyzed. "This was a very big ah-ha," says Dookeran. "When we showed it visually with a chart, people couldn't believe it. But the data was true."

To counter this, workflow was made continuous by cross-training team members and by adopting an end-to-end single-person-ownership procedure. Instead of samples being passed off at the end of each stage, they are now shepherded by one person through the stages of weighing, digesting, analyzing, and reporting. The result:

- In the case of Kourtakis's fuel cells, the new process reduced the cycle time from nine days to four days.
- For all samples, the cycle time was reduced from an average of ten days to seven.
- For 75 percent of all samples, the average cycle time dropped from 15 days to eight.
- In terms of benefits to DuPont, this project was worth $637,000 in researcher productivity gains—the ability to process more transactions in the same amount of time without adding people or spending capital.

The numbers do not reflect the benefits to CR&D scientists from getting their products to market a little faster because of the CCAS's speedier turnaround times.

The project ended well for the CCAS and for Dookeran, who was promoted.

## CHAPTER 2

HOW IT STARTS WITH REDUCING COSTS

GENERATION ONE: SIX SIGMA

The superordinate goal for DuPont, or the Y of its Six Sigma initiative, was to save $1 billion in the first 18 months, which led the company to establish several supporting goals, or the X required to achieve its Y. Those goals were:

- Tie a significant portion of each corporate leader's variable compensation to the achievement of the disaggregated Six Sigma goals
- Name and train Six Sigma Champions for each of DuPont's eighteen businesses
- Set aggressive business-level Six Sigma targets
- Install a budgeting and financial system to track Six Sigma project benefits
- Institute a Six Sigma management review system

All the launch goals had been achieved by the beginning of 2000, and DuPont was looking forward to the transition from Six Sigma installation to Six Sigma implementation. The corporate leadership team decided it needed a refreshed set of X's to drive its initiative. It also decided that these X's should be broken down into two distinct categories: those that would be driven by Holliday and his senior leaders, and those that would be driven by Champions on a corporation-wide basis.

YEAR 2000 CRITICAL X'S FOR SIX SIGMA SUCCESS

Goals Driven by Holliday and Senior Leaders

#	Goal	Rationale
X1	Nail down the delivery of goal in the strategic business units' critical operating tasks (COTs)	Make each leader accountable by integrating Six Sigma goals into the existing performance management system
X2	Define areas to increase Six Sigma competence and dedicate two days to training	Integrate the requirement to actively participate in Six Sigma into the existing training plans
X3	Ensure that each SBU starts Green Belt training using the DuPont standard training—1,000 Green Belts by year end 2000	Proliferate Six Sigma knowledge and skills beyond the Champion and Black Belt populations for enhanced synergy
X4	Tie 20 percent of variable compensation for all SBUs based on meeting Six Sigma objectives (next 5,000 people down)	Transfer the power of financial reward from the corporate leadership team to everyone in the business units who are eligible for variable compensation
X5	Visible support from the office of the chief executive (Holliday and top leaders)	Send the message to the corporate leaders and to the rest of the company that they should "practice what they preach"
X6	Continue quarterly management reviews	Keep Six Sigma on track and refine the company's capability and capacity for effectively steering its initiative
X7	Dedicate a global leadership team meeting to integrate Six Sigma into managing processes, including profit objectives	Start the process of moving from deployment and implementation to the "way we work"

Corporate Goals Driven by Champions

#	Goal	Rationale
X1	Maintain top management commitment	Continue to secure executive commitment to Six Sigma in quantum, quantifiable, and accountable terms through education and compensation
X2	Achieve bottom-line results	Perpetuate the emphasis on hard benefits that accrue to the current year's income statement
X3	Force accountability	Counter a corporate culture in which it is easy to sidestep direct accountability due to unclear lines of responsibility attached to hard performance targets
X4	Institute a disciplined approach (rigorous processes, DMAIC)	Make the Breakthrough Strategy mandatory for all Six Sigma projects
X5	Accept only a data-driven focus	Institute a culture where "we only trust in God—all others must bring data"
X6	Embody intensity/sense of urgency	Compress sense of time from the traditional rate of improvement to a Six Sigma rate of improvement (78 percent per year compounded)
X7	Make training a priority	Require every person involved in Six Sigma to complete formal training and preparation from a highly reputable source

While each of the goals was critical to success, several were pushed from the office of the chief executive. For starters, it was the goal to nail down the delivery of Six Sigma financial targets in each strategic business unit's critical operating task (COT). The specific tasks that managerial personnel must complete as important initiatives filter down throughout the corporation.

The COT process is an accountability-focused system that ties the variable pay of each senior business leader to the achievement of critical business goals. So if a DuPont business unit met its Six Sigma goal for the year, then every senior executive in that business would receive a Six Sigma–related bonus, which was weighted at 20 percent of the executive's total possible bonus. Also in the year 2000, DuPont extended the 20 percent incentive to the 5,000 people in the business who were part of the company's bonus pool.

The Green Belt training goal also was driven from the office of the chief executive. At all organizational levels within DuPont, Green Belts exist to bring added synergy and power to the project-focused core of Six Sigma and to proliferate Six Sigma competency throughout the business. Green Belts at DuPont were not necessarily required to conduct and complete formal projects as a Black Belt would, although some did.

In general, Green Belts support Black Belts in the planning, coordination, or execution of projects or autonomously execute downscaled projects within their line of sight that typically yield lower dollar cost savings than more complex Black Belt projects. A Green Belt possesses a certain Six Sigma competency and skill set but, having been trained for ten days rather than the Black Belt's twenty, does not have the scope and depth of training and insight of a Black Belt and does not function in a full- or part-time Six Sigma role.

Green Belts trained in the Breakthrough Strategy can:

- Collect data
- Execute experiments designed by Black Belts
- Conduct initial basic data analysis
- Present summary information to Black Belts

- Execute fundamental statistical process control (SPC) methods
- Perform equipment scheduling, calibration, and maintenance tasks associated with Black Belt projects and their own Green Belt projects

The subject of executive Green Belts was broached early in 2000. The company had already trained 650 Black Belts, and 1,000 projects were under way. It had achieved its preliminary financial target of $100 million in savings, and was positioned to meet its goal of $1 billion by year end 2000. Everything was going well, but DuPont wanted more from its Six Sigma initiative. It made sense that Six Sigma, as a centerpiece of DuPont's corporate strategy, would become its key transformational tool. The long-term goal at DuPont was to build a massive Six Sigma competency within the entirety of the company, so that everyone would be conversant in Six Sigma and work according to its principles.

During an "office of the chief executive" meeting in 1999, the top executives were told that the way of true culture change was to inject Six Sigma into the thinking and doing of as many DuPonters as possible. This represented a new course for DuPont. Holliday stood up and said he would be one of the first to become a Green Belt. Then COO Goodmanson said he would become one as well. The commitment from the top set the tone for the rest of DuPont's executive leaders, who all would become Green Belts and institute the Breakthrough Strategy in their own worlds as much as they would plug it into their respective organizations. The top brass would change how they did their work, along with everyone else at DuPont.

This would start a major shift at the company that would entail training thousands of Green Belts and ensuring their even distribution throughout all levels of DuPont. Clerks would become Green Belts; plant personnel would become Green Belts; supervisors would become Green Belts. So would managers, directors, professionals, staff, and executives.

At the top, this meant DuPont executives had to transition from planning and support roles to active participation. Goodmanson committed to lead a project aimed at improving safety by reducing non-event-related injuries. Though DuPont already had the best industrial safety record in the industry, Goodmanson believed the company could do better, and his project succeeded. A group vice president offered to conduct a Green Belt project for speeding up the process of replicating knowledge generated by Black Belt projects.

The next goal was to make top management commitment to Six Sigma highly visible, which meant that the top executives, including Holliday, needed to voice support and demonstrate their involvement in Six Sigma on a regular basis. It became one of the personal critical operating tasks upon which each of their annual bonuses was based. The senior corporate executives regularly included Six Sigma in their speeches, visited various locations and plants in the context of Six Sigma, and were involved in quarterly reviews at the corporate and business unit level. In these meetings, all the vice president general managers, along with their deployment Champions, met with certain members of the corporate senior leadership team (typically their group vice president) to provide a briefing on progress, problems, issues, and successes as major business units. The eighteen business units rotated through the sessions to determine the status of their progress, make proper diagnoses, draw out important learning, and keep the entire corporation on track toward its goal.

Topics covered during the reviews included progress on validated project savings to date, the status of cultural and management change, the number of projects under way, the status of Black Belt and Green Belt training, and other items that provided a window into the world of Six Sigma in each major DuPont business. During the first three years of deployment, these sessions were more structured and formal than they became later.

The senior Champion typically participated in all quarterly reviews to remain visible and involved on a corporation-wide basis. The heads and deployment Champions of each business unit were present for their respective reviews, along with various senior business-level leaders and managers. Many times business unit leaders brought along various

Champions and Black Belts to present their specific goals, deployment processes, projects, and progress.

Nylon deployment Champion Dennis Broughton recalls one review when he reported Nylon's deployment status to COO Goodmanson. It was February 2001, just after Nylon had successfully reached its year-end goal of achieving a run rate of more than $180 million of benefits from Six Sigma. He had a Project Champion present the process involved in surfacing project ideas and selecting projects. He had five Black Belts present a summary of their projects, each of which demonstrated a different aspect of how Six Sigma was working to improve the business.

At the time, Goodmanson was new to the company and new to Six Sigma. "He had been tepid to Six Sigma to that point," says Broughton. But as Goodmanson listened to the presentations, he had an epiphany. The deployment discipline, the rigor and effect of data, the sheer impact of certain projects on customers—these opened his eyes to the real potential of Six Sigma. "At the end of the meeting, he gave a monologue saying that until this point he had had difficulty in really seeing Six Sigma because he had failed to see the evidence. That day changed his mind." From that point, Goodmanson was a strong advocate of Six Sigma.

There were frequent meetings between deployment Champions and business leaders, regular conference calls among deployment Champions and Project Champions, thousands of business meetings into which Champions and Black Belts were invited for input and advice, and countless hallway and office conversations among all DuPonters about how Six Sigma would, should, or could be applied.

The reviews reflected a burgeoning culture of scrutiny and interrogation in a collegial environment. The reviews were a catalyst for fostering cultural transformation through teamwork, individual accountability, and an almost nagging attention to detail.

At the operations level, the management review process required the segments within each strategic business unit to provide a monthly briefing to their executive leaders on such topics as project selection, alignment with business goals, and the status of how each segment was meeting its designated Six Sigma financial targets. The idea was to keep Six Sigma on track and moving forward with momentum. Business heads enjoyed the opportunity to learn about problems, frustrations, victories, and triumphs firsthand from operational leaders and could provide tangible support by sanctioning their efforts, remaining plugged into their projects, and approving needed resources.

These operations-level reviews really begin at the process level, where process owners and Black Belts meet with local managers, Project Champions, Master Black Belts, and sometimes business-level executives. The focus of these meetings is to assess the activities involved in moving through the stages of the Breakthrough Strategy. The review team works face-to-face with Black Belts to evaluate the extent to which they have properly defined their project, selected and applied certain tools, improved their process, established a control plan, and so on. Initially, these reviews are conducted on a monthly basis with new Black Belts as they move through the DMAIC training cycle. They function as a steering and learning mechanism, as specific projects are subjected to the scrutiny of expert technical knowledge, and as master teachers they have the opportunity to mentor more junior Six Sigma Black Belts and help refine their work. These process-level reviews also can reveal problems and barriers to team progress that are political, organizational, or financial in nature. In these instances, the Project Champions go to bat for the Black Belts by exercising influence in the management structure.

The management review system at DuPont was designed so that everyone stayed involved, leaders could develop, and the corporation could meet its Six Sigma goals. The reviews brought a level of professionalism to this growth process with their formality and structure, and provided grounding and support. The results were available for all to see. By the end of 2000, DuPont had:

- Achieved $1.06 billion dollars in annualized hard savings
- Trained and prepared 130 Champions, 1,100 Black Belts, and 1,700 Green Belts

- Validated 3,100 Black Belt projects, each reducing operating expenses by $340,000 on average

Of all the goals DuPont had established for 2000, just two had not been achieved to the company's full satisfaction. The first was for corporate executives to define areas in which they wanted to increase their Six Sigma competence and dedicate two days to training, and the second was to dedicate a global leadership team meeting to integrate Six Sigma into the processes by which DuPont is managed. Both of those goals were an attempt to get DuPont's most senior executives directly involved in Six Sigma and move toward a state in which it is the way they do their work.

GENERATION TWO: TOP-LINE GROWTH

While the first two years of Six Sigma at DuPont were characterized by focusing inside the company on reducing cost, the next two years (2001–2002) were focused outside the company on growing revenue. Project by project, the corporation had successfully achieved and even surpassed its initial billion-dollar goal. The next task was to encompass a different thrust based more on future potential than immediate need.

That expansion required a new goal for DuPont in terms of next-generation hard benefits from Six Sigma. DuPont was now positioned to change the focus, character, and nature of its Six Sigma intervention to achieve sustainable growth and increase shareholder value.

While Six Sigma was one of the main planks in DuPont's corporate strategy, it hadn't been fully internalized as a two-pronged thrust. Productivity is mathematically displayed as a change in sales over a change in cost. Yet to this point the Six Sigma emphasis at DuPont had been on cost rather than revenue. This emphasis translated into a strong bias toward manufacturing-related projects and improvements at DuPont plants, where the principal focus was on reducing defects. Compared to transactional and service-oriented projects, manufacturing projects tended to be more concrete, easier to define, and more likely to have readily available data. It was from this platform of relative simplicity that DuPont's businesses launched and initialized their respective Six Sigma drives. If DuPont could dramatically improve its cost position, this would benefit productivity and, in turn, actualize the goals of sustainable growth and increased shareholder value.

Business by business, as the executive sessions were completed, as a critical mass of Champions was trained, and as breakthrough ideas, systems, methods, practices, and tools were integrated into the way the company did business, DuPont began to understand the power of Six Sigma. As momentum gathered, and as project successes became internally publicized, a need to definitively measure the impact of Six Sigma emerged, leading DuPont to develop SigmaTRAC, a software system specifically designed to measure Six Sigma success and enable the initiative on a global scale.

SigmaTRAC became the common language, system, repository, and tool for all Black Belts, Champions, and Corporate Leaders. Through SigmaTRAC, the Six Sigma leadership population could assess the progress toward business breakthrough. SigmaTRAC was first used to monitor such measurements of engagement as numbers of Black Belts and Champions trained and numbers of projects under way and completed. The focus was internal and on fixing processes, reducing defects, shortening cycle times, and improving product quality. But while Six Sigma projects were successful in these areas, the basic nature of the initiative changed and began to morph toward the measurement of financial benefit, with people paying much more attention to tracking hard-dollar project benefits.

The financial folks at DuPont were vigilant and systematic about not counting any Six Sigma improvement unless it brought real money to the income statement. For example, if a cluster of projects improved throughput yield and uptime of titanium dioxide production, freeing capacity to make more, the finance people would say, "Great job, good for you, but your capacity benefits don't hit the bottom line until we see the actual monies coming in from customers." The concept of sold and utilized capacity created a realization that more revenue could be generated by added capacity with no investment in facilities, equipment, or technology.

All such capacity-related improvements were catalogued in SigmaTRAC under the label of revenue, or new dollars to the top line. At the end of 2000, it became clear that completed Six Sigma projects could bring DuPont an additional $500 million in revenue if the added capacity was sold. Even though the overall initial focus of Six Sigma was on cost reduction, about one in five projects had revenue implications. This was an early clue for all of DuPont that it could take capacity improvements to customers, who could buy more products.

When DuPont figured out how to add capacity without adding fixed costs, it could derive more return per unit produced. Adding revenue through better sales and marketing, without corresponding hard investment, also would create higher margins. This was one of the key ideas that drove the Champions to reconsider the mission of Six Sigma. DuPont had extracted great benefit from Six Sigma by learning to use its ideas, tools, and methodologies for cost reduction. But the direct experience of the past two years provided a strong clue that Six Sigma could be utilized to increase growth.

Before Jeffrey Immelt became CEO of GE, he visited DuPont to discuss a concept he called "at the customer for the customer." This was GE's term for using Six Sigma to grow revenues as opposed to cutting costs. In 2001, GE completed more than 6,000 projects with customers at their sites—all focused on specific and important problems and opportunities, and all with revenue-enhancement implications.

When the Champions digested the implications of Immelt's customer-focused vision, they adopted it for DuPont. They understood that adding dollars to the top line was much different from taking dollars from the bottom line. It became clear that the Champions had to rebrand or reinvent Six Sigma, which led to the formation of DuPont's Six Sigma top-line growth network, a group of new Champions whose primary mission was to take the benefits of Six Sigma to customers.

DuPont employed a bottom-up process to establish its 2001 financial target. With at least a full year of experience under their belts, the Project Champions provided their deployment Champion with a clear view of where their respective implementation cells were headed in 2001, and how much validated and future benefits would be delivered. The benefits were a combination of cost savings and increased earnings from new revenue. Through the aid of SigmaTRAC and various meetings, they collated their estimates and passed them up to their deployment Champions. The deployment Champions organized the input and worked with their business unit executive teams to hammer out their respective next-generation Six Sigma goals. When the financial portion of each business's goals was added, the figure came out to $1.6 billion, an additional $600 million above the 2000 run rate. Although the company had created a significant increase in capacity due to Six Sigma projects, that capacity was in excess of demand due to the threatening recession. This made DuPont's earnings outlook for 2001 lower than that of the previous year, which was considered in setting the company's year two Six Sigma goal. Significantly, the Champions felt confident that they had the data required to properly configure a set of new Six Sigma goals; the senior leadership team would not have to worry about establishing 2001 Six Sigma goals, as they had the year before. This was a critical step for letting the data speak, and for the Champion network to establish the next level of autonomy and credibility for itself. It became clear that the Champions could be trusted to be aggressive with their line managers and business unit leaders in setting new financial targets. They had DuPont's best interests in mind, so no one had to arbitrarily tell them what they and their businesses could do. The approach was a distinct break from the way the company had initially approached Six Sigma goal setting. Nevertheless, Holliday's senior team said it could live with and support the new financial target and related goals.

#	Goal	Rationale
YEAR 2001 CRITICAL X'S FOR SIX SIGMA SUCCESS		
X1	Secure a $1.6 billion hard run rate and create $400 million in future benefits	Place more emphasis on projects that produce soft savings or future benefits, while sustaining the financial benefit of completed projects
X2	Create top-line growth network	Pursue opportunities to increase revenue and to renew the Six Sigma initiative
X3	Engage 1,200 Black Belts and 4,500 Green Belts by the end of 2001	Expand the capacity for doing projects (Black Belts) and build a much more pervasive Six Sigma competency (Green Belts)
X4	Institute Design for Six Sigma (DFSS) methodology and projects	Begin to target the design function, or new product introduction process, as a source of opportunity
X5	Apply Six Sigma to critical senior leadership processes	Expand the scope and depth of Six Sigma understanding and application at the executive level
X6	Continue 20 percent variable compensation	Sustaining the power of financial reward for all bonus-eligible people

What was clear was that DuPont was transitioning from a strategic focus on productivity improvement to a focus on top-line growth. For years, the company had been mounting an attack on productivity, but it wasn't until it adopted Six Sigma that it made major headway in that pursuit. Having saved about 4 percent of its cost of poor quality through productivity-focused Six Sigma projects in one and a half years, Holliday and his team became confident that the productivity assault would continue on its current course. People had been trained, systems and methodologies had been installed, and productivity-oriented projects were sure to continue multiplying in the future. It was time to redirect Six Sigma toward growth.

Holliday recalled Immelt's "at the customer for the customer" comments. By the end of 2001, GE had more than 3,000 Six Sigma projects under way in the airline industry, 1,500 since the September 11 terrorist attacks on the World Trade Center and Pentagon. GE's 2001 annual report boasted of the projects achieving $400 million in savings for customers who were contending with the crisis and change that followed 9/11, positioning the service to customers as one to "improve our long-term relationships as this key industry rebounds." GE had progressed to the point where it made perfect strategic sense to leverage Six Sigma with customers.

It was this very conclusion that DuPont and its Champions came to as well. DuPont never could have begun its initiative with a focus on growth, because it first needed to display a strong capability for leading internal change. It was difficult to conceive that Black Belts could be successful outside DuPont before they had been successful inside.

Now a great number of DuPont's Black Belts were well seasoned and ideally suited for bringing Six Sigma to customers. But there wasn't a strong Six Sigma leadership presence in the sales and marketing functions, leading the Champions to develop the top-line growth network. As the Champions led Black Belts and projects and interfaced with their management teams, it became clear that Six Sigma could be just as powerful in a customer-focused growth mode as it had been in a cost-focused productivity mode.

In addition to creating the top-line growth network in 2001, the company planned to become more aggressive with Design for Six Sigma (DFSS). DFSS is an integrated set of concepts and methods for designing quality into new products, processes, services, transactions, activities, and events. Its focus is on identifying, characterizing, optimizing, and validating designs to ensure they yield their intended "entitlement." Entitlement is a key concept in Six Sigma and can be thought of as the best you could do with your people and processes if you could improve them to the limit.

The corporate leadership team decided to expand the scope and depth of Six Sigma through a further emphasis on Green Belt training, as well as through the expanded inclusion of Six Sigma practices at the level of the office of the chief executive. While in many companies Green Belt training is reserved for those who are below Black Belts in the organizational structure, DuPont turned this thinking upside down. Its goal for 2001 was to train 3,500 additional Green Belts, the majority of whom would be from the executive and professional ranks.

None of these new thrusts for 2001 was intended to achieve immediate financial benefit. Rather, they were additions to the Six Sigma infrastructure intended to yield benefits only after an appropriate ramp-up period. Even then, in the case of many DFSS projects, tangible benefits could never be validly or reliably calculated, as their nature is to avoid future costs of poor quality. Similarly, certain other Green Belt or even customer-focused Black Belt project outcomes could not be reliably measured, although they could often be loosely connected to increased revenue growth.

DuPont's third year of experience (2001) with Six Sigma was one of a shift from the more tangible world of cost reduction into the more ethereal world of revenue enhancement. The company would continue its hard-benefit, bottom-line projects to the order of an additional $600 million during the year, but it would also initiate new projects that would yield future revenue when the market returned to its cyclical pace. In this sense, the "soft" portion of DuPont's 2001 goal would become "hard" in the future, but not before year end 2001.

Fewer Champions and Black Belts were trained in 2001 than in 1999 and 2000, and fewer straightforward productivity projects were defined and completed. But dramatically more Green Belts were trained, and more growth- and design-oriented projects were initiated and completed. The envelope of Six Sigma expanded to include many more executives and business leaders at DuPont, selected customers, and various suppliers.

To set the year four Six Sigma goals, DuPont surveyed the corporate officers and Champions during the fourth quarter of 2001. The survey asked the business leaders and Champions what they were trying to accomplish with Six Sigma, how intensely they planned to implement it, what key opportunities were present, and what hazards were in the way. The data were needed to develop sound goals that would become the critical X's for Six Sigma success in 2002.

YEAR 2002 CRITICAL X'S FOR SIX SIGMA SUCCESS

#	Goal	Rationale
X1	Continue quarterly management reviews	Discuss performance, identify issues and barriers, and solidify commitment to Six Sigma
X2	All director-level personnel and above to have a Six Sigma critical operating task	Drive the desire to become personally involved in Six Sigma within the business leadership ranks
X3	Provide full resources for top-line growth plans, including DFSS projects	Create more leadership force behind the top-line growth focus
X4	All SBUs complete critical-to-quality flow-down and capability flow-up	Migrate the deterministic and probabilistic thinking from the process to the operations and business levels
X5	Validate (final) pretax operating income benefits of $800 million in 2002 (3 percent of 2002 revenue)	Level the playing field regarding Six Sigma contribution, and narrow the variance of contribution from business to business
X6	Institute "corporate-group-promotable" policy by May 2002	Push the requirement for promotability up to the corporate level and further solidify Six Sigma as the way DuPont does work
X7	General business promotional requirements set by year end	Saturate the salaried workforce with Six Sigma concepts and tools, and further solidify Six Sigma as the way DuPont does work
X8	All corporate officer group executives will be Green Belt–certified by year end	Create a personal experience and common understanding of Six Sigma for the top seventy executives and thereby speed the migration to Six Sigma as the way DuPont does all its work

Two critical X's that popped out of the process were related to strengthening senior leadership commitment to Six Sigma. The first was to continue quarterly reviews in a standardized but flexible manner. Historically, each business unit head would sit down with his or her boss, one of the corporate officers, for the express purpose of discussing Six Sigma. While these sessions were structured in terms of who had to attend and what had to be discussed, they weren't so structured as to entail a formal agenda. The key purpose of these reviews was to discuss performance, identify issues and barriers, and generally solidify commitment to making Six Sigma work the way it was designed to.

The second executive-leadership-related X pertained to the way business leaders got rewarded for directly supporting Six Sigma. Prior to 2002, corporate officers, business unit heads, Champions, and all other bonus-eligible employees were compensated for Six Sigma success as a collective whole, not as individuals. If the financial targets were met, bonuses were paid to all who were eligible. After studying critical data and listening to Champions, it became clear that commitment to Six Sigma at the top was not as strong as it could be. Only 60 percent of the company's executives at director level and above had a Six Sigma–related critical operating task (COT) in 2001. A significant number of executives were delegating Six Sigma but not practicing it themselves.

Therefore, the executive reward structure was changed in 2002 to become individualized, and it was expanded to include all director-level personnel and above. All directors and vice presidents would be accountable for their individual involvement in Six Sigma, and they would also be eligible for the associated individual reward.

Every director-level-and-above employee had to tie at least one of their five required COTs to building some type of Six Sigma competency in themselves and their organizations. For example, someone might go through Green Belt training, or become a process owner for a Green Belt project in the area of top-line growth. Or maybe a business leader would commit to having twenty top-line growth Black Belts in operation by year end.

This reward applied to director-and-above-level Champions as well. However, in their case, several of their five COTs might be related to building Six Sigma power and competency. Depending upon a Champion's level of direct involvement in Six Sigma, between 20 and 80 percent of variable pay could be tied to Six Sigma–related tasks.

The next critical X was to fully resource top-line growth plans, including Design for Six Sigma projects. DuPont already had introduced top-line growth as a subset of its Six Sigma initiative. Every DuPont business now would have to establish a top-line growth financial target, a plan for training top-line growth Champions and Black Belts, and a plan for selecting and executing top-line growth projects. The intent was to elevate the top-line growth emphasis from great idea to corporate imperative.

DuPont's Six Sigma strategic planning consisted of a "critical-to-quality (CTQ) flow-down," coupled with a capability flow-up. The CTQ flow-down is a way of breaking high-level goals into lower-level objectives in a cascading manner, according to the idea of determinism, or "Y is a function of X." At the same time, capability is determined for each critical-to-quality characteristic in the entire system, and these capabilities are cross-multiplied to derive system capability estimates. As flow-down objectives become matched with flow-up capabilities, all the way from the strategic intent to the singular CTQs, there is a clear picture of where performance gaps are. This provides a rational framework from which to select projects, allocate Black Belts, and focus resources to optimize the probability of moving the needle of capability at the strategic level of a corporation, which is discussed in much greater detail later in the book.

The next critical X for 2002 Six Sigma success was to validate pretax operating income benefits of $800 million, roughly 3 percent of DuPont's overall revenue. The $800 million figure was arrived at by applying a simple 3 percent formula for all revenue-generating businesses. So if a business brought in $1 billion in revenue, for example, it would be asked to contribute $30 million in validated savings, either cost savings or revenue increase.

The intent was to narrow the variances in how each DuPont business did its work. There was still a good deal of variation among the business units in their Six Sigma contributions as a percentage of their revenue. Eleven of DuPont's eighteen businesses were falling short of the 3 percent benchmark, while one business had saved, or earned, almost 5 percent of its revenue using Six Sigma.

Several DuPont organizations, such as Legal and General Services Business, had no revenue, but they did have costs, which could be decreased through the systematic application of Six Sigma. In calculating the $800 million, it was estimated that about $100 million in 2002 savings would be provided by these nonrevenue groups.

There were several critical X's related to building Six Sigma competency to make Six Sigma the way all DuPonters do their work. In 2001, DuPont required all CG4s—those in the managerial and professional ranks who have been earmarked as future business leaders—to become certified as a Black Belt, Master Black Belt, or Champion to keep their status as promotables. In 2002, DuPont raised the requirement up to its director-level corporate promotables, called CG3s, requiring them to obtain a Black Belt, Master Black Belt, or Champion certification to retain their status.

DuPont then required its entire salaried workforce to become Green Belt–certified (vice presidents and directors in 2002, managers in 2003, professionals in 2004, and all others in 2005). Approximately 20,000 DuPont employees are salaried, and at year end 2001 there were 6,000 Green Belts working throughout the corporation, most of whom were salaried. The requirement to train and certify 20,000 employees represented a tripling of the Green Belt saturation at the time.

In particular, the requirement of Green Belt certification for all corporate officers, presidents, vice president general managers, and functional corporate vice presidents by the end of 2002 was designed to more deeply ingrain the Six Sigma way of thinking into the minds of the company's leaders. During the first three years of deployment, Holliday and the other corporate officers were highly involved in and committed to Six Sigma, with a healthy portion of their variable pay attached to achieving Six Sigma financial targets. Some officers and senior executives even became certified as Green Belts and led projects to improve management processes. But by the end of 2001, only 10 percent of DuPont's top seventy leaders were Green Belt certified.

John Hodgson, who became COO in 2002, after Goodmanson was named CEO for DuPont Textiles and Interiors, became Green Belt certified and led a project to identify the critical X's related to the corporation's capability for growth. Hodgson had to learn to speak the language of Six Sigma, asking all of his business unit heads what their Y's and X's of growth were, and to use such tools as a CTQ flow-down. Hodgson then led other top executives in personally understanding and applying Six Sigma to their own critical operating tasks.

GENERATION THREE: THE DUPONT SIX SIGMA BRAND

The process involved in evaluating how well DuPont met its 2002 Six Sigma goals, or critical X's, fed directly into the process of establishing goals for 2003. In conducting this evaluation, we administered a survey to all Champions. In addition to the data generated from the survey, we relied on such metrics as validated top-line growth project dollars, number of executive Green Belts, and so on.

By the end of 2002, 70 percent of DuPont's top seventy leaders were Green Belt certified. While this was not completely at goal, the critical mass was set. The pressures of managing the day-to-day business and the choice of some projects that needed some time to get data was the cause. Within the next year, all corporate officers met their obligations. Their projects ranged from increasing Green Belt certification numbers to analyzing the corporation's capability for increased growth. As a result of executive Green Belt certification, DuPont corporate executives are now using common tools, language, and methodologies, forcing Six Sigma into the company from the top.

In 2002, with certification as a condition for promotion, DuPont trained 10,000 Green Belts, 4,000 more than had been certified by the end of the prior year, reflecting the intent to saturate the salaried workforce with Six Sigma concepts and tools and further solidify Six Sigma as the way DuPont does work. In addition, 20 percent of corporate promotables had become certified as either Black Belts or Champions by the end of 2002.

As for the critical financial goal of adding another $800 million to DuPont's total Six Sigma run rate, 2002 performance was a mix of good and bad news. The good news was that the target had in fact been exceeded by $90 million. The bad news was that there was still a good deal of variability from business to business. Going into year five, there were certain pockets of DuPont that still didn't get Six Sigma.

As the Champions looked at 2003, they still viewed 3 percent of revenue as a viable lower limit for Six Sigma benefit. It was reasonable to expect each business to add 3 percent of revenue to its profit margin, through either cost reduction, revenue enhancement, or some combination of both. It was the same goal that had been established the year before, with one modification: In 2003, each business would be held to a 3 percent minimum contribution, and the business-level leadership teams would tweak global variable compensation as much as 25 percent based on performance. In addition, each business unit head had to designate this 3 percent benchmark as one of his or her critical operating tasks for 2003. By doing so, these leaders would tie about 20 percent of their variable bonus pay to the achievement of this benchmark.

Also in need of more support was the 2002 objective to fully resource top-line growth plans. In 2002, there was no specific dollar figure attached to top-line growth, and at year end top-line growth projects accounted for only a very small percentage of the growth targeted by the corporation as a whole. The Six Sigma top-line growth focus needed new energy for 2003.

- More top-line growth Champions and Black Belts were needed to complete more projects.
- More DFSS projects were needed to take hold and produce financial benefits.
- More dollars were needed to be added to the top line.

The only missing ingredient was a designated top-line growth financial target. The Champion network had proven itself capable of setting aggressive and realistic Six Sigma financial goals in the past, and had also proven itself capable of delivering the targeted results. But these goals had been segmented by organizational level and segment, not by type of project. Now it was time to put some traction on top-line growth projects, calling them out as a priority. The same bottom-up process was used, with each business having to commit to a certain contribution based on its size and its capability for securing new top-line growth dollars. The process was facilitated by the top-level Champions as they met with their business leadership teams.

The final commitments that were made fell into a normal distribution—a few leaders, a few laggards, and a larger group in the middle. There actually was a correlation between the nature of a business unit's lead Champion and the magnitude of the top-line growth commitment: the more aggressive the Champion, the more aggressive the goal. The Champions who would "get in the face" of their business unit leaders were those who would walk away with a great goal. Other Champions were less confrontational and, therefore, less effective in challenging their leadership teams. With the overall financial target for Six Sigma fixed at the lower limit of at least 3 percent of revenue for all revenue-generating businesses, DuPont would add at least $850 million to its Six Sigma benefits in 2003, assuming $25 billion in revenue. When combined with the progress already made, this would bring the company over the $3 billion mark of benefits from Six Sigma since it was brought online.

Six Sigma is really a ten-year journey. Although there was resistance to Six Sigma at DuPont in the beginning, this decreased as results became visible, and the slope of Six Sigma's success curve has increased with each passing year. Along the way, DuPont morphed its Six Sigma initiative from one of a basic productivity capability to a machine for driving top-line growth.

DuPont is aiming to integrate Six Sigma thinking and practice into the cycles of business activity at all levels. Management processes, all the many cycles of operation, the multitude of processes and actions that transform lower-value inputs into higher-value outputs—this holistic focus is now the next characterization of Six Sigma at DuPont.

DuPont Six Sigma is:

- The name for where the company has arrived and the name by which all DuPonters have come to characterize the initiative
- Not just for Black Belts and Champions, but for executives, directors, managers, and process owners
- Not just a manufacturing improvement tool, but a globally applicable system of breakthroughs that can be applied in any manufacturing, service, transactional, or engineering environment in any type of industry
- Not just statistics for the tech-heads, but concepts and methods for business leaders
- Not just a way of doing work right the first time, but a philosophy, a pervasive way of thinking that transforms corporate consciousness as much as it transforms corporate performance
- About the big ideas and valuing the power of those ideas
- About a systematic framework and methodology for assessing customer needs and achieving entitlement value in everything everyone in the company does
- About designing a corporation for world-class performance
- About building a cascading system of determinism and measuring all critical quality characteristics in the entire value chain
- About finding leverage and understanding how to properly count opportunities
- About thinking in terms of transformation, understanding the nature and impact of error, grasping the importance of probability, and increasing business power

DuPont Six Sigma is a well-defined way to do work that has some lofty attributes tied directly to DuPont's people and core values. Some of these attributes are accountability, fact-based and data-driven decisions, rigorous disciplined processes, focus on the bottom line, a sense of urgency, and following the voice of the customer.

These were the descriptors on DuPont's Six Sigma Web site, along with the critical X's for 2003, after they had been approved by the DuPont officers. Of the 12,000 people directly involved in Six Sigma, 2,600 hit the Web site within twenty-four hours and 6,000 people hit the site within forty-eight hours. Six Sigma has become a critical part of how DuPont does business.

YEAR 2003 CRITICAL X'S FOR SIX SIGMA SUCCESS

#	Goal	Rationale
X1	Continue quarterly management reviews	Discuss performance, identify issues and barriers, and solidify commitment to Six Sigma
X2	Continue competency-related critical X's: • Corporate promotables must become certified as Black Belts, Master Black Belts, or Champions to retain status • Personnel at the next level down (managers, scientists, and professionals) become Green Belt certified • A small percentage of top executives remain to become Green Belt certified	Further solidify Six Sigma as the way DuPont does work by: • Continuing to push the requirement for promotability up to the corporate level • Continuing to saturate the salaried workforce with Six Sigma concepts and tools • Creating a personal experience and common understanding of Six Sigma for the top seventy executives
X3	Each strategic business unit has a lower specification limit of 3 percent of revenue (totaling $1 billion)	Level the playing field regarding Six Sigma contribution, and narrow the variance of contribution from business to business
X4	$1 billion in annualized, validated top-line growth revenue will be secured by year end	Place an imperative on the need to secure top-line growth using Six Sigma

ONE DUPONT PROJECT: SHIPPING AND TRANSPORTATION

DuPont Titanium Technologies (DTT) makes white pigment from ore and coke at its plant in DeLisle, Mississippi, where 750 people work. DTT has a process by which it extracts titanium dioxide from the ore, using coke as a combustion element, to make the pigments that go into such products as coatings, plastics, and paper.

The company transports railroad cars full of ore from a harbor right to the DeLisle plant thirteen miles away. Coke also is delivered by rail car from the supplier. In between lies a staging yard, where other rail cars for DuPont come in from various locations throughout the United States.

The ideal situation would be to transfer the ore directly from the rail cars into the manufacturing process, but this wasn't always possible because titanium-dioxide-bearing ore is a rare commodity that DuPont bought whenever it could, allocating the ore among five plants—three in the United States, including DeLisle, one in Taiwan, and one in Mexico. So the flow of ore into the pigment-manufacturing process was based on supply, not demand. Sometimes more ore would arrive than could be used immediately, and so the ore would remain in the rail cars in the staging yard. As a consequence, the DeLisle facility was having trouble controlling its demurrage costs—the amount of money charged by the rail company for holding cars at the staging yard beyond an allotted amount of time. In some cases, cars would sit for months at a time, incurring demurrage charges of up to $50 per day per car. When added together, these costs reached $750,000 a year, so significant that many people and teams had tried to solve the demurrage problem over a long period of time.

Laura Burton, assistant buyer, was chosen to become a Black Belt back when the organization initiated Six Sigma in 1999. Burton had worked in procurement for DTT for seventeen years. Her first Black Belt task was to solve the demurrage problem.

"I had some feelings of not being prepared to meet such high expectations," says Burton, "especially about working on a logistics problem outside my normal area." As a Black Belt, Burton had to start from scratch in terms of managing a team and leading a new project in an area that was not her own. "I was honored that management would choose me, but compared with anything I had done in the past, I knew this assignment would be tough," she says.

Burton's first task was to define and measure the demurrage problem. People in the group had been living with the issue for a long time, and different attempts to solve it had failed. They had seen improvement thrusts come and go, falling short of their promises, time and time again. They already were very busy, and in some cases they actively resisted Burton and her agenda. They would say they didn't have time for meetings, and they were reluctant to give information to Burton. "It was not sabotage, but information was slow in coming," she says.

For example, at the beginning of the project, Burton was told that the raw materials "releasers," the clerks who track and release the rail cars and then authorize payments to the railroad for the demurrage, would only be available to meet on Saturdays. "Once we began to work and do the process mapping, everything totally changed," she says.

One of the fundamental challenges of the project was that all of the ore planning and procurement was done by a buyer and a planner at DuPont headquarters in Delaware. The DeLisle site had no input as to how much ore it was to receive. The ore sent to DeLisle came from a Florida plant owned by DuPont. Since there was no storage at the Florida site, all of the production from that site would come to DeLisle and have to wait in the rail cars.

With some help from her Champion and Master Black Belt, Burton got all the necessary operations people at the table to map the ore and coke transportation process.

- What are the critical process steps?
- Where and when do we make critical decisions?
- Where are the critical "risk points" in the process?

It wasn't until she started working with data that Burton made her big discovery. She collected and sifted through reams of data about rail cars—the number of days they were held, the product they contained, the cost of demurrage per car per month or per year, and so on. "I really tortured the data, or it tortured me, for a good period of time before I began to actually make important discoveries," says Burton.

As she made her way through the analysis phase of the Breakthrough Strategy, she found the critical causes of the demurrage problem: There were scheduling and timing issues related to ore coming from Florida by rail, and there were commodity storage utilization issues at the DeLisle plant. However, there was one underlying problem bigger than all the others.

"I had the railroad invoices for every month for several years," says Burton. "I discovered that somewhere along the line, the demurrage condition changed dramatically. The railroad made a change in their billing that was not in our contract."

Because the purchasing was done elsewhere, the releasers assumed the price had been renegotiated and their sole responsibility was to verify that the material had arrived, after which time they authorized payment.

"It was assumed that the new rate was negotiated by the central buyer," says Burton. "At the meeting with the railroad you could cut the tension with a knife."

Because the fleet of rail cars numbered about 200, the $50 per day per car added up quickly. At about the same time, DuPont had been exploring other types of facilities, such as a pipeline, that would have eliminated the need for the railroad. During the negotiation for a settlement of the demurrage problem, the railroad put the pipeline issue on the table. As part of the settlement, the railroad wanted DuPont to delay the pipeline for a number of years, to which DuPont agreed. In turn, the railroad agreed to increase from two to four the number of days a car could stay in the staging yard before demurrage charges would begin to accumulate.

Each successive discovery made Burton feel more confident as a Black Belt. The tools and the data bridged her transformation from feeling a little out of place to feeling at home with leading process change. "There were an awful lot of ups and downs," Burton says about the two months she spent digging for data and tracking rail cars day in and day out. "One day I would be thinking this is never going to work, and the next day I'd see how it might work."

Some of Burton's key discoveries were made possible not so much by the power of Six Sigma tools but by the discipline of the DMAIC process. Sometimes critical X's were found simply by collecting and eyeballing data.

One of Burton's discoveries accounted for two-thirds of the project's $750,000 in validated annual demurrage cost savings. "We had a defect, really, and we looked for the root cause of that defect until we found it. Doing so required me to stretch, which I did, in a very short period of time. I didn't thoroughly enjoy it at all times, but it was very good for me."

Since her demurrage project, Burton has solved other problems within DTT. In one case she achieved significant results in a technical field much more removed from her procurement background than even the rail car project was. Her advice to others is simple: "Learn the tools and apply them. All the power is in the tools."

After two years as a Black Belt, Burton was promoted to be a business Process Owner for the titanium dioxide's SAP implementation team.

ONE DUPONT PROJECT: SALES

DuPont's Elvanol business has been supplying polyvinyl alcohol (PVA) to the U.S. textile industry for more than thirty years. Elvanol, the trade name for DuPont's PVA, is combined with ingredients such as wax and starch to create a substance that is used to strengthen yarn for weaving and then removed from the finished fabric.

DuPont sells its Elvanol to textile manufacturers that use it to make what is called "mill blend" themselves, and it also sells it to resellers that combine it to make blends that they sell to many of the same customers as DuPont. The U.S. textile industry had been under enormous pressure from foreign textile competition with much lower labor and operational costs, and the industry had been shrinking about 10 percent a year since the mid-'90s.

Growing revenue had been difficult, a problem faced directly by DuPont Elvanol salesman Leo Singleton. One day in 2001, Singleton was called to meet with one of his customers at Mt. Vernon Mills. Headquartered in Greenville, South Carolina, Mt. Vernon Mills is one of the largest privately owned textile companies in the United States, with annual sales close to $1 billion.

At the meeting, Singleton was told that DuPont would be fired as a supplier. Mt. Vernon was in a supplier consolidation mode and was getting ready to sever its relationship with a number of its many suppliers, including DuPont. "Hold on, wait a minute," Singleton said. "Are you sure you know what you're doing? We are the biggest, best, and one of the small few who actually manufacture the product. Most others are just blenders or resellers."

Mt. Vernon Mills, which has ten plants around the United States, was buying 6 million pounds of PVA a year, but only about half a million of it from DuPont. The company reasoned that since DuPont was a small supplier, with revenue of only $500,000 a year from only one of the ten Mt. Vernon plants, DuPont would not consider the loss of business very significant.

Singleton suggested that the customer reconsider keeping DuPont as a supplier of PVA, since DuPont actually made the product. He also suggested that Mt. Vernon Mills could achieve better cost savings by using a single PVA manufacturer instead of multiple ones.

Mt. Vernon had a process by which it purchased PVA blends from many different intermediary suppliers and distributed them among ten manufacturing plants. Singleton figured that the key to lowering the overall cost for Mt. Vernon's mill blends was for the company to choose one supplier of PVA and one additive supplier. Then Mt. Vernon could mix its own blends, making the overall process flatter and less expensive. At a cost of around 90 cents per pound, PVA was the most expensive ingredient in the blend. The other ingredients, starches and waxes, might cost closer to 20 cents a pound.

Several months later, Singleton enrolled in Green Belt training, as required by the corporation. He knew the Mt. Vernon Mills situation remained unsolved, so he thought it might be a good idea to focus a Six Sigma project on it. "I was trying to pick a Green Belt project directly related to my annual performance objectives, and one of my objectives was to increase market share at Mt. Vernon Mills," he noted.

Singleton then set up a meeting with his customer contact at the Mt. Vernon Mills, Bill Duncan, vice president of purchasing. But Singleton did not reveal the topic until they met. "Have you heard about Six Sigma?" he asked Duncan. Yes, Duncan had heard of it and had done some reading about it, but said that his company was too small to do it.

Singleton then asked Duncan if he would like to team up on a Six Sigma project that would lower Mt. Vernon's cost for PVA. Over the course of several meetings, each lasting less than an hour, the two agreed that if they could lower the cost by at least three cents a pound, Duncan would raise the amount of Elvanol purchased from DuPont.

Singleton and Duncan developed a fishbone diagram to crystallize the potential inputs to mill blend cost. Of eighteen different possible causes, the project team determined that the dry pound cost of ingredients, including PVA, was the biggest determining factor. "We developed a measurement scheme along with a cause-and-effect matrix to make sure we knew that dry pound cost was the key," says Singleton.

If Mt. Vernon Mills could lower the dry pound cost of all its raw materials, it could achieve at least a 3.5-cent reduction in overall mill blend costs. With Mt. Vernon making its own blends, the middleman would be eliminated and dry sizing costs would be reduced. The solution was that simple, as Singleton had long suspected.

What he didn't suspect was the way Six Sigma would help make his sale. In the process of moving through DMAIC, Singleton put together a set of twenty PowerPoint slides—fishbone diagram, cause-and-effect matrix, high-level process maps, etc.—which were highly instrumental in convincing Mt. Vernon Mills to change its procurement model.

Singleton loaned the slides to Duncan, who used them to communicate with his bosses. "My charts became his charts," says Singleton. "Each time I put together a set of charts, I would delete the DuPont Six Sigma logo, put on the Mt. Vernon logo, and give a set to Bill. Everything was an open book."

Singleton came up with even more data by having fifty-pound bags of samples sent to DuPont from each of the ten Mt. Vernon plants from all over the country. A technical director of DuPont then had each of the contents analyzed at the DuPont labs to determine the exact contents of all of the blends. It turned out that the blends varied and that the customer ultimately was paying dearly for combined contents that did not include the expected amount of PVA.

As noted, Singleton had had ideas for Mt. Vernon right from the start. But his hunches hadn't been enough to catalyze the reaction he wanted from his customer. It was Six Sigma that finally sold Duncan on exploring Singleton's ideas further. Before the Six Sigma project, Singleton simply had a good idea with no structured data support.

The power of Six Sigma turned out to be key in convincing all ten plants to choose one PVA supplier and one ingredient supplier.

Anyone in procurement knows how difficult it is to get plants in different geographic locations to commit to using the same one or two suppliers. People have strong, trusting relationships with their current suppliers. They have standards they've worked hard to clarify. And sometimes they simply don't like people telling them how to run their plants.

But Duncan had what he needed to make the case to the CEO for procurement and operational change at Mt. Vernon Mills. The data showed the clear benefit of blending additives with PVA in-house: an average dry pound cost reduction of 13 cents. When added up over the course of a year, this represented $1.1 million in cost savings for Mt. Vernon Mills, far exceeding any original expectations on Duncan's or Singleton's part.

After the various sizing blends were tested and accepted at each manufacturing location, DuPont signed a three-year contract with Mt. Vernon Mills to be its only direct supplier of PVA. DuPont so far exceeded Duncan's expectations that he gave Singleton 100 percent of his direct PVA business. For DuPont, this represented a considerable increase in revenue, with several million pounds to be purchased, instead of the original half million. The total hard annualized revenue increase to DuPont represented more than $2 million.

"I can pretty much get an appointment with anyone just by saying I work for DuPont, but Six Sigma gave me more credibility," says Singleton. "I just sort of sold Six Sigma like I sold Elvanol, because Six Sigma was something of value, and my job was to bring more value to customers and to DuPont."

## CHAPTER 3

HOW DUPONT ORGANIZED FOR SIX SIGMA

D uPont's leadership realized it would require a significant amount of support to reach its aggressive corporate Six Sigma goal.

As we've seen, DuPont's Six Sigma structure was not superimposed on its existing organizational structure. Every Six Sigma Champion and Black Belt reported to a DuPont business leader, a line manager, or a supervisor who had a clear line of organizational accountability in that business.

Each of the eighteen separate DuPont businesses had a full-time Six Sigma leader, or deployment Champion. Each had a staff of other full-time and part-time Six Sigma people, including Project Champions, Master Black Belts, and Black Belts. Each had a substantive Six Sigma competency in its network of Green Belts. Regardless of their extent of involvement, the people implementing Six Sigma at DuPont were part of a network of specialists integrated into the existing organizational structure.

As the senior Champion at the top of this network, I reported to DuPont's senior leadership. Beneath me were the twenty-two deployment and functional Champions, who were ultimately responsible for about 180 Project Champions who worked out of their respective business units.

By year end 2000, 147 Master Black Belts were underneath the Project Champions. That number grew to 200 by the end of 2001 and 254 by the end of 2002. Below the Master Black Belts were 1,100 Black Belts by year end 2000; there were 1,300 by year end 2001, and 1,800 by the end of

2002. Green Belts were not included in the formal reporting structure at DuPont.

Project Champions functioned as operational leaders—they uncovered project opportunities, coordinated training for Black Belts, broke down organizational barriers for Black Belts, and handled various logistics to support Six Sigma aims. Master Black Belts were technical leaders who understood and could apply Six Sigma methodologies. It was they who conducted most of DuPont's ongoing Black Belt and Green Belt training. Black Belts served as project leaders.

In essence, DuPont's integration of Six Sigma into its existing organization was done in a fixed yet flexible manner. The hard reporting lines remained connected to the business structure, while soft reporting lines were connected to the Six Sigma network. The businesses drove, directed, and controlled Six Sigma within their particular organizations, but they received guidance, and sometimes policy, from me, as the corporate Six Sigma Senior Champion, and from the business-unit Champions.

The chief Six Sigma executive reported directly to Chad Holliday's office. Six Sigma policies were created by the twenty-two Champions, led by me. We would go to Corporate for approval and then back to the Champions for implementation. The deployment Champions then worked directly with the business-level leadership teams to enact corporate policy in their businesses. The business-level teams were made up of multifunctional teams who ran the businesses. For example, a team might include a director of research and development, a director of marketing, a director of finance, and a director of HR.

All policy decisions made by these business-level teams were carried to the general body of twenty-two deployment Champions, who would debate their merits and shortfalls. The Champions, functioning like a senate, would come to a final decision. After formalizing our position, we would present it to Chad Holliday and DuPont's other top officers for veto, modification, or approval before it was made into global policy. In most cases, the CEO simply provided a stamp of approval, with little debate.

While there were some key dictates from the top in terms of how Six Sigma would be installed and deployed, far more decisions were left open for local configuration and implementation. The overall intent was to push decision making, autonomy, and control as far down into the businesses as possible, consistent with DuPont's culture, which had for years been moving toward a decentralized structure. Each DuPont business was self-sufficient in terms of engineering, manufacturing, marketing, and sales, and the leader of each business acted almost as a mini-CEO. The decentralized Six Sigma structure was just a continuation of DuPont's corporate culture. In fact, I was the only Six Sigma–related executive on the corporate staff. Everyone else, from Champions on down, were embedded into the various businesses. As a result, employees, budgets, accountability, and benefits were handled in the businesses, and the results accrued back to the businesses. Every Six Sigma person housed within a strategic business unit reported to a line leader or manager and was paid by that unit, which reaped the benefits and rewards of their labor. One small exception was that initially the funding for training thirty Black Belts, along with the associated executive and Champion training sessions, came out of the corporate budget. But the laptop computers, the SigmaTRAC software, Green Belt training, and all other expenses were paid for by the business units.

Of DuPont's twenty-two deployment Champions selected to lead the installation, deployment, and implementation of Six Sigma, eighteen of the deployment Champions were assigned to the business units; four functional Champions focused on all businesses. These four functional Champion leaders established and deployed five system-wide, cross-business networks that identified critical success factors related to training, information technology, finance, human resources, and communications and developed standardized company-wide policies in these areas. DuPont already had various cross-business, functionally based networks in operation, but they were preoccupied with various agendas and activities. The Six Sigma networks were able to be more focused on the new tasks at hand. In addition, the company instituted a sixth network solely devoted to building the DuPont Six Sigma community.

From a staffing perspective, each deployment Champion volunteered to serve on at least one of the five networks. The network leaders and the deployment Champions populated the various corporate policy-making bodies while remaining inside their business structures. This would provide balance between corporate control and local operations. For example, Mary Ruth Johnson led the communications network while still working in the Polyester business unit.

The network structure provided the framework for instituting disciplined command and control over deployment Champions and business leaders. From an operations or business unit perspective, the structure provided uniformity throughout the company. For example, the structure was inflexible on the Black Belt training curriculum and certification requirements (regulated by the training network). Also, for all the people embedded in local operations and processes (Project Champions, Master Black Belts, and Black Belts), there were certain global, local, and even team policies with which they had to comply. For example, as previously noted, HR instituted a policy that all CG4 employees—those considered to have high potential—must serve as a full-time Six Sigma Black Belt, Master Black Belt, or Champion to keep their promotability status.

As a specific illustration of how these networks communicated, installed, and monitored compliance with the policies throughout DuPont, the training network began to formulate policies to get the right knowledge to the right people at the right time in support of Six Sigma goals. First, after conducting due diligence, they decided to use the Six Sigma Academy for all their training needs, as DuPont lacked the ability to conduct it internally. This is typical, as a corporation initially implementing Six Sigma usually does not have the internal infrastructure—the trainers, content, knowledge, and so on—to train a large number of people on Six Sigma. In DuPont's case, once a business defined the number of Black Belts it needed, the Academy then trained those individuals.

In the first year of training by the Academy, DuPont spent about $10 million, which came out of its corporate budget. This covered:

- Eighteen executive sessions, one for each business unit
- Six Champion sessions

- Six Master Black Belt training sessions
- One Black Belt class for each business, training thirty Black Belts (additional training would be paid for by the businesses, though it would be coordinated at the corporate level)

In the first year of its Six Sigma journey, DuPont made about $20 million from Six Sigma projects, which equaled a slight profit overall. While this number seems small compared to the big goals of project savings, the answer lies in the accounting of the project benefits. The projects had a recurring benefit over time and the annualized benefit was recorded. The actual benefits hitting the income statement during the last few months of our first year actually paid for the program and created "in-period" profit. It more than covered the training costs. After the first year, the corporate training budget was reduced to $5 million annually, as the individual businesses picked up the cost of their own training. By the third year, DuPont became self-sufficient in its training; the training and consulting fees it paid to the Six Sigma Academy were totally eliminated.

The Six Sigma Academy had been hired to set up a world-class training process during the first and second years of implementation. The Academy's expertise lay in its ability to:

- Identify and define the specific training for each position (Black Belt, Master Black Belt, Green Belt, and Champion) in support of DuPont's global Six Sigma goals
- Deploy that training according to a wide array of local circumstances
- Target course content to improve project and business unit objectives, and determine who needed to attend the classes
- Assign and deploy instructors to deliver that content
- Ensure that the system was working as planned

To implement its Six Sigma training at DuPont, the Academy employed its plan-train-apply-review (PTAR) cycle to teach the measure, analyze, improve, and control stages of the Breakthrough Strategy: learning in the classroom for a week, then applying for a month what was learned, and so on.

At the project level, training was used as much as an implementation tool as a learning tool. Black Belts at DuPont could not graduate without having completed two projects yielding a total of at least $350,000 in validated savings.

But DuPont was not willing to entrust its Six Sigma training destiny entirely to the Academy. DuPont oversaw every wave of executive, Champion, and Black Belt training on a corporation-wide basis. The eighteen strategic business units and more than eighty business segments within those businesses all needed the right knowledge at the right time. People had to assemble and deliver that knowledge in a compressed schedule.

THE TECHNOLOGY BEHIND TRACKING SUCCESS

DuPont created a Six Sigma information technology (IT) network to develop and deploy hardware and software standards for tracking Six Sigma–related progress. The network was initially led by Dave Andrews, the executive who missed his family ski trip to become one of the first Six Sigma deployment Champions. At the time, Andrews had been working on the company's Y2K preparedness projects (projects associated with the technological hiccups companies expected when the calendar year switched from 1999 to the new century). His new task became to create an IT support structure to be used by executives, Champions, Master Black Belts, and Black Belts throughout DuPont as they managed and implemented Six Sigma.

DuPont considered it critical for IT to be intimately involved in the planning and deployment of Six Sigma. "The IT component is so pervasive that it must be at the table," said Andrews.

Andrews was given four main objectives:

- Develop and refine the SigmaTRAC software, inherited from the Specialty Chemicals people who developed it, to meet the needs of all DuPont businesses and the thousands of users within them.

- Develop a digital dashboard so the corporation could monitor key indicators of Six Sigma performance.
- Configure and deploy laptops and software for use by Six Sigma Black Belts and Green Belts, as well as install a training help desk.
- Design and implement Web- and server-based systems to support the objectives of the other networks (training, finance, HR, and communications).

One of the first steps Andrews took was to form a broader IT network than the existing one, which included a staff of four Champions. He had each of the Champions go to the CIO of their respective businesses and secure an IT person to work with in managing all the particulars of the Six Sigma IT systems within their unit. Andrews also established a steering committee within the larger IT department at DuPont that was solely devoted to refining the SigmaTRAC application.

The core IT systems, and SigmaTRAC and the digital dashboard, were at the heart of DuPont's Six Sigma drive. Around those two systems were two additional systems, called Navigator and MINITAB. Navigator was a repository of Six Sigma materials that could be used as reference material. MINITAB is a statistical software package used for doing simple and complex statistical analysis and graphing.

The digital dashboard was essentially a portal to SigmaTRAC. The technical hierarchy gave DuPont a way to categorize IT systems from a Six Sigma user's point of view.

DuPont set out to install its Six Sigma IT systems in the most efficient, user-friendly, and standardized way possible. The adoption of Six Sigma IT systems was done globally, not through the local business units. When it came to IT, corporate standardization was essential. Predictably, Six Sigma had major ramifications for the entire IT infrastructure of DuPont, affecting its accounting systems, materials planning systems, human resources databases, customer-related IT systems, and PC-based software.

DuPont needed an IT architecture that had the capability and capacity to sufficiently support its ambitious Six Sigma aims. The architecture had to be user-friendly to thousands of employees throughout DuPont, and robust enough to withstand the variable needs and requirements of the local business units.

Specialty Chemicals was the first division at DuPont to create a Six Sigma–related system. At first SigmaTRAC was a PC-based system linked to Lotus Notes. After it was tested and successfully used by Specialty Chemicals, it was migrated to the Web.

"A lot of training had to go on," says Gary Lewis, Specialty Chemicals Champion. "SigmaTRAC runs on a server; Lotus Notes makes up the front end, so people had to be trained on Lotus Notes."

SigmaTRAC uses a linked network of servers, with each strategic business unit able to capture its own project data and organize and report it as desired. In addition, SigmaTRAC could be used to aggregate data according to specific parameters so that all manufacturing project results worldwide could be combined and quantified.

Within a few months of its adoption company-wide, every DuPont business was using SigmaTRAC. Within a year, the details of more than 4,000 Six Sigma projects had been entered into the system. And by the end of the third year (2001), SigmaTRAC was capturing, organizing, collating, segregating, and aggregating data from more than 7,500 projects system-wide. SigmaTRAC became the second most widely used IT system in all of DuPont, behind Lotus Notes. Six Sigma Champions and the corporate officers used it to:

- Provide executives with aggregate project benefits by strategic business unit, by region, or by function
- Show how much money a business unit saved through its Six Sigma projects completed in the current quarter as well as preceding quarters
- Categorize Six Sigma project results
- Monitor the progress of the various projects that impact the lines of responsibility, with each Champion able to look at his or her entire area of responsibility

- Get an aggregate view of the execution of all the Black Belt projects to see how many were under way, what the nature of those projects was, and the dollar impact of those projects
- Record and store the data collected and analyzed during the life span of an individual project, including team member profiles, team meeting agendas and minutes, tools used, the details of a project's progress, conclusions reached, results achieved, and their financial impact
- Organize all administrative and technical aspects related to a project according to the five phases of the Breakthrough Strategy (define, measure, analyze, improve, and control)
- Provide Master Black Belts with the technical information, such as project cycle time data, to effectively support and intervene in projects when necessary

In general, the higher a user is in a given organization at DuPont, the more access that person has to various data and information. For example, the corporate Champion could look at the roll-up of the entire company. A Champion could see the detail in his or her area only, while a Black Belt might only be able to see titles of various projects that were under way.

DuPont set certain policies relating to IT globally:

- Every Black Belt and Project Champion was issued a laptop computer loaded with SigmaTRAC, MINITAB, Navigator, and Lotus Notes.
- The look and feel of the software was standardized across the board.
- Standardized training was provided to all users of SigmaTRAC, MINITAB, and Navigator, along with Six Sigma training.

Executing these IT policies sometimes was difficult, given the varying factors for the individual business units, each one's relations with its suppliers, the volume of product produced and sold, and delivery, timing, and configuration requirements. But while the basic policies were mandated, local business units could supplement them according to their needs. For example, some business units decided to equip their Black Belt laptops with Microsoft Scheduler or Planner or Visio graphics, in addition to the other applications. One unit was using a process-mapping software program and had its people trained in that software. When the corporate standard came down, the group was allowed to keep its software and then merge it with SigmaTRAC, MINITAB, and the others over time.

Andrews's team had to figure out which PC products were necessary for Six Sigma–related work and which should be optional. Then they had to test the software for applicability, negotiate corporate licenses for its use, and get them loaded onto laptops into a standard configuration.

For one wave, they might need twenty laptops configured with the standard Black Belt tool kit, five of which would also need Microsoft Planner. Due to the fast pace at which the initial Black Belts were trained, the demand was often for immediate delivery to a classroom location. Some Black Belt candidates walked into their training session to see their laptops up and running, displaying the words "Hi, welcome to Black Belt training!"

For training and support, the IT network relied on outside vendors. These vendors provided training in basic Microsoft products for those who needed it. Training was generally conducted in advance of a Black Belt class, often on a Sunday before the Monday class. The specialized software programs were taught as part of Champion and Black Belt training.

The IT network's next job was to support the development of a corporate Six Sigma Web site, as well as a server-based Champions network, called S2C2 (Six Sigma Champions collaboration). This network served as a way for Champions to work together across divisions, enhancing problem solving. The IT network collaborated closely with the Communications team to get the site up and running before handing over the entire responsibility of the site to communications. (The contents of this site will be discussed in more detail later in this chapter.)

Andrews outlined several CTQs (critical-to-quality characteristics) for those who spearheaded IT in the context of Six Sigma. Among those CTQs:

- A robust IT infrastructure is an essential condition for Six Sigma success.
- There must be a budget for creating the Six Sigma IT infrastructure.
- IT support people must connect themselves to their internal customers—always listening to their problems, feedback, and needs.

The IT network met formally twice a month during the buildup period and quarterly later. After the initial intense work of installing the Six Sigma IT systems, their ongoing maintenance and improvement became decentralized.

ESTABLISHING THE FINANCE NETWORK

Next, DuPont had to figure out how it would count the financial benefits delivered by Six Sigma. This was the responsibility of the finance network, which was given four objectives:

- Establish a standardized definition of hard payback on Six Sigma projects, along with the metrics that would embody that definition.
- Define and install a system for validating hard Six Sigma savings.
- Develop the course material and train the finance people who would provide the actual validation of Black Belt project savings.
- Complete its own host of Six Sigma–driven projects organization to make dramatic improvements in such core functions as taxation, treasury, auditing, and corporate accounting.

The head of the Six Sigma finance network was Joe Fanelli, who became one of the four corporate functional Champions to serve alongside the eighteen deployment Champions. To achieve the above objectives, one of Fanelli's first moves was to build a finance Six Sigma network, supported by Lotus Notes. He relied on that network to install the Six Sigma financial infrastructure, including validation criteria and the mechanisms by which it would share learning.

The representatives from each strategic business unit who formed the finance network defined the criteria for "hard Six Sigma benefits"—quantifiable enhancements to revenue or reductions in cost or working capital. Such costs could be related to overhead, materials, head count, cycle time, capability, and other factors, but they had to be validated as hard benefits to the income statement (i.e., project savings achieved as a direct result of a Six Sigma project and verified as line-item operational cost reductions or revenue increases for six months).

Cost-related breakthroughs, such as eradicating waste, reducing inventories, correcting process inefficiencies, eliminating defects, decreasing energy consumption, or reducing overhead or labor costs, were the easiest Six Sigma savings to quantify. One project, for example, focused on reducing natural gas consumption in DuPont's bio-based materials business.

Process or operational improvements that would reduce future costs were not counted as hard savings. Nor were projects to improve yield and throughput, which provided more capacity to produce product without additional capital investments. These were not considered hard because they did not impact the bottom line of DuPont. Increases in a factory's capacity, for example, mattered little to the income statement until additional products were actually sold as a result of its increased capacity and registered as actual revenue.

DuPont's global policy was to only count real dollars on its income statement. The finance team installed a system so that all the thousands of projects could be documented in SigmaTRAC in this manner. It also developed a validation process using SigmaTRAC so that the company or an individual unit could consistently confirm and capture all the hard benefits accruing from Black Belt projects.

The financial validation process was made up of two key steps:

- *Initial validation.* A finance specialist worked with a Black Belt or Project Champion to establish baseline performance measures for the project at hand. Those measures were translated into economic terms, to account for the cost of poor quality. The finance person computed the expected savings based on the findings in the analysis phase of the Breakthrough Strategy. If the projection was significant and certain enough, the project proceeded to the improve phase of the Breakthrough Strategy. For example, it would be enough for initial validation if the Black Belt could show that DuPont was overfilling bags of a certain product and that by filling the bag with exactly the right amount, the company could avoid shipping extra product without getting paid for it. This initial validation would be enough to go ahead and do the project knowing exactly how much could be saved.

- *Final validation.* This occurred after the last phase of the Breakthrough Strategy, after a project had been completed for at least six months and after directly traceable financial results had consistently accrued during that time. Such a rigorous final validation process minimized the risk of viewing gains as long-term when they were only short-term in nature. The same example of filling the bags with the right amount shows how the system worked. If a project put in an exact measuring device to deliver exactly the right amount every time, the Black Belt would put the project into the control phase and for six months the financial analyst would watch the savings. After it was proven to be statistically valid and the savings were real, the project would be finally validated. DuPont learned that most projects were finally validated at an amount greater than the initial validation, due to the conservative nature of the analysts.

At DuPont, a certified Six Sigma finance specialist was usually assigned to participate on each Black Belt team, particularly in the early stages of a project, when the risk of making inaccurate financial assumptions was high. There were instances when Black Belt teams created their baseline metrics during the annual down cycle of a seasonal business. Such a baseline would be skewed, and the ensuing project results would be inflated due to seasonality. DuPont's financial specialists prevented this from occurring, and served as a balancing force for maintaining the integrity of Six Sigma financials.

DuPont developed a Six Sigma Financial Analysis course, a four-and-a-half-day program that prepared internal business analysts, who generally work within the strategic business units to support management with budgeting, forecasting, and financial measurement, to perform the role of financial consultant and project validation expert. Eventually, 500 business analysts completed the course and were prepared to function in a Black Belt team setting.

The finance network functioned as a flow-up system, so that business analysts in a particular business unit could forward questions and concerns to their Six Sigma finance representative. If the answer or resolution was clear-cut, the representative addressed it directly. If the issue had wide applicability or if the finance representative didn't have a good answer, it was posted inside Lotus Notes for all eighteen finance network representatives to see and respond to.

Overall, the tone set by the finance network was one in which business analysts were Six Sigma participants, rather than just gatekeepers. The result was that a core of specialists—Black Belts and Six Sigma finance people—spoke the same language. It's an example of how process-focused projects improved the financial position of DuPont.

THE HUMAN RESOURCES NETWORK: CHANGING THE COMPENSATION SYSTEM

When the human resources (HR) network was established in 1999, led by Dennis Broughton, formerly the head of DuPont's Nylon business, the Six Sigma compensation system at DuPont had yet to be established. It quickly became the network's central issue.

DuPont found it beneficial to make compensation a matter of corporate policy and recognition a matter of local autonomy, allowing the latter to be much more fluid. This balance of control and empowerment drove the effective development of leadership at all levels within DuPont's Six Sigma structure. The Six Sigma reward system was covered at some length in Chapter 1. Here, we will explore exactly how they came up with that system.

At the corporate level, the overriding concern was to install reward and recognition enablers in a manner that would energize the Six Sigma initiative. While motivating people was the goal (the Y's), the reward and recognition enablers were the key factors (the X's) by which to achieve that goal. Culturally, they wanted these enablers to send a clear message to all employees that Six Sigma was a corporate strategy that was at DuPont to stay.

The HR team brought in a handful of respected advisors from throughout the HR community in the various DuPont businesses to serve as a decision-making body for guiding the deployment and implementation of HR policy and practice.

At the earliest stages of Six Sigma implementation, compensation issues were limited to a relatively small number of individuals. At the senior executive level, compensation was relatively simple, with about 10 percent of variable pay allocated against achieving the corporation's initial Six Sigma goal. If DuPont realized its initial Six Sigma financial goal, the executives received that portion of their bonus. The deployment Champions were also compensated for their collective contribution to Six Sigma; they were awarded a one-time, discretionary variable compensation by the heads of their respective business units. Each SBU head gave a dollar amount to his or her deployment Champion based on whether the business unit met its overall Six Sigma financial target.

Once Six Sigma had been rolled out corporation-wide, DuPont had to develop a much larger-scale compensation plan to fuel the ongoing empowerment of the initiative. The HR network recommended that the corporation adopt an across-the-board policy for compensating the overwhelming majority of people who were directly or indirectly responsible for Six Sigma deployment and implementation on an ongoing basis.

The system was attached to DuPont's existing compensation system so that everyone already in the variable compensation pool would be eligible for an annual Six Sigma bonus. The office of the chief executive set that amount at 20 percent of each person's available total variable pay. This meant that approximately 5,000 of DuPont's top people would have 20 percent of their variable compensation tied to whether their business unit met its annual Six Sigma goal.

By 2003, all business unit heads were required to commit themselves to capturing 3 percent of their revenue in financial benefit through Six Sigma. If they did, their eligible people would receive that 20 percent of their variable compensation. All the business unit heads designated the 3 percent benchmark as one of their critical tasks for 2003.

The corporate Six Sigma compensation system was based on the reporting numbers in SigmaTRAC. At the end of 2003, the deployment Champions took the total validated Six Sigma project savings for their respective businesses and entered them into the corporation's Six Sigma HR system, which determined the size of the bonus for all eligible people that year. All employees who received a variable compensation that year participated in the 20 percent pool. DuPont also agreed to award team members and Black Belt leaders between 1 and 2 percent of their project's validated savings or revenue.

To level the playing field, so that some business units would not grant more options for the same work as others, the HR network proposed that all Black Belts throughout the corporation would be eligible for stock options upon certification, which was defined as the successful completion of training and the delivery of two projects that together came to more than $350,000 in validated benefit.

The recognition system was much more flexible than the compensation system, allowing different local businesses, functions, plants, and departments to recognize, in their own ways, employees who made significant contributions to achieving Six Sigma goals. The only corporate guideline established was to encourage the business units to recognize Six Sigma people and, in turn, have them encourage all the organizations in their domain to do the same.

For example, the Nylon business held several Black Belt certification events at DuPont's hotel in Delaware. All Nylon Black Belt honorees were brought together from around the world to engage in two days of advanced training. On the evening of the second day, during a fancy dinner, a top DuPont executive addressed the group, offering praise and encouragement.

This prestigious event tended to make a lasting impression on the honorees. Broughton often got notes from Black Belts after such events were over, saying something to the effect that "I've worked for DuPont for seventeen years, and that was the most moving event I've ever been a part of in my entire career. I felt more appreciated and valued than ever before."

Broughton sent a letter to all his Black Belts' spouses and families thanking them for their support and sacrifices. With the letter, Broughton included a certificate giving the Black Belts and their spouses a night on the town.

At the local level, Nylon and the other business units employed many different forms of recognition. Memos from superiors, special plaques, lunches, and congratulatory phone calls from the business unit head were woven into the ways the local business units expressed their thanks. It became common to have Black Belts present their projects to the highest level of local management after the projects passed through final validation. At these meetings DuPont business leaders expressed their appreciation and support for what their Black Belts had done.

In addition to bonuses and recognition, the Nylon business at DuPont instituted a scoring system during training by which Black Belts were evaluated every week. When they demonstrated that they had successfully learned the Six Sigma methodology and tools and properly applied them to their project, a process that usually took about four months, they received a "technical registration" signed by Broughton and the individual Master Black Belt instructors they trained under. It was a way of providing immediate recognition, since formal Black Belt certification typically takes at least a year to achieve. The Black Belts seemed to appreciate the immediate reinforcement after four months of intense training, high expectations, and often painstaking application. It showed they had been able to stand up to the intense pressure of the training process.

One of the most powerful forms of recognition was a promotion. More than three-fourths of the original deployment Champions eventually were promoted to positions of management.

KEEPING 80,000 EMPLOYEES INFORMED

The communications network played an active role in aiding and advising the business units as they established Six Sigma throughout their businesses.

Since DuPont had no corporate Champion with a formal communications background, the leader of the communications network had to be chosen from among the Six Sigma deployment Champions. The person DuPont chose was Mary Ruth Johnson, a longtime DuPonter with a formal background in accounting and business leadership. Johnson was a deployment Champion in the Polyester business.

Johnson's main responsibility was to communicate the global policies and guidelines consistently, clearly, and effectively to DuPont's 80,000-plus employees, explaining the whys and wherefores of Six Sigma. Johnson tried to make clear throughout the company that Six Sigma was not just a program but the way DuPont worked.

But no one was a bigger proponent of spreading the word about Six Sigma than CEO Chad Holliday, who reinforced it at every possible opportunity.

When DuPont's senior leaders first agreed to commit the corporation to full-scale Six Sigma deployment, Holliday wrote a two-page letter articulating what Six Sigma was, why the company was pursuing it, and how he would personally manage its installation and deployment. In part the letter read:

> I'm confident that this business management process will deliver not only significant bottom line impact to DuPont but will create a culture that will better define how we do our work. Six Sigma is not a program

of the month; it is a key part of how we will do our business well into the next century. It is the foundation that will enable us to achieve our mission of sustainable growth.

In a follow-up letter Holliday wrote several months later, he told employees:

It's been three months since I last talked to you about Six Sigma. The one thought that comes to my mind is that we're off to a fast start. We selected and trained 23 Six Sigma Champions, one from each SBU, as well as finance, information technology, operations and corporate research. These Champions are working with their leadership teams to take each SBU through Six Sigma training.

As of this writing, we have sent Specialty Chemicals, White Pigments, P&E, Nylon, P&IP, Fluoroproducts, Polyester and Dacron through this leadership training. These SBU's are naming project Champions and Black Belts, and are sending them to specific training. Remaining SBU's will start the process by September, and we'll have over 600 Black Belts by the end of the year.

I look forward to learning the details of each project. As we build a database of results, we will share it across the company. As we strive for sustainable growth, the tools of discipline and business processes, Six Sigma will firmly establish our horizon and position delivering solid financial results, enabling our leaps to horizon two and three. I appreciate your support for this critical journey.

These kinds of communications, along with all the other e-mails and documents, fixed Six Sigma in the minds and consciousness of all DuPont employees. Holliday also conducted town meetings via live video broadcasts with all employees globally. Holliday used the town meeting format quarterly after corporate earnings were released to give staff members the chance to ask questions about whatever was on their minds. Here are some of the questions asked by employees, along with Holliday's responses, at the time the company launched Six Sigma. Note his focus on the Six Sigma methodology.

Do we see Six Sigma presently returning to the company what you expected?

More, more. I visited GE, I visited Allied, I went to the Six Sigma Academy. I saw everything that everybody was doing, and what I've seen is that DuPont has just taken to this better than any other place. And that's absolutely no exaggeration. I'm usually very complimentary of DuPonters, but I'll guarantee you we are doing it. . . .

I thought that Six Sigma would do a lot to improve our working capital, reduce our costs, but I just didn't visualize what it could do on the growth side. And I think the greatest potential might be in . . . growth. . . . So I'm quite encouraged about what Six Sigma is going to do. It's a great technology, we have to keep working, we have to get better, get more people trained, get more people working in teams.

With regard to the financial performance of DuPont, what decisions have you made during your tenure as CEO that you're most proud of? Can we learn from these decisions and improve our financial performance going forward so we can take advantage of the economy when it comes back?

In a company as broad as ours, with 18,000 customers, 2,000 trademarks, and I could go on and on with the complexity, what you find is that most of the decisions are made by everybody else, not the CEO. And what will make us strong is those other people being right. But I, along with some others, do make one-tenth of 1 percent of the decisions that are pretty important, too. The decision to focus our company on growth, the decision to go forward and add new technology to this company, I'm very proud of because it wasn't easy. And you get criticized when you bring in new technology and it doesn't always pay off right away.

I used to think about how Mr. Carothers, inventor of nylon, must have felt in some of those early days. We've been focusing on productivity, Six Sigma, and how taking Six Sigma across the company was a big decision, because we all like to do things our own way. I've learned in my 30 years that we all like to do it our own way. But if we use one common way to look at the data—not politics, not the organizational position but real data to make decisions—and if we use that data with teams of people across this company, what a difference that can make.

You closed out your comments about growth, and you've been talking a lot about growth. What do you think we can do to get growth rates that are challenging the organization to deliver?

We've got to go about it differently. It's a competitive world out there, and if we're only selling the same products we've been selling for 30 years, it's not going to be right for us. But if we keep looking at how we can add to that product with knowledge, this is how we can grow. The product is a key part of the offering, but we've got to put in more as we go forth. And you tie that to Six Sigma top-line growth where we get the data and do it right, we can get there.

How can each of us contribute?

Eliminate waste. We have made great progress over the years eliminating waste across our company, but we must continue doing that. There are Six Sigma programs going on throughout our company to eliminate waste—participate in those. It is unbelievable what 90,000 people can do, all saving a little bit a day, and how it can add up over time. So don't think what you do is not important.

One of the communication team's first tasks was to develop statements about Six Sigma that anyone anywhere in DuPont could use to communicate with their various constituents. Because of the tension between global and local needs, the communications team had to make sure everyone delivered a consistent message, while allowing that message to be adapted when necessary to local concerns.

The imperative for consistency was nowhere more crucial than at the very top of DuPont, where management made a point of discussing some aspect of Six Sigma in every major communication. Their goal was to inject Six Sigma into every organization, channel, and aspect of doing business throughout DuPont.

The communications team recommended to senior executives that top management at every opportunity reinforce that:

1. Six Sigma is important and will touch everyone at DuPont. It is a fundamental change in the way the company works.
2. Six Sigma is an accelerated, proven process for improving DuPont's business.
3. Six Sigma has never failed when implemented properly. If DuPont stays the course, it will be successful.
4. Six Sigma may have the solution to that chronic problem employees face at work.
5. Seek out Black Belts, Champions, Master Black Belts; begin a conversation with them.
6. Find out about Six Sigma projects, DMAIC, and the Breakthrough Strategy. It is the way line-of-sight work gets done.
7. Six Sigma is not a magic panacea. Its success is the result of disciplined hard work. It reduces defects and will improve the quality of DuPont's business and processes.

The communications team developed PowerPoint slides and videos for use throughout DuPont to build awareness and educate the workforce about Six Sigma.

One corporate video was based on an address General Electric CEO Jeffrey R. Immelt made to DuPont's senior leaders. Immelt talked about GE's general experience with Six Sigma, Design for Six Sigma (DFSS), and the role of Six Sigma in driving overall business growth.

DuPont produces a highly read e-mail newsletter called "DuPont Network News" that goes out to everyone in the corporation with access to the Internet. "Network News" carried messages about Six Sigma to DuPont and its people. Next, all of DuPont's strategic business units integrated information about Six Sigma in their communications.

The Polyester business, for example, produced and distributed a separate quarterly Six Sigma newsletter listing training schedules, recognizing people who became Six Sigma certified or who completed a Black Belt project, summarizing project successes, providing educational material on how to use various Six Sigma tools, and the like. Tapes & Films, another DuPont business, integrated similar material into its regular "monthly report." Still other businesses, such as iTechnology, created their own Six Sigma Web sites.

The communication network conceptualized and developed a Six Sigma corporate Web site communications network to provide news, information, inspiration, and education. The site highlighted pictures of the deployment Champions, a list of all the Project Champions with their contact information, a glossary of Six Sigma terms, and other informative content.

While the Six Sigma message was being successfully communicated within DuPont, it also needed to be conveyed to such outside audiences as shareholders, the media, customers, and suppliers. In particular, shareholders and Wall Street analysts were interested in Six Sigma from the standpoint of return on investment. Given that Six Sigma is by nature a vehicle for improving financial performance, it became necessary to develop and deliver key messages to these audiences on an ongoing basis throughout the initiative.

Chad Holliday and his corporate staff decided that it was much better, and safer, to talk about Six Sigma with these groups only in the context of what Six Sigma had *done* for DuPont, not in terms of what they expected it to do. In other words, internally the company was open, visible, passionate, informative, and forward-looking. Externally, it was cautious, selective, and circumspect, referring to what it had accomplished as opposed to what it was undertaking.

One of the earliest statements DuPont made to the financial community about Six Sigma was on the cover of its 1999 annual report. The cover simply listed DuPont's three major strategic focuses, the last of which was "productivity gains using Six Sigma." In other words, the company was not shy about publicizing its commitment to Six Sigma. After all, Six Sigma was a key corporate strategy alongside DuPont's drive to become an integrated science company and a company that made its living through knowledge-intensive products and businesses. But DuPont didn't talk about specific goals or targets.

By virtue of including it on the cover of its 1999 annual report, DuPont was asserting that Six Sigma was a key vehicle for improving productivity and reducing costs. The report suggested that Six Sigma would become more focused over time on growth and revenue enhancement, consistent with DuPont's forward-looking emphasis on economic value creation and sustainable growth.

THE NETWORKING NETWORK

One final network task was to create a global community that could work through important problems and issues and share Six Sigma learning across organizational boundaries.

Among the Six Sigma networks at DuPont was one set up for Black Belts, one for Master Black Belts, and one for deployment Champions. The deployment Champions, for example, met quarterly for two days. The Master Black Belt network met once every other month. And Black Belts met as needed within the structure and requirements of their local organizations.

Within these networks, smaller communities sprang up. For example, several DuPont businesses created a network of Black Belts assigned to one of DuPont's local plants in LaPorte, Texas. The Black Belts working in the plant benefited from each other's insights and solutions. Such smaller, more homogeneous networks can become a way to pass on highly specialized learning and replicate solutions to common problems.

The overall idea was to create as many networks within the larger ones as necessary to ensure Six Sigma self-sufficiency. DuPont's intent was that there would be a forum for various groups to interact with each other, based not on their organizational affiliation but on their Six Sigma affinity.

With enough collective learning, collaboration, knowledge transfer, and professional development, DuPont would no longer need to depend on outside sources to sustain its Six Sigma initiative.

Deployment Champions, Project Champions, Master Black Belts, Black Belts, and Green Belts all heavily participated in the various Six Sigma networks, despite the fact that they were housed and run by the business units.

DuPont also set up a corporate intranet, accessible only to DuPont employees, to allow the free flow of information across businesses in a message-board type of environment. Accessed through Lotus Notes, it is today used by anyone who is a Six Sigma Champion or Black Belt. A Project Champion in France who needs to improve the quality of raw material might post a question about what project selection criteria to consider. Other Champions, Black Belts, or Master Black Belts can then respond with their experience, thoughts, and ideas.

The system ultimately functions as a promotional site for Six Sigma, more than a strict tracking or data-management site. It is a place where people go to look up Six Sigma terms, find out what a Black Belt is and does, read about a particular success, get the information and help they need, or simply become more educated about Six Sigma.

THE MASTER BLACK BELT NETWORK

By the end of 2002, there were 254 Master Black Belts in DuPont (up from 200 in 2001 and 147 in 2000). This growing community had access to a separate Master Black Belt network, established in 2001 in order to:

- Promote the development and improvement of Six Sigma methods, tools, and practices
- Support the training network by maintaining the Six Sigma curriculum and determining the best way to teach it
- Leverage effective projects, processes, and practices across business lines

- Support the continuing education and development needs of Master Black Belts
- Foster two-way communication between Project Champions and Master Black Belts

The Master Black Belt network became a mechanism for sifting through best practices, organizing them, and distributing them when and where they were needed.

THE TOP-LINE GROWTH NETWORK

A final network, called the top-line growth network, was established two years into the implementation of Six Sigma. Its emergence represented a shift in thinking about Six Sigma and its application. As discussed in Chapter 2, prior to 2001, DuPont's Six Sigma focused on cost and capacity improvements. But in the process of systematically applying the Breakthrough Strategy, and as a by-product of learning Six Sigma through application, Black Belts began to take on top-line growth projects that were less tangible and thus more difficult to define, measure, analyze, improve, and control. For example:

- One Black Belt reduced monthly average invoice undercharges by 70 percent in North America—resulting in an annual revenue increase of $1.5 million.
- A Black Belt reduced the cycle time for metals analysis testing from an average of eleven days to an average of four days.
- A Black Belt project tackled the problem of how to grow revenue for Lannate, an insecticide, in the Kyushu district of Japan.

When growth was targeted as a new strategic thrust, a highly respected sales or marketing person was chosen from each of DuPont's eighteen businesses to create a top-line growth network. This group was then trained in DMAIC and, in some cases, design for Six Sigma. The DuPont line was that the company wanted not just to meet customer requirements with good products at a good price but to enhance the value of their relationship through a knowledge-intensive exchange. If the customer had a problem in her business, then DuPont had a problem in its business. If a customer was struggling with a given performance characteristic and a DuPont product was involved somewhere in the value chain, DuPont would send over a Black Belt to help get it figured out. DuPont would solve its customers' problems, at no cost, and in the process secure their goodwill and make their operations more profitable.

For example, a Champion might figure out that the reason a customer was not purchasing more of a DuPont product was capacity constraints. DuPont helped the customer remove those constraints, thereby enabling the customer to use more of DuPont's product to fulfill its stepped-up production capacity.

It became the equivalent of giving customers a rebate in the form of intellectual capital—offering hard dollar savings for their business in exchange for buying DuPont products. And as Champions and Black Belts became involved with customers, the vision of top-line growth became clear and tangible.

While defects could be reduced only to zero, there was no limit on how much DuPont could grow its revenue. It was this sense of possibility that drove the TLG network to adopt Six Sigma to help solve its customers' problems.

DuPont saw connecting with its customers as attempting to help them understand what the miracles of science could do for them. It meant breaking these needs down into specifics by identifying, optimizing, and validating the critical X's related to meeting customers' requirements. For example, rather than saying a customer needed a new, clear coat of paint, the performance coating team would establish all of the properties needed to formulate a new product to meet the customers' specific needs. The difference in the approach is to drill down to the individual attributes and understand the interdependences so that the right formulations can be created.

Through the use of DFSS (Design for Six Sigma), through solving customer problems with the Breakthrough Strategy, and through the use and standardization of tools such as quality function deployment (QFD), DuPont could figure out what made their customers tick, and could, by helping them, increase its own revenue.

To this end, the TLG network assembled a top-line growth tool kit—an intranet-based package of materials aimed at helping marketing and salespeople understand what Six Sigma is, why it could generate top-line growth, and how certain methods and tools could be employed in the interest of generating more revenue.

One DuPont business took up the revenue-generating cause by conducting a Black Belt project aimed at improving sales force effectiveness. The in-house study looked at specific data for Nomex, a fire-resistant fiber used in industrial and fire service applications, under specific conditions and circumstances. The essence of the project was to sift through forty-three possible reasons why a deal was closed and an order completed. The Black Belt project team figured out which of the reasons were "critical," or exerted the most leverage in getting deals closed quickly.

For example, one critical X was entertaining the customer. Project data revealed that if salespeople entertain the customer, they have an 86 percent chance of closing the deal. If they don't entertain the customer, their chance of closing the deal drops to 43 percent. But if entertainment is key, what kind of entertainment is best? The data showed there was no significant difference between taking a customer to a NASCAR race, buying him or her lunch, or having a picnic under a big shade tree. It wasn't really the kind of entertainment that mattered; it was the relationship—trust and bonding—that ensued.

The output of the project was a little pocket brochure with twelve things for people to do while selling Nomex. These were the critical variables that, if well done, improved the Nomex sales hit rate. Nine months later, the average sales per salesperson for Nomex had risen by 110 percent. On an individual basis, some salespeople's revenues went up more than 500 percent.

The top-line growth network drove the emergence of Six Sigma as a tactic for achieving sustainable growth, DuPont's overriding mission. They did this by getting the word out about the possibilities involved with top-line growth to all corners of DuPont.

ONE DUPONT BUSINESS: THE CASE OF NYLON

Nylon's Six Sigma journey began immediately after its deployment Champion, Dennis Broughton, returned from training in Scottsdale. Before being chosen to lead the Nylon Six Sigma charge, Broughton was the operations director and plant manager of the Victoria, Texas, plant, which was then, and still is today, one of DuPont's largest and most competitive manufacturing facilities, supplying more than 2 billion pounds of products annually to other DuPont businesses, as well as to many outside customers.

The first task facing Broughton was committing to a financial target for savings in the Nylon business. Based on the size of the business, the appropriate number would have been $120 million. But Nylon's leaders didn't consider $120 million to accurately reflect the amount of opportunity. While he didn't have any hard evidence of a higher or lower cost of poor quality than other DuPont businesses, Broughton was convinced that a first-phase target of 4 percent of revenue was achievable. This made the savings target for Nylon $180 million through 2000, a period of about 18 months into the deployment.

If $180 million was the goal, then Nylon needed 180 Black Belts, or one Black Belt for every sixty-seven employees, a more concentrated dose of process leaders than the normal 1:100 ratio. Broughton believed the commitment to greater Black Belt density could only help its chances of generating breakthrough operational power. The hard part was figuring out how to allocate Black Belts, training, projects, and support among 12,000 Nylon employees in four separate operating units with twenty-one locations worldwide.

Broughton and Nylon's leader, Don Johnson, relied on their existing knowledge and performance data to disperse the Black Belt positions.

Their chief concern was to allocate slots according to a logical scheme for addressing known operational problems, such as improvements in throughput, facility uptime, process yields, and product quality, while making sure that Black Belts were distributed proportionately across all implementation cells.

Aside from management, sales, and finance facilities, most of the sites in Nylon were manufacturing plants, located throughout North and South America, Asia, and Europe. Some locations existed to manufacture products and provide support to a specific sub-business, while others supported many businesses and sub-businesses. Some plants manufactured products and provided support to a specific market segment, such as carpet yarns, while others supported multiple segments, such as industrial and apparel.

Johnson and Broughton began dividing Black Belt slots among the sites, considering the nature and intensity of work at each, the extent of implicit opportunity, and the potential magnitude of financial impact. They tried to be prescriptive about how many Black Belts each Nylon location, region, and business would develop. For example, two large, complex intermediates plants in Texas were allocated a larger number of Black Belts due to the volume of production and the costs of raw materials used in the process.

"We believed the critical X's, the things we had to do, were to pick good people, give them world-class training, demand that the projects have a financial payoff of greater than $200,000, and provide discipline and robust follow-up after training to see that the projects stayed on track," says Broughton. That translated into sixty-five Black Belts from the intermediates business, fifty-seven from the flooring business, thirty-seven from apparel, and twenty-four from industrial. The total number was 183—three more than Johnson and Broughton originally thought they would need.

The configuration of the Nylon implementation cells formed the structural basis for monitoring and managing the initiative. Johnson and Broughton reasoned that if Six Sigma was the way to do business, then it should correspond perfectly with the existing business structure. That led to eleven implementation cells, one for each of Nylon's business segments, each led by a Project Champion:

- North America: one Champion from each of Nylon's four business areas (intermediates, flooring, apparel, industrial) overseeing manufacturing-oriented Six Sigma projects, and one Champion based in Delaware overseeing all transactional projects for all four businesses
- Europe: one Champion from each of the four businesses overseeing manufacturing-oriented projects in Europe, and one Champion based in Geneva overseeing all transactional projects for all four businesses with a presence in Europe
- South America: one project Champion overseeing all projects, both manufacturing and transactional in nature, enacted in that region of the world
- Asia: no project Champion designated, because there was only one Nylon manufacturing plant for one business in the entire region

For the next ninety days, Johnson and Broughton officially launched the Nylon Six Sigma initiative by traveling to each of the eleven implementation locations, to galvanize the operational and process leaders around Six Sigma as a key strategic thrust for Nylon.

They spoke with the groups of the need for Six Sigma, the intensity and pace with which it would be installed, the basic concepts of breakthrough, and the terminology of Six Sigma. They also discussed how much money each segment would be expected to contribute to the $180 million target. They required each cell to earmark one of its best senior people to become the Project Champion, and several of its very best managers or professionals to become Black Belts.

With 180 Black Belts, each working on an average of two projects simultaneously, and an average of five members per team, as many as 1,800 (15 percent) of Nylon's 12,000 employees were actively working on Six Sigma projects in the early phase of the deployment. This percentage would increase when Green Belt deployment began in year two. Black belts trained their team members in the methodologies and tools to the extent required to allow the team to complete the project work.

With approval from the corporate level, Nylon instituted a reward program distributing 1 percent of project savings back to project team members. For example, if a project saved $400,000, the team would have $4,000 to split among themselves, but with rules:

1. Project savings must be officially validated by finance after approximately six months of realized project savings.
2. The Master Black Belt mentor, Champion, and/or Process Owner must recommend what percentage of the overall award should go to the Black Belt or project leader (Master Black Belt).
3. The Black Belt project team leader recommends what percentage of the remaining dollars should be allocated to each individual team member based on the extent of their individual contributions.
4. A request form is completed, which triggers a financial review process.
5. Checks are cut, and a senior business manager and Champion call a meeting of the team, thank them for their work, tell them how much they are appreciated, and hand each of them a check.

One team of eight was awarded $140,000 for completing a very impressive project, which resolved a long-standing process problem in a chemical reaction step.

In other cases, Black Belts received individual awards greater than $30,000, and team members received individual awards of more than $20,000 per individual. The average team awards ended up being in the range of $4,000 to $8,000 per team, with average project savings of $400,000.

"Saying thank you can be very hollow, but everyone knows how much an organization hates to write a check," says Broughton. "So people felt,

if you write a check, 'I know you really appreciated what I did.' "
Awarding team members went a long way toward softening the impact
of an increased workload.

Actual implementation of Six Sigma at Nylon began in June 1999 with
two waves of thirty Black Belts each, and two more waves of thirty each
in August. While these first two waves were generally performing well in
their respective locations, Broughton noticed certain pockets of weakness
and found that there was too much variability in the skill sets and competency levels of Black Belts. Broughton then standardized all Black Belt
curricula across all business segments within Nylon. Nylon enhanced its
voice-of-the-customer module with examples from service and transactional environments, such as credit, sourcing, engineering, and contract
services, and it added more training course examples related to sales and
marketing after top-line growth became a corporate priority.

While deploying Six Sigma, Broughton was also considering the first
rounds of projects for the Black Belts to tackle. He turned the actual job
of project selection over to the network of new Master Black Belts.

"Don and I did not, and in fact could not, know where all the big financial opportunities were in our business," says Broughton. "We had to rely
on the dispersed knowledge of 12,000 employees to find the problems."
As long as projects saved at least $200,000, they were deemed by Broughton
to be sufficiently valuable to assign a Black Belt. Examples included increasing the throughputs of various production units that were in sold-
out positions, improving the yield and quality of yarn offerings, reducing
energy consumption, and improving product distribution costs.

Broughton held regular conference calls with all his Champions to discuss progress and problems and to provide support. Topics included project identification and selection, financial validation processes, Black Belt
and Green Belt curriculum development and revisions, and, most important, Black Belt selection and productivity.

He met three times a year with the eleven Champions, though he regularly monitored Six Sigma activity and results through SigmaTRAC.
Broughton developed a simple but effective communications plan, includ-

ing Nylon's own Six Sigma intranet Web site as a resource for those involved and those who wanted to learn more.

Nylon made it a policy to include at least one article on Six Sigma in every monthly newsletter. The articles educated people about the concepts and tools of Six Sigma and featured Six Sigma success stories, each of which described a recent successful Black Belt project and recognized the Black Belt and team members. Six Sigma was part of the agenda anytime an operations executive visited a plant or location.

In its second full year of Six Sigma implementation, the overall size of Nylon had been reduced, as two of its four major business segments were moved to other organizations as part of a strategic restructuring initiative. While the intermediates and flooring segments remained, the apparel segment was combined with the Lycra business, and the industrial products segment was moved to a joint venture. Even in the midst of this major organizational change, Nylon continued the momentum of Six Sigma. Using the same density formula of about one Black Belt per 67 employees, Nylon retained 120 of its 183 original Black Belts and targeted $120 million in Six Sigma benefits for 2001.

In 2001, DuPont added the top-line growth plank to its Six Sigma strategic platform, focusing on areas such as sales and marketing. "We started driving top-line growth, but it wasn't a big deal," says Broughton. "We already had Black Belts working in marketing and sales, so it was just a matter of giving these folks a revenue project instead of a cost project." The next year, Broughton's organization validated $215 million in direct benefits from Six Sigma projects, $65 million greater than its target of $150 million.

Within sub-businesses of Nylon, there could be many Six Sigma projects at one location. For example, one business segment, Nylon Intermediates, Specialties, and Polymers (NISP), which produces intermediate chemicals and polymers used to make carpet fiber, air bags, industrial yarn, and other products, had been trying for many years to reduce manufacturing costs. As more costs were cut, it became more difficult to find more costs to cut, especially in a tough economy.

Mark McPherson, one of Nylon's eleven Project Champions and a former operations manager who had worked under Broughton, was given responsibility for projects that would be executed by thirty-one Black Belts for $31 million in hard benefits to NISP, about 20 percent of the total goal for Nylon. The task of identifying projects and Black Belts to do those projects was handed to McPherson during Project Champion training with the Six Sigma Academy. After spending five days learning about Six Sigma, McPherson held a session with the three site managers of the plants to select the initial projects. The guiding principle during this process was that only people who were intimately involved in various operations, such as key operations and technology managers and scientists, were qualified to identify viable project opportunities.

The hard criteria for selecting these first projects were:

- Each targeted project had to deliver $200,000 in pretax benefits.
- Each project had to be manageable in scope.
- Each had to address a defect, which NISP defines as a problem that has yet to be solved. This could come in the form of an operational issue failing to meet manufacturing specifications or customer expectations.

McPherson ultimately selected fourteen Black Belts for the Victoria, Texas, plant; twelve for the Sabine River Works plant in Orange, Texas; three for the Maitland plant in Ontario, Canada; and two who were dedicated to R&D projects housed at the Delaware business office.

The Victoria, Texas, plant had operations devoted to making Adi-pure, DuPont's brand of an organic acid that is used for adhesives, coatings, synthetic lubricants, and hydraulic fluids. There were five Black Belts working on improving the process throughput, yield, quality, uptime, and energy consumption of the area.

Four Black Belts were assigned just to the operations of HMD, a chemical used in epoxy curing agents, petroleum additives, resins, adhesives, inks, fibers, scale and corrosion inhibitors, and water-treatment chemicals.

Here the Black Belts focused on increasing throughput, reducing raw material and catalyst consumption, reducing energy consumption, and improving product quality and uniformity.

They also devoted two Black Belts to improving the processes and operations that made the intermediates used to produce adhesives, corrosion inhibitors, fibers, polyester coatings, and epoxy resins.

Within its Adi-pure acid and HMD operations, projects focused on improving yield and decreasing energy consumption, while in C-12 operations, Black Belts focused on capacity and yield improvement, with a secondary focus on reducing energy consumption. One of the C-12 projects addressed the problems associated with a certain impurity that was forcing a process to run more slowly than it otherwise could. While the process was not producing defects, it was running at reduced rates to compensate for the impurity. By reducing the level of impurity and its variability, the plant was able to increase production.

C-12 is a high-performance intermediate chemical used in synthetic lubricants, coatings, adhesives, pharmaceuticals, and fragrances.

In all, the Victoria plant completed twenty-nine Black Belt projects in these three areas during the first eighteen months of Six Sigma.

Within NISP and the Victoria plant, certain projects were also focused on improving purchasing, accounting, inventory management, engineering, maintenance, and so on. One such project homed in on the cost associated with maintaining rail cars for shipping material out of the plant. Through benchmarking data and a failure mode analysis, it was determined that the time-based rail car maintenance schedule was too frequent, resulting in higher costs. The maintenance schedule was changed to one that was based on actual rail car mileage logged, resulting in $400 million in savings.

Another project was enacted on behalf of the Victoria plant by a Black Belt in the R&D group in Delaware. A business such as NISP has to constantly make sure the catalysts it uses are the best for the given application. There are processes and equipment involved in doing so, and both vary to an extent that impacts the validity and reliability of conclusions.

This project did not produce any immediately recognizable dollar savings; it fell more into the category of future savings or cost avoidance. Therefore, while it was positive, it did not count toward McPherson's $31 million target. The idea within Nylon was that such projects were undeniably good for business and for customers, but they could not be counted as hard, immediate savings for the purpose of tracking Six Sigma impact.

Project selection and execution was sometimes a painful and difficult process. At times, people would resist the idea that they could improve their operations any more than they already had, especially without any capital investment. It was hard for them even to conceive that there might be some unrealized opportunity in the inner workings of their processes and operations.

But McPherson helped them work through their resistance and, while he didn't prescribe projects, he did ask managers and process owners to tell him what was most important and what they were having the most trouble with. The organization then set out to determine which could be translated into projects that met a minimum requirement of $200,000 in payback.

There were also cases in which certain projects had to be reduced in scope or abandoned altogether when data revealed that the financial value of the improvement opportunity didn't justify the resource commitment. But the process worked, and McPherson and the Black Belts exceeded their $31 million target contribution.

ONE DUPONT PROJECT: QUALITY CONTROL

When it comes to paint, the DuPont SmartPaint symbol stands for quality ingredients, high standards, and stringent quality control through world-class technological processes. When customers buy paints with the DuPont SmartPaint symbol, they are assured high performance and quality. They can expect decorating to be easier because DuPont SmartPaint co-branded products have superior adhesion to interior walls, woodwork, and interior metal surfaces, even radiators.

However, DuPont neither manufactures nor distributes paint under its DuPont SmartPaint brand. Independent producers make the paints and other firms distribute and sell it. All that DuPont sells are the white pigments that go into the paint made by the independent suppliers. DuPont sets the performance standards, monitors production, and tests the product for compliance. DuPont also provides scientific capability and quality assurance in exchange for brand royalties.

All this was fine until certain DuPont SmartPaint colors sold by the UK home-improvement chain B&Q under their B&Q Colours brand started fading or changing color when exposed to extreme heat. This wasn't good for customers, and it wasn't good for DuPont either, given its reputation as a leader in scientific solutions. To make matters worse, at the time the paint-fading issue came to light, DuPont was planning a major launch of new paints with similar characteristics, which meant that they might have had the fading problem as well. To maintain the integrity of the DuPont SmartPaint brand, the fading problem had to be fixed fast.

This DuPont SmartPaint problem occurred right when Dave Mukoda, market development manager and chemical engineer, became a Black Belt—and it was one of his first projects. Why were certain colors changing when subjected to excess heat—coming off, for example, a radiator? This was the question Mukoda and his team set out to answer.

Mukoda had been part of the original team that launched the DuPont SmartPaint brand, so he knew its chemistry and its customers. He'd started in R&D, worked in manufacturing, and then moved to the Coatings Technical Services organization in support of Ti-Pure titanium dioxide customers. In this role, Mukoda had many responsibilities, not the least of which was to solve customer problems. If for any reason DuPont's product fell short of customer expectations, or entitlement value, Mukoda was involved. For the six years prior to becoming a Black Belt, Mukoda solved complicated quality problems for the titanium technologies group, working with customers in Europe, Russia, Japan, the United Kingdom, North America, and South America.

"My job was to ensure DuPont products possessed more value than those offered by the competition, and to make sure customers understood this," says Mukoda. Sometimes Mukoda helped customers figure out how to use less DuPont product to accomplish the same operational objective. Other times he helped them improve their designed experiments and testing methods so they could properly assess the quality of DuPont products. Customers frequently came to Mukoda because he had a reputation for helping them create more value using DuPont knowledge and products.

Mukoda had functioned like a Black Belt before becoming one, and he already had a good handle on the use of statistics in conquering the technicalities of quality and performance problems. As part of his Black Belt training, Mukoda worked closely with John Miller, a DuPont statistician who helped him with his heavy statistical lifting. "Statistics is a lot of compounded calculations," says Mukoda. "Before Six Sigma, I would spend maybe two weeks with John, but now maybe I spend about four hours with him for any given Black Belt project."

Black Belt training made Mukoda more capable of recognizing certain types of problems and gave him the tools for their remedies, including software that does all his number crunching. "Once you automate this, and you learn the rule sets of which data goes with which tools, you don't need as much professional statistical help," says Mukoda.

Mukoda's project of fixing the fading paint entailed a number of analytical breakthroughs leading to a solution. The fading problem was first identified in June 2001, via customer complaints. B&Q had its own quality system that was investigating the matter when Mukoda was called in to help.

"We had an independent lab in London test the paint and found that yes, there was a real problem here," says Mukoda. "We looked at what it was being painted on, like a wall, and we ran experiments to determine if the problem was caused by an interaction with what it was being painted onto."

The DuPont laboratories had to develop a test to reproduce the fading on a faster basis. So they created a process of baking the painted material. Using this process, they tested the paint on glass and found that certain colors of the paints still faded. This eliminated the interaction between the paint with other materials, such as walls or wallpaper, as a potential cause.

Mukoda's team determined that fading was a problem with only three of the nine primary pigments used to make all the different DuPont SmartPaint colors. The group then conducted many statistical experiments to find the problematic variables that caused these certain pigments to fade, such as light exposure, surface temperature, and type of surface.

Paint is made of pigment and resin, which holds the pigment to the wall. The resin is what gives DuPont SmartPaint its superior qualities. Mukoda found that when the paint resin was heated to certain temperatures on certain surfaces, it interacted with the three pigments to cause fading.

Mukoda never really discovered exactly how the pigments and the resin interacted to cause the problem, but it didn't matter. Once he figured out the conditions under which the problem was occurring, they could quickly work toward a solution. Since the resin was so integral to the quality of the paint and the properties DuPont promises to customers, it made sense to replace the three problematic pigments with others that were more resistant to resin interaction under high-temperature conditions. "Once we found the problem, the solution was fairly easy," says Mukoda. "We simply asked the paint manufacturer to come up with three pigments that would work with our resin." DuPont then had to create paint with the three replacement pigments and test those under the same conditions to ensure that they would not fade as well. The issue was totally resolved by August, two months after the problem was identified.

During all this testing, B&Q had stopped selling the fading paint, virtually halting all revenue to DuPont from the product line. In addition, an entirely new product line set to launch had been at risk, to the tune of almost $1 million a year. Total Six Sigma revenue—that is, sales that could now occur because of the fix—came to $1.8 million a year.

CHAPTER 4

DUPONT SIGMA AT THE BUSINESS LEVEL

Although DuPont took great pains to properly organize for its Six Sigma initiative and create a corporate environment that would encourage its acceptance, introducing it to the rest of its employees was another challenge altogether.

To the outside world, DuPont appears to be a single company, with revenues of $25 billion. In reality, it is a compilation of many more or less autonomous parts. Its businesses have revenues that range from $500 million to $4 billion, and each business unit or division has anywhere from 500 to 8,000 employees. As noted earlier, each business unit is run as if it were a separate company. What each business has in common, though, is a firm commitment to DuPont's core values: safety, health, and the environment; integrity and high ethical standards; and a culture of treating people with fairness and respect. Each business unit also pushes authority and accountability as far down each chain of command as possible. DuPont approached Six Sigma the same way, with the goal of getting each of its people to take Six Sigma personally.

While the general implementation template of Six Sigma was set by corporate headquarters, each business unit adapted Six Sigma according to its own unique trajectory. As described earlier, leaders from each DuPont business attended a week of Six Sigma training. Following that, the business units set their individual goals. Each session was attended by the business unit's president, vice president, and general manager, and his or her direct reports—typically ten to fifteen people representing all functions and geographical regions. When the savings goals of each of the divisions were combined, the total contribution was $920 million, just $80 million short of the $1 billion in savings that CEO Chad Holliday had targeted.

With this $920 million goal DuPont was on its way to progressing from a company that operated according to the status quo to one that was set on adopting sweeping change.

As all corporations intuitively know, it is one thing to institute strategies and issue global directives from up high, but another to enact those directives where real people live and work. The localized stories of embracing Six Sigma are the real stories of change, because they tell how Six Sigma created one breakthrough here and one breakthrough there throughout DuPont. As a result, Six Sigma changed the way the work got done at all levels—the process level, the operations level, and the business level.

TAKING SIX SIGMA PERSONALLY

The key to successfully adopting Six Sigma at any level is to take Six Sigma personally. No one can delegate the responsibility for leading Six Sigma to someone else, and no one can lead a corporate initiative that he or she believes lacks business power. At DuPont, we simply had to be deeply convinced that Six Sigma was the right initiative to undertake before we committed a good portion of our lives and careers to it. As the Champion of Six Sigma at DuPont corporation-wide, I had to take Six Sigma personally before I could help to install Six Sigma properly.

Each of DuPont's strategic businesses was run by a team of executives whom Chad Holliday and I knew could benefit from taking Six Sigma personally themselves. They would be responsible for installing Six Sigma in their business unit, and they would be accountable for the results generated by their Champions and Black Belts. We had to work with the leaders of each business to:

- Inform them how the corporation would actively pursue Six Sigma, and make it clear that no business would be exempt

- Request that the top leadership team of each business or unit commit itself to realizing a designated part of the total corporate Six Sigma goal
- Make it clear that the business-level executive teams were wholly responsible for realizing their respective Six Sigma financial targets
- Train the business unit team so that they could be successful within the confines of DuPont's corporate policies and procedures
- Provide them with the ideas, structure, systems, knowledge, methods, and tools they would need to be successful
- Empower them with the autonomy needed to effectively implement Six Sigma in accordance with their unique circumstances and needs

Chad Holliday made it clear to DuPont's top 200 business leaders that he was completely committed to an ambitious first-year Six Sigma goal of $1 billion in savings. But as he acknowledged, he did not know how much of the goal would fall on the shoulders of each individual business. Nonetheless, he guaranteed that each business would be responsible for some of the corporate goal, based on its inherent capability for making a significant contribution.

Such an open-ended directive was a modification of the typical top-down formula for successfully deploying Six Sigma. This top-down formula would normally entail a very tightly controlled and mandated goal-setting process. Each leader would receive a preconceived goal and then would have to figure out how to make it. Everything would add up and then deviations would be managed. Consistent with DuPont's more consensual culture, Holliday decided to deviate from the traditional formula to one that better fit the company's management style. In doing so, he introduced a certain amount of risk in its launch of Six Sigma. What if the individual businesses, when they configured their respective contributions, fell far short of the $1 billion goal?

In part to offset this risk, DuPont sent each of its business leadership teams to Scottsdale for training under Mikel Harry and Rich Schroeder at the Six Sigma Academy. Those of us at the top felt that the business-level leaders would have a better chance of success if they were exposed to the Academy's no-excuses approach to aggressively adapting Six Sigma and extracting its benefits. The deployment Champions had already been to training, as had DuPont's top corporate leaders, and of course, the leaders of Specialty Chemicals, our test division.

DuPont's business leaders traveled to Scottsdale in waves for their Six Sigma baptisms. I traveled with each team, as I was the person who would have to renegotiate the business-level contributions if, in the end, the business units came up short on the overall goal. It was an approach that respected the consensual nature of DuPont while holding fast to aggressive Six Sigma performance benchmarks.

TRANSFORMING THE BUSINESS LEADERS

In the executive sessions, Harry covered the theoretical and mathematical underpinnings of Six Sigma—effectively creating the basis for a dramatic shift in thinking among DuPont's business leaders. As companies such as GE and Motorola had already shown, there was a different and better way for DuPont to do business. It was Mikel Harry who explained *why* those companies were successful, and how DuPont, by setting its targets very high, could do the same.

Rich Schroeder played the role of hard-core business diagnostician. We often met with Schroeder before an executive session to give him the data about that business's strengths, weaknesses, quality levels, market share, operating margins, types of products, number of plants, number of employees, revenue, and so on. In the space of about an hour, Schroeder would dissect the business from a cost-of-poor-quality perspective. After reviewing the number of plants, product areas, geographical mix, and financial performance, he would offer recommendations on how to begin cutting the costs of poor quality. In a meeting with the polymers managers, for instance, he built a case that they should look first at their polymer compounding business.

As another example, looking the leaders of a particular business in the eye, he would ask: "What are you going to tell Mr. Holliday you're going to commit to? What's your piece of the pie?"

They might say, "Forty million dollars."

"Not enough," he would reply. "You are capable of much more than that. Your goal should be $70 million in the first 12 months, and these are your critical tasks. You'll need seventy Black Belts, ten Champions, and three Master Black Belts. I'd put thirty Black Belts in North America, and I'd concentrate them in your Texas clothing factory. There, you'll need ten Black Belts focused on transactions, ten on scrap reduction, and ten on improving the tensile strength of your fibers. For now, I'd forget about Europe, but I'd bring your Brazil operations online after you deploy your first wave of Black Belts in the United States. When you do this, they will need six Black Belts and one Champion."

Schroeder would go on like this until he was finished with his interrogation, diagnosis, and prescription. The executives in each session were usually shocked—and impressed—at how knowledgeable he was about their businesses, compared to other outside consultants. After he left, the team would engage in its own assessment and come up with their goals and deployment plan. Interestingly, they were always very similar to what Schroeder had recommended.

There were certain cases, however, when Schroeder would leave the session in disgust. That was simply part of his style in conveying how serious he was about what we were undertaking. One time he went through his diagnosis, then asked all the team members who were "with him" to raise their hands. When nobody raised a hand, Schroeder went off like a Roman candle. "What the heck are you doing here?" he asked. "I'm giving you the benefit of all of this knowledge in unrolling Six Sigma. I'm telling you this works, the recipe works. What more do you need?"

The financial person for that business raised her hand and said, "We need to go back and look at the data and understand the implications and financial ramifications of implementing this in our business."

Schroeder replied tersely: "You don't have to look at any data. I've been doing this for six years, I know what the data are. That's what you're paying me to do. So sign up and do it."

Then he asked if anyone else was unwilling to raise a hand. Someone else said, "Well, we're a very process-oriented business, and we make our decisions by consensus. We need to decide together what we're going to do in our division."

Schroeder cast a piercing glance at the president of the division and said, "Are you going to do this or not?" The president, a well-respected senior leader, honored the DuPont way of making decisions by saying he and his team would have to work through their own process to come up with their goals and deployment plan.

Schroeder put on his cowboy hat, donned his sunglasses, and marched out of the room, saying he would have no part of their mediocrity.

As the room went silent, I said, "And that brings the provocation portion of the meeting to a close." Everybody burst into laughter, easing the tension in the room. After Schroeder had left, the leadership team rolled up its sleeves for the rest of the day and came out of the meeting with a terrifically detailed and promising deployment plan, setting a goal of $50 million. They wanted to get 50 Black Belts started on the compound business Schroeder had mentioned as a priority.

Ironically, the team came up with a deployment configuration that was very close to the one Schroeder had recommended. But they did it their way, and that was important to them, as it was throughout DuPont. Schroeder did his job by provoking them to think outside the box. In essence, he helped establish the tone for those who would lead the Six Sigma charge. DuPont's Six Sigma initiative would be a relentless drive for perfection. It would be led by people who were unafraid of sticking their necks out further than they had ever done before.

As with the corporate executives, there were some business-level executives who fully believed Six Sigma could deliver on what it promised. Others were undecided. Still others were basically convinced that Six Sigma would not work. Even after two days in Scottsdale with the

Academy, the business unit executives essentially fell into the categories of yea-sayers, fence-sitters, or nay-sayers.

Because these business-level leaders were not initially required to tie a portion of their variable pay to achieving Six Sigma goals, some were not eager to be the first to adopt Six Sigma. Some were doubtful that Six Sigma would play out the way it had been described to them. If the initiative was likely to fall apart quickly, as many others had, it might be best to not get involved in the first place, they reasoned. Conversely, the most optimistic and eager executives signed up to be early pioneers. They were among the first to get Six Sigma religion. As a result, they were well into the throes of implementation before other business units had even bought in.

Once the early adopters became successful in improving quality and achieved increased financial gains using Six Sigma, the laggards began to take notice. It wasn't long before they began asking to be the next in line. The success of those who went first became a learning experience for those who came after.

A SEAMLESS DRIVE

There is a great deal of crossover between the responsibilities of a deployment Champion and the operating unit executive teams. For example, Six Sigma financial targets mirror the business unit's financial targets. Given that, Six Sigma training should be a business goal as much as it is a Six Sigma goal.

Six Sigma was attached to DuPont's business structure so that it would transform the way everyone in the company thinks and works. DuPont business leaders became Six Sigma leaders, and Six Sigma leaders became business leaders. DuPont was careful to recognize the highly synergistic nature of its business goals and its Six Sigma goals, to the point that the two sets of goals were indistinguishable.

Clearly, not all businesses are alike, and this is true for DuPont as well. But this joining of Six Sigma goals and business goals functioned as a double-edged sword while the various businesses at DuPont were negotiating their respective Six Sigma contributions. Some businesses were in fairly dire shape in the marketplace. For example, strong leadership in the Specialty Chemicals business to tackle the cost of poor quality was a key strategy for this business. As a result, they set aggressive goals. They had increasing costs, their competitors were more global in their presence, and they were losing market share. If the average benchmark for attacking poor quality through Six Sigma was 4 percent at DuPont, some of the businesses wanted to go after 8 percent. They viewed Six Sigma as an opportunity to quickly and aggressively turn around their cost structures.

Such an aggressive target required more Project Champions, Master Black Belts, and Black Belts and a greater initial commitment of resources. As a general rule, the business units required one Black Belt for every $1 million they targeted. So if a particular business went after a cost savings of $100 million, it would need 100 Black Belts to realize its goal. It would also need about five to six Project Champions and four to six Master Black Belts.

A SECOND CHANCE

In setting business unit targets, some businesses were more aggressive than others. Some executive teams decided that they would simply match the cost-of-poor-quality percentages of the corporation. If the corporate target was to save 4 percent of revenue, then they too would commit their businesses to 4 percent of their respective revenue. No such cookie-cutter approach was, of course, suggested or recommended. But these leaders decided that they would best serve their interests by mirroring the norm.

Lou Savelli, the leader of one business, Performance Coatings, a paint business, was in the midst of a major acquisition. He claimed that his organization was already attacking the cost of poor quality at a 4 percent rate, so he didn't think Six Sigma would help his cause. Nonetheless, he brought his team to its Six Sigma executive session with an open mind. He reasoned that the corporation was providing free training for thirty Black Belts in each business, so why not take advantage of it and see what they might have to offer?

This group vice president's time with Harry and Schroeder provoked him to make a speech to his group before they'd actually hammered out their Six Sigma commitment. He noted that very few times in life do you get a second chance, and this was one of those times. His business had done an excellent job in the early 1990s of improving quality and managing its processes, but it had slid back quite a bit since then. Now Chad Holliday was offering up Six Sigma to each of DuPont's businesses on a silver platter.

The group vice president, Savelli, was so convinced of the effectiveness of Six Sigma as a world-class methodology that he immediately proposed a goal of $100 million for his business, about a 4 percent cost of poor quality. His team was extremely surprised at this. They had thought that he was positioning Six Sigma as an incremental add-on to the business, at best. But now he was treating it as if it were the Holy Grail and suggesting that they commit to substantial savings. Nonetheless, a year later, this business exceeded its $100 million goal and began to apply Six Sigma methodology to its various acquisitions as well, including its European paint plants.

The more reserved businesses felt that the Six Sigma Academy was giving them a high-level song-and-dance act. "Who are they to tell me how to run my business?" they said. "I've been working on quality for the last ten years, and we don't have that kind of margin of error." The net effect of such thinking was that these leadership teams tended to set their contributions far lower—at about 2 percent.

In these cases, we sat down with the deployment Champions for those businesses and told them that they would likely hear from CEO Chad Holliday. They were told, essentially, that they would have to be more aggressive in their goal setting and bump up their target. We might accept a slightly less than average target if there was a suitable explanation (an emphasis on growth in the business, a superior cost position, a new acquisition, etc.). But 2 percent was unacceptable.

Generally speaking, the DuPont businesses went to Scottsdale and returned home with an aggressive goal. All the while, I kept a running total of the combined target savings in my head—a couple of businesses committed to 8 percent, most committed in the 4 to 7 percent range, and a few committed to less than 4 percent.

GOING ON FAITH

After the businesses had completed their time in Scottsdale and finished their goal-setting process, we looked at the sum total of their intended contributions. As noted, it came in at $920 million, $80 million short of the company's $1 billion goal.

Some might have viewed this shortage as a cause for alarm; we, however, viewed it as a brave commitment of the businesses' serious intent. Those at DuPont had a reputation for erring on the side of caution. This would have been true even with the most aggressive campaign, which Six Sigma was. We believed so much in the Six Sigma methodology and in the abilities of our deployment Champions that we felt there was more to be gained by accepting $920 million rather than squeezing further to make up the $80 million shortfall. If we tried to go back to renegotiate the targets or force an artificial number on certain businesses, they wouldn't own their goal anymore. Meddling with the goals could pose a much greater risk than simply letting the businesses run with their own targets. We signed off on this, however, with the expectation that some businesses would probably exceed their original projections. We had faith in our people and in Six Sigma, which held us back from making public the fact that the business-level targets did not add up to their intended sum. We simply kept this fact to ourselves, hewing to the spirit that Six Sigma was more about achieving goals than about establishing them.

After the top leaders of the eighteen division platforms had completed their training with Harry and Schroeder and established aggressive but achievable financial targets, DuPont's business unit leaders began their collective and personal Six Sigma journeys. All had their own visions of how far they would go and how fast they would get there.

There was a strong correlation between those that went to Scottsdale sooner rather than later in the scheduling sequence and the DuPont businesses that set aggressive goals. It was very much as though the aggressive businesses viewed Six Sigma as an opportunity for meeting their business goals. For these businesses, Six Sigma was a badly needed and powerful change agent that would help them propel their organizations up the performance curve. For example, the titanium technology business, led by Jeff Keefer and Championed by Mike Edenfield, used Six Sigma as the change agent to improve uptime and yield as well as save capital spending.

The other businesses played a corporate waiting game. Some thought, "We know that we must and will do Six Sigma, but we can't do it now because of other pressing concerns and priorities." Others decided, "If we wait long enough, this Six Sigma thing might just go away, like so many other initiatives." In either case, the businesses that were scheduled later in the year tended to be less aggressive in their targets—clearly a sign of their hesitation to jump on board. Also, businesses that started Six Sigma early had more time to achieve their initial Six Sigma targets.

By mid-2000, all the DuPont businesses had embarked on Six Sigma. The deployment Champions had been trained and were deeply involved in establishing a Six Sigma infrastructure. All the necessary Six Sigma leaders had been selected and installed. It was now time to push Six Sigma down from the operational level into manufacturing and processing facilities, the research labs, and all the other organizational segments of the company.

INITIATING PROJECT CHAMPIONS

White Pigments is a $2 billion DuPont business unit. It was engaged in reinventing its technology and processes at the time it launched Six Sigma. Six Sigma was embraced by the top leadership of White Pigments as a critical strategy to achieving business aims.

Just as a business-level deployment platform has a Champion leader (a deployment Champion), so does each operations-level implementation of Six Sigma, via a Project Champion. With the top-down support of his business's leadership team, White Pigments deployment Champion Mike

Edenfield went about selecting and developing the people he needed to set and keep Six Sigma on course in his organization.

Edenfield believed in moving quickly in installing Six Sigma, utilizing people capable of leading culture change in a large, complex organization. In selecting Project Champions, he tapped those who already had a deep functional knowledge of the business and who had established a strong leadership track record. He also decided to select and develop only two Project Champions, a very small number for a business the size of White Pigments.

In general, Mikel Harry and Rich Schoeder recommended having one Project Champion for every ten to twenty Black Belts. At White Pigments, each Project Champion would oversee more than a hundred Black Belts. Edenfield also decided to select and develop thirteen Master Black Belts. His thinking was that this leadership configuration would provide more technical support than managerial support, which would be a better fit with the highly self-directed and scientifically oriented White Pigments culture.

In such a technical environment, relying on only two Project Champions made sense. They would work closely with the White Pigment leadership team and Master Black Belts to manage the integrity of project selection, Black Belt training, and project implementation. Edenfield and his business unit leader selected one Project Champion, Rob Johns, to oversee all manufacturing projects, and one, Fred Michaels, to oversee all transactional projects. Both Champions were highly motivated, credible performers who had been in the business at least six years.

White Pigments was one of the first DuPont businesses to deploy Six Sigma. Their Project Champions attended the White Pigments executive training session at the Six Sigma Academy in April 1999. Edenfield wanted the two Champions to be exposed to the same education the White Pigments leadership team experienced. He and the Project Champions also attended the Academy's five-day Champion training, where Six Sigma experts covered the Six Sigma Breakthrough Strategy and dissected change management and other aspects of leading and executing Six Sigma.

Like their executive leaders, the Project Champions were particularly taken with the bottom-line focus of Six Sigma, as well as its reverence for discipline and data. White Pigments had always had a similar focus, so Six Sigma seemed tailor-made for the organization.

White Pigments' Project Champions also participated in Black Belt and Master Black Belt training; Edenfield was determined to do everything possible to maximize their chances of success with Six Sigma and minimize the risk of failure. He and the Champions learned, alongside the Black Belts, about how to map processes, reduce variation, conduct designed experiments, and use Six Sigma Academy MINITAB software and a host of other tools.

They also became deeply involved in helping White Pigments' executive team establish its financial validation system, which analyzed the cost savings of each Six Sigma project and which later became the system adopted company-wide. The Project Champions helped to develop a better understanding of the relationship between operational excellence and financial performance. Understanding how projects impact the earnings sheet is key for all who participate in Six Sigma.

Overall, White Pigments' Project Champions experienced both bottom-up technical training and top-down managerial guidance. At DuPont, Project Champions were midlevel Six Sigma leaders: They were and are the glue that binds operational goals to people and projects. The opportunity they had also led to personal career development. In most cases, they later moved into positions of greater leadership.

PREPARING THE TROOPS

Once the leadership had been trained, Six Sigma had to be implemented at the process level. Essentially, this is the handoff of responsibility from the Project Champion to individual Master Black Belts, Black Belts, and Green Belts. It was they who were primarily responsible for executing projects that improve the way products are made and business is conducted on a day-to-day basis.

One of DuPont's smaller businesses, Surfaces, makes Corian and Zodiaq countertop products at its two plants in Toyama, Japan, and Buffalo, New York. Although Surfaces is one of DuPont's smaller businesses, its Buffalo plant, the larger of the two, produces more than ten miles of Corian a day.

Overall, the greatest issue for Surfaces to solve was one of capacity. It had been enjoying eight years of annual growth of between 12 and 18 percent. But the increasing demand the business was experiencing could be met only if it had the capacity to do so. The Surfaces leadership team's concern was how to get more capacity from its existing plants without spending money to build a new one, which would cost about $125 million. It was in this environment that Paul Brown, a manufacturing technical support engineer, was asked to be a Master Black Belt and drive and manage projects within his manufacturing sphere of Surfaces. The Surfaces business already had a Project Champion, but it also needed a manufacturing-oriented Black Belt. Brown first functioned as a Black Belt, working on individual projects; when he became a Master Black Belt, his responsibilities shifted to overseeing the work of others.

Brown oversaw a cadre of seven Black Belts working within the Surfaces manufacturing operations. Surfaces also developed one additional Master Black Belt to oversee five Black Belts engaged in improving nonmanufacturing processes and operations, such as order entry and accounts receivables.

Because of its small size, Surfaces' total initial Six Sigma goal was to contribute $12 million of savings. For an effort on this small a scale, we didn't feel Surfaces needed the services of a deployment Champion. A Project Champion and two Master Black Belts were sufficient in terms of the Six Sigma management structure.

Brown's duties as a Master Black Belt mirrored those of others at DuPont. As was the case for most Master Black Belt candidates, Brown had a strong technical background as well as good people skills. He had held various management positions within different operations and technology areas, where he had honed his abilities to solve problems and mentor people.

"I have always been a data wonk who loves numbers," says Brown. "It's just that before Six Sigma I didn't understand the statistics and how powerful they can be."

Over time Brown completed many successful projects and mentored the Black Belts in his area. But he didn't start out with such enthusiasm for Six Sigma. When his deployment Champion first asked him to devote himself full-time to Six Sigma, he was nervous. He reasoned, "Let's see, my management want $12 million they didn't have before, and they want me to get it for them. I don't know anything about Six Sigma. And it sounds a lot like the many initiatives we're tried in the past."

To Brown, Six Sigma sounded much more like a risk than an opportunity. It was as though he was being asked to come to the aid of his company at his own expense. He recalled, for instance, his involvement in the Operational Excellence initiative, involving "high-performance work teams" and "Deming-style SPC [statistical process control] which he considered to be feel-good initiatives. He would come to realize Six Sigma had a deployment approach and infrastructure the earlier program lacked. But he didn't know that when he was called into service.

Unlike many Master Black Belts, Brown did have the luxury of time, in that his business unit would not begin Black Belt training for four months. He put this time to good use by implementing the organizational changes necessary to make Six Sigma successful in Surfaces. First, he promised his old job as a technical superintendent to a woman he had been developing for about a year and a half. With his old job filled, there was no turning back for him.

Brown also selected the Black Belts he wanted from the best manufacturing people in Surfaces. As he and his deployment Champion negotiated with the plant managers in Buffalo and Japan and with their operational managers, it became quite a tug-of-war. The people he had brought on board had to be the best in terms of their leadership skills, maturity, demonstrated technical ability, and sheer presence in the workplace. At the same time, the positions they vacated would *not* be backfilled. That was the practice set by the Six Sigma Academy, and the various DuPont businesses insisted on adhering to it.

This helped make it clear that DuPont was "serious about Six Sigma to the extent that we will take your best people and make them Black Belts." It also became clear that Six Sigma was not a quality initiative led by quality engineers but, rather, a business initiative led by the most financially minded and technically capable people in the organization. Brown says that he didn't get every one of the people he wanted for Black Belts, and in some cases the people he got didn't last. In general, however, his negotiations yielded the right pool of people, even if their bosses gave them up reluctantly.

DEVELOPING BLACK BELTS

Black Belts begin their Six Sigma trek much the way Brown did: wondering if their assignment will be a boom or a bust for their careers. In any organization, Black Belts who get started later in a Six Sigma initiative are much more likely to hit the ground running, as their doubts and fears about how their assignment will affect their careers have been answered by demonstrated results in other parts of the company.

In the beginning of their Six Sigma journeys, Black Belts rely on their instructors and Project Champions for guidance and insight. They work through existing data—charts, graphs, and other materials—that help to explain the phases, concepts, technologies, and tools of the Six Sigma Breakthrough Strategy.

That's exactly how it turned out for Paul Brown and his Black Belts. In the beginning they "had no clue" about how to identify and define projects. They did know that the overriding goal for their section of the Surfaces business was to achieve a 10 percent increase in capacity, but beyond that the details were sketchy. With the help of the Academy instructors, they came up with projects that would help them to achieve those goals, based on the data they had or could quickly get their hands on. They identified projects focused on eliminating process defects in their manufacture of Corian sinks and countertops; they developed projects that would speed up certain production lines without compromising quality. With each project, they waded through the phases of define, measure, analyze, improve, and control to achieve their project goals. This represented the best possible learning opportunity for Black Belts—experience. By simply sticking with the task at hand and methodically moving through the fixed structure of the Breakthrough Strategy, Black Belts were able to solve difficult problems that, in the absence of Six Sigma, would have remained unsolved.

- They characterized processes as they existed before running statistical experiments. This meant quantifying the actual output of a process in terms of good output versus defects.
- They gathered data from their customers on products and specifications.
- They improved their ability to measure problems and analyze causes of problems.
- They developed an understanding of the difference between primary outcomes, Y's, and secondary Y's or X's (inputs).
- They ran any number of experiments to isolate the variables that mattered most. For example, they tested one variable against another to see which one had a greater impact in causing the defect. And the list goes on and on.

Over time, as they defined, measured, analyzed, improved, and controlled performance problems, DuPont's Black Belts picked up a rich array of information about which measurement devices would let them prove whether a process was in control or not. They began to see problems with new eyes, developing the confidence to solve critical issues that had stumped their organizations or manufacturing engineers for a long time, such as improving product quality purity beyond what had been tolerated by the business for years. One Black Belt, after a series of experiments, came up with the settings for the manufacturing process that all but eliminated a trace element impurity, opening up new markets for their products. Over time, they developed a certain impatience and intolerance for people who acted as if they knew the root of a particular problem or performance shortfall when they clearly didn't. Where were their data? How deep was their understanding of variability in the process, or the nature of what was causing the problem? Could they speak the language of statistics?

Brown's personal Six Sigma epiphany came in working on his first project—a relatively complicated study of how Surfaces could speed up a production line for Corian without compromising the properties important to customers. Manufacturing said that speeding up the line could be done; R&D said it couldn't be done. The technical staff fell somewhere in between. Only an in-depth measurement and analysis of the production line yielded Brown the answer. Yes, he found, certain equipment could run 10 percent faster. As a result, the line could produce more product in the same amount of time.

After the project was concluded, the data showed that the improvements made were returning an additional $4 million to the Surfaces income statement. Those kinds of experiences give Black Belts confidence that they can do anything. "Show me any business out there and I'll go in there and save you money," says Brown. He completed another project during his first year as a Black Belt that yielded another $4 million in validated annualized savings, through capacity gains on another Surfaces production line.

Several key process-level leadership lessons emerged from the Surfaces experience. First and foremost was that everything is a process. "It's fundamental stuff," says Brown. "Everything is a process with inputs and outputs, and once you understand this you can even improve transactional processes that seem to be invisible." Black Belts are trained to take this thinking to the extreme, as they intensely define, measure, analyze, improve, and control the relationships between critical outputs and inputs —what are called critical-to-quality (CTQ) characteristics and critical-to-process (CTP) characteristics.

While these lessons vary across the many DuPont locations and operational specialties, the experience of Surfaces serves in many ways as a proxy for all. Eight respected and talented Black Belts became better leaders than they'd been before, thanks to their Six Sigma training and experience.

YOU DON'T KNOW SQUAT

Another leadership lesson that we learned at DuPont was to trust only data. Data cut through the ambiguity so typical of organizational life. Data at DuPont have become the weapon of choice—a stun gun for debilitating those who would offer opinions based on intuition or anecdotal experience. "When you have legitimate data and you use DMAIC, people stop developing hurt feelings when their opinions are upended. Their self-esteem isn't dashed when you tell them they don't know what they are talking about," says Brown.

When Brown conducts Black Belt or Green Belt training at DuPont, he typically tells the trainees: "I was you once. I thought I knew everything and had the answers, but I'm here to say you don't know squat." These few words speak volumes about the transformation that takes place over time as one becomes a Black Belt and then a Master Black Belt.

Brown had gone from intellectually grasping Six Sigma and hearing about it from others, to experiencing it himself. In months, he went from struggling to come up with project ideas to having to turn them away because they poured in with such fervor and frequency. It was then that he knew Surfaces had gone from learning about Six Sigma to leading Six Sigma, and that Six Sigma was at DuPont to stay.

As Black Belts implement successful projects, they become stars of sorts and establish a reputation for solving problems. As a result, Brown has been asked by many different departments and functions within Surfaces to help with problems. When that happens, he explains, you can't say no; he regularly gives on-the-spot advice and helps others with statistical tools and software. All these informal consultations, says Brown, although they have nothing to do with regular projects, are an opportunity for learning more about oneself and growing as a leader.

One of the first things Brown does in developing Black Belts is to make them mentors to Green Belts. His approach goes back to the idea that you learn best when you have to teach something. As Black Belts teach Green Belts, they witness someone else internalizing Six Sigma and

DMAIC. This has been a powerful experience in furthering Black Belts' belief in and understanding of the Breakthrough Strategy. Just the simple task of teaching a basic tool, such as the fishbone diagram, can open the eyes of the Black Belt to different questions. In a fishbone diagram, the head of the fish is the Y, or the outcome. Each of the bones is a possible cause connected to the basic backbone. This cause-and-effect diagram graphically shows what does and does not impact the outcome. Deciding what grouping to use to cluster ideas as bones can help a Black Belt learn to master the process.

"Six Sigma changes the way people think," says Brown. It is truly about cultural change.

PROCESS OWNERS

The Process Owners—the managers, superintendents, and technical specialists who are responsible for running the thousands of processes in a corporation the size of DuPont—were critically important for the Six Sigma success. If a plant manager is in charge of everything that comes into and goes out of the plant, then a Process Owner is in charge of everything that comes into and goes out of his or her process. Process Owners are also responsible for the elusive aspects of what goes on in between—the space in which value is created for commercial gain.

Process Owners are generally required to participate on any Black Belt teams executing projects on their processes. In many cases, Process Owners are Green Belts, while in other cases they are not. Regardless, their participation is mandatory, since they are ultimately accountable for the performance of their processes.

To foster this accountability, and to maintain the seamless integration of Black Belt interventions and ongoing operations, all Process Owners in Surfaces are Green Belts. Also, they are involved in the initial validation of project savings during the measure phase of the Breakthrough Strategy. As the project moves through the analyze and improve phases, Process Owners remain involved. During the control phase, as the work comes to a close and resulting gains become more critical, Process Owners take an even more active role. In the Surfaces business, while the Black Belt is responsible for improving the manufacturing process, the Process Owner is the manufacturing director held accountable for the final outcome.

In Surfaces, all Process Owners make a formal presentation to the leadership team before the completed Six Sigma projects are submitted for final validation. These meetings, called project turnover and notification, are effective because the Process Owners accept responsibility for the results and control plan. Brown says the system "works like a top" because "it's hard to be down on something you are in on."

Brown says there were many people in DuPont who didn't initially accept Six Sigma. Many were skeptical due to lack of exposure and involvement, as only a small percentage of the company was directly involved as executive advocates, Champions, Black Belts, and Green Belts.

But when their Process Owners stepped up and validated what Six Sigma was achieving, it cut through a lot of the doubts. Here were people connected to the business in operational leadership roles saying that Six Sigma worked and was good for all. By actively participating in the projects, Process Owners secured greater acceptance for Six Sigma thinking.

ONE DUPONT BUSINESS: THE CASE OF GLOBAL SERVICES

While Nylon and other groups around DuPont were quickly racking up immediate and significant wins from Six Sigma, another group was struggling to find its way with Six Sigma.

With 5,000 employees, Global Services provided DuPont with more than 3,000 offerings in areas such as human resources, business consulting, finance, information technology, facilities management, engineering, purchasing, sales, hospitality, and safety. Global Services was a demand-driven business that worked on a fee-for-service basis, so the many DuPont businesses could pick and choose what they needed from Global Services and pay only for what they used.

At Global Services, it was beginning to look like the common misconception that Six Sigma was just for manufacturing would be proven true.

Unlike some Six Sigma Champions, Joanne Smith at least knew the arena when she became the Six Sigma Champion for Global Services, having been a business manager in the division's engineering practice, a group with 500 consultants and 500 capital management experts.

Smith was familiar with the success of the Six Sigma pilot at Specialty Chemicals and had heard all the stories of Six Sigma success in industries outside of DuPont. She also knew that Global Services, like all organizations, had defects that needed to be fixed.

After the official Six Sigma kickoff and training, Smith and her superiors agreed to tie 40 percent of their variable compensation to the achievement of their first annual Six Sigma financial target, which was $45 million. Until then, variable-compensation-eligible people in Global Services had been paid an average of what their counterparts received in the profit-making businesses throughout DuPont, since Global Services was not a revenue-generating business unit. Smith was convinced it would be better for Global Services to control its own variable-compensation amount, rather than having it determined by others.

Although Smith viewed Six Sigma as the hardest thing Global Services would have ever had to do, she was optimistic, at least at first. But she and her team weren't so pleased with their initial progress after their first waves of Black Belts, forty-five in all, went to work. As good as her team was, it was struggling to identify projects and having trouble completing the ones they did identify.

"We went through some pretty scary and frustrating times, especially since we were on such a high before we ran into these problems," says Smith. "The training and all the examples were geared toward manufacturing, so we had to learn everything the hard way."

Global Services had chosen six Process Champions, defining the boundaries of its six implementation cells:

- Sourcing, logistics, and South America
- Engineering
- Facilities services, finance, and hospitality
- Business, consulting, customer care, certain other functional areas, Canada and Mexico
- Asia Pacific
- Europe

The organization mixed nine business units and four continents to make six independent implementation cells. Six of its very best people were selected to lead the cells. But Smith, the Champions, and the Black Belts hadn't fully comprehended how difficult their $45 million financial goal would be to attain. Global Services is highly fragmented, both functionally and geographically. Often, it coordinates service delivery with outside providers and requires the coordination of data and efforts across several outside organizations. There was a general dearth of data and measurement capability in Global Services. In many cases there weren't even hard, documented process flows for many of its more creative and consulting-type services.

"It was intimidating, because the organization as a whole didn't know how to deal with data and wasn't used to measuring or being measured in terms of process or performance effectiveness," says Smith.

Global Services found that it was more difficult to inject Six Sigma into an organization without data or a strong measurement capability, and decided that they would need more time and effort to define and measure phases of the Breakthrough Strategy. This deflated the spirit of the group. Other DuPont businesses were getting quick, big hits on yield and capacity, which made Global Services feel isolated. Their problems were different from those faced by the other business units. While the other businesses were sharing and learning from each other, Global Services was in many ways alone.

In the midst of these negative feelings, Smith took on a Six Sigma project to focus on their problems with project identification and long project cycle times. She brought in one of General Electric's original Master Black Belts, Susan Beauchamp. Together with their team, they installed a more disciplined project identification workshop process and more disciplined project operating procedures.

The old mind-set had a primary focus on searching for projects that met the criterion of $175,000 in savings. Beauchamp helped change the focus so that it was more on the customer than on the money. They attempted to identify what was critical to meet customers' needs.

Smith and her team applied a formalized idea-generating technology to identify problems and opportunities. They set Six Sigma aside for a moment and brainstormed a long list of items the business needed to address in general.

They then separated the issues into two basic buckets:

- Objectives you just go do as a business leader with no special methodology or support
- Objectives you need Black Belts to accomplish

This integration of project selection into the business fabric made all the difference. It integrated the voice of the customer into the organization, created team alignment, and surfaced great ideas for projects.

Part of the problem had been that people wouldn't speak up about certain problems or opportunities because they didn't imagine their ideas could save at least $175,000. With the barrier removed, ideas flowed freely and took on a life of their own as they combined with other ideas to spawn still more ideas. Smith's new approach was the change that revived Global Services' Six Sigma spirit.

Some big project hits were made, and the mood of Global Services shifted from one of pessimism and fear to one of great accomplishment.

- An HR project to study health insurance benefits focused on claims DuPont was covering that were paid to ineligible employee dependents. For example, a child would reach the age of coverage ineligibility, but the parents didn't recognize this and did not remove the child from coverage. Savings to DuPont: $2.4 million.

- A procurement project began with the voice of the customer regarding PC user requirements. Most DuPont business units were using many different brands of PCs with more capacity and capability than they needed. The project team standardized requirements across all eighteen major units and set itself up for leveraged buys during its PC-upgrade cycle. Savings to DuPont: $4.5 million in the United States alone.

- One of the first Green Belts in Global Services was its vice president, Al Titus. He led a project that improved the organization's financial reporting system. Savings to DuPont: $60,000.

- One early sourcing project brought a pool of 150 suppliers down to just two, with 66 percent of DuPont's major businesses standardized on these two suppliers. Savings to DuPont: $6 million per year.

It was projects such as these, and many others in the $200,000 to $500,000 range, that turned the tide for Global Services. They were back on a high, based on real results and money in the bank.

In addition to its six Champions, seven Master Black Belts, forty-five Black Belts, and more than 250 line managers, Global Services provided Six Sigma awareness training to more than 700 people within the first six months of implementation. Global Services finished 2000, its first year of implementation, having achieved a $30 million run rate of savings from Six Sigma, about $6 million over its goal.

By the end of 2001, Global Services added another $47 million to its Six Sigma run rate, for a total of $77 million in the first two years of implementation. In the first two years, an additional $8 million was delivered in one-time savings, and working capital was reduced by $71 million. Within two years, Global Services' sourcing organization alone saved DuPont $50 million.

Also at the end of 2002, Global Services instituted the requirement that 50 percent of the next-generation Black Belts would already be functioning in leadership roles or would be on the group's promotables list (the top 10 percent of all employees)—a change that shifted the Black Belt pipeline from one of anyone available to one of top-notch people.

Global Services made this change in Black Belt selection because it had become apparent that strong leadership skills were critical to achieving results. They wanted to embed Six Sigma into their culture, and choosing Black Belts from among the division's future leaders was a way to do this. Ultimately, Global Services ended up with a balance of extremely strong career Black Belts (to maintain continuity of progress) and two-year-tenure Black Belts (who learned, delivered results, and then moved back into leadership roles to further institutionalize Six Sigma).

In addition, and just as significant, Smith and her Champions realized the need to improve the knowledge transfer process to Green Belts. To accomplish this, Smith once again relied on her contact with the GE Master Black Belt Susan Beauchamp, who agreed to develop a customized sourcing approach for DuPont. Smith, sourcing Process Champion John McCool, and sourcing Master Black Belt Tom Tumlin met with a GE team to discuss the details. McCool and Tumlin continued to work with GE and, together, eventually upgraded its original work.

For training, a set of strategic pillars was established to guide the knowledge transfer process to all Green Belts throughout Global Services. The pillars were:

- Customer satisfaction
- Growth
- Best-in-class business strategy
- Alliance and supplier performance
- Change management

After each phase of the Breakthrough Strategy, the work of Green Belts was reviewed to establish its connection with each of the five pillars. The review process was directly linked to the pillars, asking:

- How does your project enhance customer satisfaction?
- How does it contribute to growth?
- How does it promote best-in-class business strategies?
- How does it improve partner and supplier performance?
- How does it get more of DuPont following established best practices (change management)?

These questions were the guiding lights by which instructors configured their course material.

Before the first year of Six Sigma was over, Global Services had become one of the top DuPont business units in terms of delivering results.

CHAPTER 5

ENTERPRISE-LEVEL Q&A WITH MIKEL HARRY AND DON LINSENMANN

1. How does a senior executive leadership team determine if its company needs Six Sigma, and if it does, how does the team establish the direction of the Six Sigma deployment?

While profit is always a key driver, most companies have other high-level goals as well. Today, DuPont's value of "the miracles of science" is what shapes its behavior and drives its growth.

Six Sigma is a slope changer. It is a wedge that you drive into your culture, your communications, your systems, and your executive leaders. It is a disruptive and dislodging intervention that reaches management where it lives. Six Sigma is a means for uprooting old practices and replanting, not for perpetuating the habits and patterns of the past. A company is only ready, therefore, if it decides that it must change dramatically, and that it is willing and capable of making that change.

In making this decision, a corporation must look both inside and outside. It looks inside at how it is performing relative to its aspirations. Are the shareholders and officers satisfied? Does the corporation and its major units have clearly defined strategic and financial goals? Are there visible and pervasive diagnostics for assessing performance? Has the company fallen short of its goals year after year? Or have the goals been set too low? These are some of the questions an executive team needs to ask as it looks inward for the reason and will to do Six Sigma.

At DuPont, there'd been five consecutive years of basically flat earnings growth while targeting 10 percent growth. There was a clear historical pattern of falling short of that corporate metric. The company did have a vision that was populated with various success factors—but many of these factors were either poorly defined or did not have a clear scale of measure. In that sense, the company's future was a cloud, with only loose form and ethereal promise.

That very cloud was an indication that maybe DuPont was ready for Six Sigma. It had a vision and goals, and it had a historical performance continuum. But it was clear the company would not achieve its vision and goals at the rate it was going. There was a need for something different, and that need grew out of dissatisfaction with the status quo. This was the pure and simple basis by which DuPont made a break with its past.

But a look outside can be just as powerful in terms of finding a reason for enhancing quantum change in a corporation. Sometimes it's difficult, even for executives, to determine or admit that their company isn't as strong as they think it is relative to others. It's human nature to think you are the best, especially in the business world. This is why benchmarking is essential. Not the kind of benchmarking that encourages making trips to other companies, conducting a few meetings, and coming home with some global "ideas." That's not benchmarking. That's a feel-good, collegial, networking, field-trip time. The way to approach benchmarking is with a rigorous, data-drive, Z-score, T-test technical dialogue between people who speak the language of business capability, capacity, and capital. DuPont did not know how to do this at the beginning. Only when this is defined can a corporation begin to assess its need for Six Sigma.

Without the external view, a company cannot determine its business entitlement in any intelligent way. At the beginning of DuPont's Six Sigma journey, the limited external view came from GE and Allied, though more on a personal level, between the leaders of those companies. Nor can a company purport to know if it can or cannot benefit from Six Sigma. A classic example of this is a highly successful company with first-to-market technology, an 80 percent market share, and great earnings growth. The question is not about how much money the company is making or about how many customers it has. The question is about how much money it's leaving on the table. That's where the opportunity lies, especially in a corporation that is far and away the leader of a self-feeding market.

Proper benchmarking can strip away your fantasies as you discover that your 80 percent market share is a function of four-sigma performance. How much money are you leaving on the table in the cost of poor quality? That number, which typically runs about 20 percent of a corporation's revenue, is why an external assessment of a corporation's need for Six Sigma is often more valuable than an internal one.

Corporations are like people in that they have to look outside themselves to capture a better vision of what could be. Driven by the realization that there is a better life outside the confines of one's hometown, the young person goes to college. Paradoxically, the more we look outward, the more we are forced to look inward. The same is true for corporations, which, because they are a collection of human beings, tend to behave like them.

In addition to benchmarking, some corporations look outside to their customers for feedback about quality, or lack of it. A good example is when Motorola thought it was the world's benchmark for certain products and processes, as it had made some fantastic advances. Fortunately, the company was smart and brave enough to ask customers what they thought, and usually humble enough to accept what it heard. Motorola's perception of itself and reality were not quite aligned.

These, then, are the moments of truth when corporations decide they need Six Sigma. Either through internal inspection, outside exploration, or a combination of both, the leaders magnify their dissatisfaction to the point where they realize they need and want significant change. Having done this, they scan their options with the objective of locking in on the best possible means for moving their corporation in the right direction.

After having determined the need for Six Sigma in this way, a senior corporate leadership team must set the direction for its installation, deployment, and implementation. This is done by establishing the company's business entitlement in quantitative terms, which we can tell you is between 15 and 25 percent of revenue. In a corporation the size of DuPont, that comes to about $6 billion. Once the bogey is out there, you then have to cut through all the myths and excuses about why the number is too large.

A big reason for the usual skepticism among the executive ranks revolves around their past experience with classic quality or improvement initiatives. If your target is to improve your income statement to the order of $6 billion, it becomes pretty clear that these sorts of initiatives won't do it. You need a huge culture change, a wedge that is large enough to change the slope of past performance. And you need to drive that wedge deeply into your company, beginning at the very top and not stopping until it has reached each and every employee.

In practical terms, this means Six Sigma is more akin to revolution than evolution. As a leadership team, you have to be ready to lead the revolution with all the will and fortitude you've got. Therefore, rather than spending energy on thinking about all the particulars involved in doing Six Sigma, a leadership team is better served by asking itself one simple question: Are we ready to lead a revolution?

The final aspect of assessing readiness involves an evaluation of a corporation's capability, capacity, and capital for doing Six Sigma. Do you have the money and people you need to lead a revolution? It can cost millions of dollars for a large company to get started, much of which involves the outside expertise of consultants, the training of executives and managers, creating systems to track progress, and creating Champions, Black Belts, and Green Belts. Six Sigma is not a benign intervention or a topical treatment; it is invasive surgery. So a corporation must ask itself if it at least has the people who can become

Six Sigma leaders with the proper training and preparation, and the capital to make that happen. External benchmarking can be key. Meet with others who have changed their continuum through Six Sigma, and see what they have to say.

2. How does a senior executive leadership team focus and energize a Six Sigma initiative in light of other corporate priorities and initiatives?

The short answer is that Six Sigma is an umbrella for other corporate or even locally focused initiatives. This is because Six Sigma is entirely impartial to the philosophy or even objectives of such initiatives as Baldrige, TQM, operational excellence, or whatever. It is also impartial to initiatives that have more of a business focus than a quality orientation, such as e-commerce and the like.

Raining down on the Six Sigma umbrella are all the macroeconomic and competitive dynamics that exercise influence over a corporation. For example, increasing global competition, currency swings, and increased energy costs were some of the forces impacting DuPont. It is the combination of these forces, along with the current feeling about how the company is performing and has performed, that determines how Six Sigma will be set up and deployed at a company. Ironically, it is also this very impetus that can be the litmus test for whether the current initiatives are accomplishing what they are supposed to accomplish.

If a corporation wants to improve business performance in terms of growth and profit, then the initiatives it adopts should directly feed that goal. Period. There can be no exceptions or fancy philosophical tiptoeing around why certain initiatives are good for the company and customers, despite their apparent lack of impact on the bottom line. In the cases where a corporation's initiatives are making a demonstrable impact, the task for senior management is to quantify that impact and determine if it is sufficient to reach their goals. Six Sigma speeds this determination.

We raise this point with full knowledge that some might assume all executive leadership teams are highly disciplined in the way they set goals and regularly evaluate their progress. But this is not the reality. Working with thousands of executives over the years, we have more often than not interacted with CEOs, COOs, CIOs, CFOs, and other chiefs who set goals and invariably fall short of them, year after year, despite their initiatives.

Just for the sake of argument, what if a corporation did meet its goals year after year? We might be inclined to think it was setting its sights too low, as the role of business has always been to actualize in the present what was unthinkable in the past. Still, we acknowledge in theory that a corporation might not have a need for Six Sigma and, therefore, would not be concerned about how to position it in light of other priorities. The more likely case, however, is that it would simply not be aware of its need for Six Sigma, or would think that some point in the future is a better time for undergoing its rigor.

The more compelling case is when there is a burning platform for change in a corporation due to the weight of competition, the reality of poor performance, or the imperative to keep up with emerging forms of economic opportunity. In the case of DuPont, the burning platform for change was a new economic order with a focus on science-based solutions organized around customers. In such a world, what a corporation needs most is a built-in capability and capacity for rising to any challenge, not a battery of initiatives, even though it does need these. It needs a new genetic structure that can meet new expectations and demands.

When the bridge is burning, there tends to be a certain sense of urgency involved in efforts to keep it from crumbling. We make judgments very quickly, ruling out what doesn't work and rapidly implementing what does. This was the case with Motorola in the '80s. It was the case with many other U.S. companies during that time, whose bridges were burning under the Japanese threat.

Even if the way we make money has changed since the '80s, the basic goal is the same. In the short term, we do business to bring in cash. In the long term, we aim to bring in more cash by changing what we do and how we do it. In both cases, we are examining our entitlement and asking ourselves if we are satisfied. If the answer is no, then we can be pretty sure that our existing initiatives are not yielding what we need or want. This simple realization can go a long way in determining how to position Six Sigma in light of other initiatives.

When you total all the resources dedicated to corporate and business initiatives in a major corporation, such as those that had once been tried but were now gone from DuPont, it is not unusual to see the immediate opportunity for, say, $500 million. The people are there, along with the will to improve. What's missing is the organizing principle by which the various people can be pulled together and focused on achieving the primary aim of a corporation: to make money.

Six Sigma is not just one more initiative cluttering up the corporate plate. Whether you're doing SAP, JIT, TQM, or any of the rest, Six Sigma forces them to produce cash results or be discontinued.

Six Sigma is much more a *how* than a *what*. Executives ask, "What is Six Sigma?" The answer is that Six Sigma is like the company that doesn't make the golf ball but makes it go farther. This is what Six Sigma does, and this is how it should be positioned.

3. How can a senior executive leadership team measure the global effectiveness of its Six Sigma initiative and assess its momentum?

Overall, this has to be done in terms of activity and results, inputs and outputs. In Six Sigma language, we'd describe this as the measurement of CTPs (critical-to-process characteristics) and CTQs (critical-to-quality characteristics) providing the basis for analyzing and improving a process. This is Six Sigma as a process system. Why should Six Sigma as a management system be any different? The Six Sigma management system moves through various stages as it matures and gathers momentum.

It its early stages, a senior leadership team can best focus on Six Sigma by tracking indicators such as number of training classes, number of Black Belts and Master Black Belts, and number of projects completed. If the immediate goal is to reduce the cost of poor quality, as it should be for all corporations pursuing Six Sigma, then these activity-based indicators are the best gauges by which to assess momentum toward that goal. As a matter of reference and benchmark, such initial activity should be heavily monitored during the first year or two of deployment, depending on the scale of the initiative.

As a $30 billion company, the scale of DuPont's deployment was massive. There were eighteen major deployment platforms and about 150 separate deployment cells within those platforms. Because of the size of its effort, DuPont's major businesses did not launch their respective Six Sigma thrusts simultaneously, but did so one after the other in tightly staggered fashion.

Once the basic resources and infrastructure of Six Sigma are installed, a corporation begins to reap certain tangible benefits. The inputs yield outputs, and the initiative clearly progresses beyond its infancy. There is a period of about six months when all of the infrastructure gets put together to scale up with the deployment. After this start-up period, early project successes start to hit the bottom line. It was this phenomenon that allowed DuPont to actually show a slight profit from Six Sigma in the first years, despite the consulting fees and start-up costs. Typically, as DuPont's experience corroborates, this begins to occur between four and six months after the first Black Belt waves are trained. The early project successes are quantified and validated, and are publicized throughout the corporation and via local organizations.

If deployment is properly planned, paced, and supported, project successes start to accrue into visible aggregated net benefits by cell and by platform. At this stage, typically after at least one year of deployment and implementation, a corporation should begin to seriously monitor net project savings and annual project savings run rates. In DuPont's case, each of its eighteen major businesses had a run rate goal that was to be met eighteen months after the first business began Six Sigma. It also had an aggregate figure that was simply the sum of all businesses, $920 million of individual goals supporting the top-down goal of $1 billion of projects in SigmaTRAC either initially or finally validated.

At this stage of Six Sigma, the company's consciousness shifts from activity to results, even though a senior leadership team should still pay great attention to both. But the time for judging efficacy and momentum based on activity alone has surely passed. Now it is significant and visible results that drive the bandwagon forward, as activity alone cannot propel a corporation into the next phase of Six Sigma development and maturity. In the event that such results are not realized, a company may be set up for a Six Sigma reset.

If this is required, it is better to recognize the need sooner rather than later. In any case, we cannot overemphasize how difficult a reset can be. When a Six Sigma thrust does not yield its intended results, there are likely shortfalls in resources, management commitment, structures, systems, curricula, or consulting help. Overcoming these shortfalls and starting over is literally one's worst nightmare when it comes to Six Sigma. The failure has been set, and now Six Sigma has become part of the baggage of the past.

With the proper attention, however, such a negative scenario can be avoided. DuPont escaped this by learning the lessons from those before it and making sure there was buy-in from the top down, as well as dedicating DuPont's best and brightest talent to Six Sigma. After a year or two, net projects savings become noticeable on the income statements and balance sheets of a corporation's various businesses and profit centers. At this point, Six Sigma typically begins to make another turn, from a focus on the cost of poor quality to a focus on growth. The idea is to maintain momentum by shifting the focus of Six Sigma from the bottom line to the top line.

DuPont began this shift when it instituted its top-line growth network after reaching its first major milestone of $1 billion in hard Six Sigma benefits. The company's unwavering focus on Six Sigma activity had led it to its focus on Six Sigma results. In turn, this focus enabled

DuPont to alter its vision of Six Sigma to be much more inclusive of projects that improved relationships with customers and generated more sales and revenue.

Monitoring the productivity-related benefits of Six Sigma, a senior leadership team can begin to assess its momentum by watching its stock price and P/E premium. In terms of timing, this forward-looking focus becomes realistic after about three to five years of consistently accruing benefits to the balance sheet. It is only after a corporation changes the trajectory of its past performance that Wall Street begins to project and price that momentum into the future.

A corporation's P/E premium, therefore, is the ultimate metric for assessing the efficacy of Six Sigma. In the infant stages, a company measures Six Sigma activity because it has to realize the thinking, methods, and tools of breakthrough. When quick and continuous results build to critical mass, this creates the platform upon which Six Sigma is integrated into a company's genetic code and becomes the way we work. When capability rises to this level, Six Sigma becomes a primary vehicle by which a corporation achieves any strategy.

The company culture also plays into the success of Six Sigma in any organization. In the case of DuPont, there was a set of core values around safety, respectful treatment of people, and stewardship of the environment. It regularly measures performance against these values, just as it measures a host of business values such as return on invest-ment, productivity, profit, and so on. DuPont also has enabling values for viewing its business in terms of process, speaking with data, and measuring all things important—all key tenets of Six Sigma.

Examples of other enabling values are automation, which was big in the automotive industry at one time; digitization, which is espoused by many corporations today; and outsourcing, which gained favor among many large corporations. The key point to make is that digiti-zation and automation are inherently good for a corporation, as is Six Sigma, given the current business environment. As such capabilities become fused into a corporation's genetic code, it leverages them across a wide range of business objectives and concerns.

It is not uncommon to suppose that Six Sigma should become a core value alongside others that a corporation may have espoused for decades. But this is not the goal, as the role of Six Sigma is to simply become the way a company does business.

In the event that Six Sigma does become institutionalized, it should strictly enable the achievement of all goals and the realization of all core values at the business, operations, and process levels of a corporation.

4. How can global performance measures be used to guide a Six Sigma initiative and ensure its continued progress?

Most corporations do not revere the idea and practice of measurement as an enabling value. As a class, they are very good at regularly examining such Y-related measures as costs, revenue, earnings, and profit. Likewise, operations managers look at such performance metrics as cost per unit, productivity, and so on. At the process level, the focus is most typically on key product or service characteristics that are desired by the customer.

But most companies are not so good at measuring and monitoring problematic variables, or X's. They are focused at all levels on the Y's, not the X's. The entire science of Six Sigma is predicated on the principle that Y is a function of X. It is this very deterministic reasoning that enables a corporation to change the way it does business and reap the rewards of improved performance.

If you look at DuPont's history, you see a corporation not unlike others in that it had been preoccupied with measuring its Y's. The company had certain business values, such as profit, that it monitored religiously. It had certain core values, such as safety, that it also measured regularly. You can look around the company and find people who are well aware of how many employees are injured each month per 100,000, or some such number. This is the Y.

But such attention does not mean the company has always had a deeply ingrained value for measurement. It simply means that DuPont has been good at counting frequency numbers, much as a person balances a checkbook at the end of each month.

A corporation can value productivity, growth, or profit. It can value innovation, as 3M has. It can value accountability, as has General Electric. It can value the ethical treatment of people, a sentiment we see at virtually every corporation. But where are the values that drive the wedge that lifts the rock? Where are the values for statistical thinking? For problematic reasoning? Fact-based decision making? Mining for leverage? Empowering questions? Measuring the immeasurable?

These are just a few examples of enabling values—X-weighted thrusts that actually contain the power to move the Y's in the desired direction. As DuPont experienced over the last few years, when a corporation shifts its focus from the Y side of the performance ledger to the X side, good things happen. The X's get defined, measured, and analyzed. Then they get improved and controlled, which in turn drives the Y's where they need to go. Y is a function of X.

In the history of civilization, there is no better principle by which to guide directive action. It is the root of the scientific method, therefore, that guides and drives progress at large, and certainly guides the progress of Six Sigma. When the Y's are systematically connected to the X's at the business, operations, and process levels, it becomes clear which levers need to be pulled to get results. So concerning injuries at DuPont, as previously discussed, the actual number of injuries was very small compared to the total number of hours of opportunities for injuries. DuPont learned that major impactful X's on safety include extensive safety orientation, training, measurement, and personal accountability supported by leadership.

The Black Belts have the methods and tools to bring the principle that Y is a function of X to bear on the fundamental performance of a corporation. They actually set the system in motion by connecting the X's to the Y's at the basal level of what a corporation does each and every day to make a living. In doing so, they discover the all-elusive transfer functions that govern the efficacy of how value is created throughout a corporation—the true relationships between process-level X's and Y's. The transform function is the causal relationship between inputs and outputs, defining the predicted output from known inputs. An example of a big Y at the strategic level at DuPont would be year-over-year revenue growth. For DuPont, the goal is 6 percent. The X's include new-product introductions, price increases, sales force effectiveness, new geographies, new customers, and so on.

This builds a growing cache of confidence that more transfer functions can be discovered, improved, and controlled. The thrust continues until so many little gears of change are turning that the value of measurement and data becomes contagious, even in areas that reside toward the end of the controllability continuum. Confidence translates into such areas as finance, communications, public affairs, marketing, and sales, where transfer functions are more difficult to measure but, nevertheless, are there.

Having run this gamut, a corporation begins to internally experience the power of measurement, and it then drives that enabling wedge even harder than it had before. For DuPont, after being initiated from the top, the wedge was most definitely driven from the bottom as Black Belts gathered great enthusiasm for what they could accomplish.

To ensure entitlement, or to secure the most shareholder value possible for each dollar invested in a business, you have to measure what you value, and you have to do so in a way that leaves no room for ambiguity or disconnection. Therefore, if your current metrics meet these criteria, keep them. If they don't, then you'll have to reconfigure them, add new ones, and discard the ones that don't connect—if you're aiming to do Six Sigma the way it's supposed to be done.

The reason a corporation decides to install Six Sigma is that its leaders are dissatisfied with the company's current performance. And if a corporation's performance is ailing, it's most likely due, in large part, to a lack of connection between its goals and values (Y's) and its processes and practices (X's). Recognizing that X's become Y's at successive levels of activity, the simple solution is to respect this inescapable phenomenon by building a system of connected dashboards throughout a business enterprise. Then the system should be relentlessly reinforced and utilized to guide a Six Sigma initiative and ensure its continued progress.

5. How does a Six Sigma deployment platform derive quantum improvement in harmony with corporate goals and objectives?

Six Sigma is like a mechanical system in that overriding aims are achieved only to the extent that its working parts function in a holistic, synergistic manner. Building such connectivity and synergy, however, is usually much easier said than done, and only a properly guided initiative can do this.

There are two key ways in which a deployment platform derives quantum improvement in harmony with corporate goals and objectives. There is first a short-term thrust, motivated by personal gain, such as individual bonuses, which flows down the goals of the corporation along with the values, or big ideas, that enable the achievement of those goals. After this, there is a bubbling-up effect by which the various deployment platforms begin to influence the perceptions and decisions of the corporate senior leadership team about where to direct the company next.

Six Sigma began as a method and technique for process engineers and then grew into a structure and framework for leaders. That framework is organized around the various levels of a corporate enterprise: business, operations, and process. The corporation of DuPont represents the business level; each of the eighteen major strategic business units, along with their many segments, represent the operations level; and all the processes by which the company does business represent, naturally, the process level.

If Six Sigma is to yield its intended aims, there must be an initial and powerful top-down thrust that garners its life force from a burning platform for change, a high-level financial stretch goal, and certain guiding principles, or values. In turn, such a thrust must be focused on the achievement of financial goals that are apportioned among the various segments of a corporation and are further broken down into a constellation of single Black Belt projects. When such projects are completed, they sum up to the various operations-level goals and, ultimately, to the overall goal of the corporation within a time frame of about one year.

For DuPont, this initial thrust was predicated on improving productivity mostly through cost reduction. Also, it was driven by a system of accountability tied directly to the variable pay of its top corporate officers, as well as to the variable pay of its business unit heads and bonus-eligible management population. It was further reinforced and controlled through a disciplined process whereby each of the major business units followed a disciplined and prescriptive process for calculating their expected contributions and for committing themselves to make them.

The principles and practices required to meet Six Sigma financial goals at all levels were transferred and instilled through training and other means. Six Sigma structures and networks were set up according to role (Champion and Master Black Belt, for instance) and function (IT, finance, HR, communications). Information and project review systems were installed. While the goal was for each major business unit to function as autonomously as possible, there were certain principles and practices common to all. For example, all DuPonters speak with data or else generally do not get heard. They also must document their projects in SigmaTRAC, the common database for validating and reporting project savings.

It was this balance between commonality and autonomy that drove quantum improvement at DuPont. There were certain rules and regulations, but there were many freedoms. As each successive organizational level configured its Six Sigma CTQs and commitment, law translated into freedom and freedom translated into law. For example, a DuPont vice president of a major business was accountable for delivering a piece of the financial pie. That was law. Then there were certain flexibilities in the way implementation cells were configured in a business and the way they selected Black Belts and identified projects.

Those decisions, in turn, became law for the deployment Champions, who then became responsible for certain Black Belts and projects. How exactly they enacted those projects on a day-to-day basis was open to discretion, as long as they adhered to the Breakthrough Strategy.

The net effect was that different businesses, regions, plants, and people began to share a common drive, metrics, a language, and experience of harvesting cash from the fields where they live. Critical mass builds quickly, and successively higher goals are met as a function of aggregating project results. It is the practice of what happens inside a successful Six Sigma thrust such as DuPont's, and inside others that have achieved similar Six Sigma harmony and synergy.

Initiatives such as TQM lack a holistic focus and an infrastructure to tie efforts together at the business, operations, and process levels of a corporation. They lack the dedicated resources and the unmitigated initial focus on business improvement and cash results. Because of this, TQM-type initiatives never had a chance of achieving critical mass. They didn't create a major groundswell of success that was powerful enough to capture the executive mind and heart. Such initiatives simply did not exist in harmony with corporate goals and objectives, and sometimes even opposed them.

Six Sigma has been potent enough to make a large dent in a corporation's cost of poor quality right out of the box. Once this occurs, Black Belts and Champions have the credibility and voice to begin influencing management. When Six Sigma began at DuPont, the executives determined how much money it would target, and set that goal. After the first $100 million in annualized savings was validated in the course of a few months of implementation, the Champions network had a captive audience.

DuPont's Six Sigma deployment platform's positive effects on the company were in line with corporate goals and objectives. Confidence and commitment at the top breed confidence and commitment in the middle and at the bottom. Confidence and commitment at the bottom yield project results and increasingly noticeable and dramatic financial impact in the middle. Dramatic financial impact in the middle captures the attention, imagination, and aspirations of the top. The cycle repeats itself.

6. How should a deployment platform sustain the verified gains it realizes during the course of Six Sigma implementation?

Corporate entities serve an important role in establishing direction, guiding action, and coordinating synergies among their various entities and divisions. But it's the individual businesses and profit centers that make and deliver value, both for the customer and for the company.

This principle also holds true when it comes to Six Sigma, as deployment and implementation are driven primarily by the corporation's different platforms. That is why the platforms are defined and designated as part of an initial thrust and installation effort. While a corporation takes on the strategy of installing and deploying Six Sigma, it is the platforms that do the installing and deploying, not the corporation. Only the platforms can legitimately verify and control the gains made during the course of Six Sigma implementation.

The job of validating specific financial project results is ultimately left to finance people with input from Process Owners and Black Belts. In turn, it is the Process Owners and Black Belts who install control plans to sustain the manufacturing and transactional gains made through each project. At a platform level, however, the idea of verification and control is much more associated with aggregate project savings, the proliferation of enabling values, and effective deployment practices and procedures than with one specific cost saving.

When a corporation sets about installing Six Sigma, it configures its various units into a set of deployment platforms, which are essentially major slices of the corporation separated by product, region, customer type, or existing business divisions. The purpose for such segmentation is to designate the high-level organizational units through which Six

Sigma will be installed and deployed. The idea is similar to the structuring of a military campaign that configures its deployment units on the basis of the specific objective at hand.

These are the units that verify and control the big-picture elements of a Six Sigma thrust. In DuPont's case, under the general precept of seamlessly integrating Six Sigma into its existing structure, it simply designated each of its eighteen strategic business units to be a deployment platform. DuPont did not want to upset or contradict its strong history of decentralized and self-contained autonomy.

More important than how a company might configure its deployment platforms is the idea that they exist to ensure that each installation and deployment is effective, to force accountability for results, and to manage forward momentum. Each platform is responsible for recognizing its need for Six Sigma, defining its Six Sigma goal, measuring the CTQs impacting that goal, analyzing the relationships among those CTQs, improving their capability to meet the goal, controlling the systems and practices installed, standardizing those systems and practices, and, finally, integrating them into the way the platform does business. For example, DuPont structured its deployment cells to follow the line accountability of the organization structure. Each business unit became a deployment, so the different and specific needs of each business could drive their Six Sigma deployment. So while looking for the hidden factory (a concept that there is additional capacity in your actual factory disguised by waste) with yield and uptime was important to Titanium Technologies, top-line growth led the way for Crop Protection.

This is the Breakthrough Strategy in a nutshell as it applies to a deployment platform. We are really talking about how a platform controls the gains it has made or, more specifically, the practices by which it deploys Six Sigma. This includes controlling goal setting, Champion selection, and Six Sigma management reviews. It also includes controlling the more nebulous platform-owned aspects of Six Sigma, such as communication and culture change. Following on the differential deployment strategy, each DuPont business unit was able to communicate in a way that fit its culture. Some businesses used town meetings, while others, such as Polyester, used extensive newsletter distribution. This was also true about recognitions for Six Sigma successes. Crop Protection could build on its culture by staging gala dinners for Black Belts and their spouses to celebrate certifications.

Before going into control mode, platform-level leaders begin by verifying the aggregation of project results, just as a Black Belt would verify the gains made on a single project before focusing on control.

When best practices have been defined and documented, a deployment platform is responsible for installing a mechanism for controlling them, ensuring they are consistently repeated. This can come in the form of an activity-based check sheet, just like the one a technician might use and sign off on after performing maintenance on a piece of machinery. Only here we are talking about executives and senior leaders who bring the same level of discipline to their work. If Six Sigma changes the way a company does business, then that change must be made at all levels.

If you are a business leader, you create the vision and burning platform for change. Then you sanction, formalize, and set in motion all the various vehicles and mechanisms of Six Sigma. You constantly reinforce your belief in and commitment to Six Sigma in word and action. Finally, you implement management-level controls that maintain the integrity and efficacy of an ongoing Six Sigma thrust. In this way, you sustain Six Sigma–related progress.

7. How should a deployment platform standardize its processes and practices and then leverage them in the future?

With Six Sigma, the work accomplished in one part of the total system can act as a slingshot for achieving similar goals in other parts of the system. Six Sigma can be extended through knowledge-management practices that enable similar projects to be enacted across different platforms, bringing similar results with less effort and fewer resources.

The ability for Black Belts to continue to deliver more each year is a knowledge-management issue. Using SigmaTRAC, DuPont put in a search capability to allow Champions to see what had been done before. Copying, which is more politely known as replicating, could save about 30 percent of the time to complete a project and get it accomplished for a lower cost. SigmaTRAC has become a knowledge-management tool, although it started out as a tracking and reporting tool.

The overall thrust is one of learning, standardization, collaboration, and replication. If Six Sigma itself has a learning curve, and it does, then efforts to standardize that learning must be designed by the corporation and enacted by its various deployment platforms. From a business-level perspective, a corporation can ensure the ever-increasing productivity of its Six Sigma initiative.

A corporation must establish a strong value for learning and sharing knowledge if it's going to benefit from the idea of standardization. On a smaller scale, it's the value of collaboration and sharing that drives the capability of a corporation to extend its Six Sigma knowledge.

If collaboration does not exist in a corporation, then it must be shaped and formed into existence. For example, a corporation can install an activity-based metric that requires major organizational units to collaborate. There could be a system that requires deployment Champions to share learning about practices and processes that relate to project selection, Black Belt selection, compensation, recognition, and so on.

When DuPont began Six Sigma it did not have a strongly embedded value for collaboration and knowledge sharing. The company was organized into silos around certain product lines, and the people who worked within those silos tended to keep their attention focused within.

But as Six Sigma took hold in the deployment platforms, a focus on cross-pollination began to emerge—perhaps driven by the imperative to save so much money and achieve dramatic results in such a short period of time. The need for this knowledge sharing was recognized by DuPont during the initial stage of Six Sigma installation, which is why it established various collaboration networks corporately.

DuPont even established a small network to foster and support the creation of other networks, as discussed earlier. In all cases, there was an IT component whereby the various networks had a way to document their experiences, sorting through the trivial many to crystallize the vital few and generally communicate and share. The overriding purpose was always to find ways not to reinvent the wheel. It was very common for newly appointed business unit Champion leaders to scour the Champions network looking for advice and tools.

It is vital to drive toward identifying and controlling best practices as soon and as effectively as possible. Knowledge sharing and replication have little value in the absence of a system for ferreting out what doesn't work, for establishing control over what does, and for documenting success in a format that others can use. A Champions network supported by a strong IT collaboration capability is crucial for achieving an effective deployment and implementation.

Learning begins to accrue among the leadership and deployment Champion ranks during the implementation process. "How can I best communicate the need for phases of Six Sigma deployment throughout my business? What are the criteria I should look for in selecting deployment Champions? What's the best process for determining an appropriate Six Sigma financial goal? What's the best way to break that goal down among the various locations and segments of my business? How do I secure commitment and buy-in from my leadership team?" These, as one can imagine, are only a few of the many questions a business leader might have as he or she shapes the life-form of Six Sigma in a given platform.

Similarly, deployment Champions will face a battery of questions and concerns: "Does anyone out there know how I'm supposed to interact with the leadership team of my particular platform? When it comes to Six Sigma, do they call the shots or do I? What if I run into resistance and need help? I'm having trouble getting management to let go of good people to become Project Champions; does anyone have a document that clearly delineates the minimum requirements for a Project Champion? Can someone provide a description of what happens when less-than-ideal people are selected?" Using a collaborative workspace tool, DuPont Champions can ask one another such questions in a safe place. For example, when Imaging Systems wanted to do a sanity check on its Black Belt reward system, the Champion placed the inquiry in the workspace and quickly received information about what everyone was doing on the subject. He then could use that data to redesign his system.

While the questions are limitless, the answers, in the form of solidified and documented best practices, can save a corporation millions of dollars in avoided Six Sigma sub-optimization.

In fact, some corporations have employed the services of deployment Master Black Belts, whose job it is to gather established Six Sigma learning both inside and outside organizational and company borders. These are veritable knowledge-mongers who exist to suck up as much new learning as possible, package it into a standard format, and get it into the hands of as many people as possible.

For a platform to standardize and leverage its deployment processes and practices, it must achieve critical mass and noticeable results on a platform-wide scale. It also must establish systems and mechanisms to control best practices. Its corporate parent must instill a value for standardization, knowledge sharing, and collaboration, and design a system by which best practices are cross-pollinated and pushed and pulled across organizational borders. The corporate parent also must measure the extent to which the system is working. This is how a platform realizes the value of standardization and leverages it for future gain.

8. How should a deployment platform integrate the lessons it's learned into management thinking and the strategic planning process?

The answer lies in the idea of integrating the Breakthrough Strategy into the way a corporation assesses the past and plans for the future. While corporations exist to make money, they also need to embody certain values, or X-oriented focuses, if they are to achieve their Y-related goals. Taking on the challenge of integrating Six Sigma lessons into the fabric of management thought and action lies in figuring out how to instill and cement the concept of analytically and factually determining how to do things into the minds and hearts of those who lead.

While business leaders set Six Sigma in motion and provide the required support, they are at the end of the chain in terms of their knowledge and capability for actually applying Six Sigma to what they do; they are always the last to make Six Sigma the way they do business. But this is not so much by negligence as it is by design. The cycle of breakthrough must turn at the process level before turning at the operations level, and it must turn at the operations level before turning at the business level. Lessons have been learned many times over within the body of a corporation or platform before they are learned once at the higher levels.

Once Six Sigma is set in motion, business leaders can't help but notice how it's transformed their organizations. They have committed themselves and many of their best people to the cause; they have tied a portion of their personal compensation to that cause; they have set the cause in motion and remained demonstrably attached to its ongoing development and progress. Then, when they see the undeniable financial benefit on their income statement and hear about how their people have been transformed, they too become transformed. They begin to think in terms of X's and not as much in terms of Y's. From their daily activities to the way they plan for the future, the values and behaviors of Six Sigma become at least as important as their motivation to make more money and grow the business. The questions no longer center on how the company or business platform should cut costs or improve earnings. They center on the values that will enable them to be competitive by doing what they do better than anyone else.

When this occurs, a shift in thinking and planning takes place. It becomes much more important to establish certain values and attributes in the organization than to establish certain financial goals, although the latter are necessary. Accountability, customer focus, disciplined processes, speaking with data, fact-based decisions, measurement, commitment to training, a sense of urgency, and passionate leadership become the most common topics of discussion. They become central to what a corporation deploys and implements, values and measures.

Such a value-driven strategic framework was embodied many years ago by Motorola's Bob Galvin, who was known for his insistence on covering topics such as quality, cycle time, and customer satisfaction in corporate meetings before going over such items as earnings growth and profit. By doing this, Galvin was imprinting on his leaders the idea that X's are more important than Y's. He was saying that it really doesn't matter what a corporation wishes for; what matters is how it gets what it wants. It was the drivers, the software that made the hardware go, that Galvin was seeking.

Six Sigma forces a corporation at all levels to isolate the critical X's that govern its desired Y's. Ironically, this has very little to do with the items that typically preoccupy the top brass at a large organization. If Six Sigma does anything, it enables executive leaders to focus on what they should have been focusing on all along: instilling values rather than defining goals and prescribing actions and initiatives—even though, paradoxically, Six Sigma is a prescribed initiative. But it only prescribes the methodology, systems, structures, and resources that must be mined for leverage in achieving business, operations, and process aims. At DuPont, the focus on the training and development of DuPonters through the Six Sigma initiative is a core example of centering on the company's real competitive advantage—its people. Even though DuPont started with metrics on people trained, etc., it was building the capability of its people to grow and add value. In the end, it's all about people.

As operational and process improvements are made in a corporation or platform, its leaders begin to let go of the need to control the specific activities involved in making those improvements. As a deployment matures, the leaders become more focused on the capabilities of their organization because new processes and systems are now ingrained into their organization to control the specific activities. A good example is how DuPont's Crop Protection division used an IT program to help prioritize improvement projects responding to business needs. The leaders can be strategic, because they know a project exists to deliver tactical results. They realize that their Champions and Black Belts understand those methods better than anyone, especially themselves. Freed from the need to manage the specifics of a process, a leadership team can unilaterally focus on its own role, coming up with the critical X's that determine the destiny of the overall business.

Imagine a company or platform that listens so well to the voice of its customers and to market data that it scientifically figures out that its main competitive advantage lies in its price leadership. After digging deeper, it determines that its critical X is to lead the price curve by six months, because when it does so, it reaps twice the profit in the following six months. While many corporations understand such dynamics on an experiential or intuitive basis, or even on a limited scientific level, they don't have nearly as much capability as a Black Belt to understand the critical X's driving a particular manufacturing or transactional process. Nor would they necessarily standardize that understanding and integrate it into the way they do business.

While engaged in a strategic planning session, it's common for someone in a corporation or major unit to suggest a certain goal. Someone else then asks if the goal is high enough. The reply is that it is, because it is 10 percent higher than last year's goal—a figure that seems intuitively acceptable. It's uncharacteristic for someone in this setting to challenge the proposed goal, asking how they know it's the right one. Is it wishful thinking or is it reasonable expectation? How does this goal interact with others? What is the empirical, factorial basis for that assertion? More important, what is the confidence level that a 10 percent increase can be achieved?

It's called strategy without accountability, and it's the kind of loose thinking and lack of discipline over which a Black Belt or plant manager would lose his job. But executives somehow get to keep their jobs by integrating what is palatable, often to the exclusion of what is practical or what actually works. In the absence of an ability or cultural imperative to speak with data, they default to experience and intuition, or to what they can get away with in negotiation. In the end, they get a set of compromised goals that everyone can live with.

There is the rare CEO who says something like, "In the strategic planning process we'll focus on dramatically improving the *process* of business. In fact, I will install a strategy that will help us do just that, and that strategy is Six Sigma. But bear in mind that Six Sigma will force us to interrogate what we do like never before. We won't be able to say we value integrity, or we treat our people well, or we know we can be a leader in our industry—nebulous assertions won't fly. Only that which can be recognized, defined, measured, analyzed, improved, controlled, standardized, and integrated belongs on the docket of this corporation."

If this sounds familiar, you're probably a Champion or a Black Belt. As such, you personally understand the power of discovering the critical X's associated with the operations and processes you have improved. It is this same power that ultimately drives the wedge of change among the leaders of a corporation and its strategic business units.

ONE DUPONT PROJECT: PRODUCTION

DuPont's Cyrel business makes special printing plates out of polymers that feel like soft rubber. They sell the plates to printers, who use them to create vibrant packaging. Known as flexography, the printing process enables consumer product companies to enhance their images, sharpen differentiation of their products, and improve shelf impact.

But in order for Cyrel to make its flexographic plates, it needs a thin (0.13 mm) layer of polyester film on which to bond its thicker (about one-eighth of an inch) putty-like polymer. The thin layer of polyester film is supplied to Cyrel by DuPont's Teijin Films (DTF). DTF is the world's top producer of polyester films under various trade names such as Mylar and Melinex, with combined sales of more than $1 billion and production capacity of more than 300,000 tons per year. In addition to Cyrel, DTF supplies its film to outside companies, who use it in many other diverse applications.

But Cyrel noticed a problem with the film it was getting from DTF. Some of the film Cyrel received did not meet its tight specifications for UV optical density, a technical term for the amount of ultraviolet (UV) light that gets absorbed by the film during production. Such optical density determines the quality of the final plate assembly and its ability to deliver the properties required for high-quality printing.

To DTF's Six Sigma Champion, the mission seemed simple enough: improve the optical density capability of the film. At least this is what Mike Bachmann, Ph.D., physicist, and Master Black Belt, thought at first. Bachmann was among the first wave of Master Black Belts at DuPont, having come to the company from Imperial Chemical Industries' polyester films business, which DuPont purchased in the late '90s. Bachmann had a strong background in statistics and statistical concepts.

When he was first selected for Six Sigma Master Black Belt training, he did not understand why he should commit two weeks to learning a lot of statistical concepts and tools. But his bosses explained that Six Sigma wasn't all about statistics, but that it was about leadership and implementation and about getting everyone on board together, doing business more systematically.

"The tools were not challenging to me, but the methodology is what got me, and especially the way it was all brought together," says Bachmann. "The overall methodology sums up all the parts for you, and forces a very logical structure on what you do." Bachmann says that before Six Sigma, plants did not really define or set limits for their process X's but only their performance Y's. As a result, people would solve problems in more of a shotgun fashion than in a systematic way.

For example, engineers would jump into analyzing available data to solve a problem before properly defining and measuring the problem. This undercut the power of their analyses and limited their potential to achieve a breakthrough. Bachmann discovered that Six Sigma was much more disciplined and thorough, beginning with defining customer needs and concluding with sustained breakthrough (control).

The polyester film that DTF manufactures absorbs ultraviolet light at a specific wavelength. The film is provided in the form of large rolls of 4,000 feet. At the customer's plant, UV light was passed through the film during production to get proper bonding with a top layer of thicker, putty-like film. The only way to control the degree of bonding was to control the amount of UV absorbed at a specific wavelength in the base film. Bachmann's mission was to ensure that the absorption capability of his product dramatically improved.

As Bachmann and team worked through the Breakthrough Strategy, they found all kinds of issues and problems that potentially could limit UV density. Chief among them was the measurement capability of DTF's and Cyrel's rudimentary, low-resolution, offline testing equipment. Through a series of measurement system analyses, and a lot of effort in trying to calibrate three different sets of equipment in three separate locations around the world, Bachmann realized that they needed better measurement equipment.

Coincidentally, an online spectrometer had already been ordered and was in the process of installation when this project started. When the new system was installed at DTF's Hopewell, Virginia, plant, an interesting phenomenon came to light. Every ten minutes, there was a cyclical variation in UV optical density, which showed up as a regular peak and a valley on a control chart. It was obvious to see with the new equipment. The old equipment and measurement method were not set up or scaled to detect this pattern.

"The new equipment opened up new vistas," says Bachmann. "We could see the properties we were studying at a tenfold improvement in resolution, and we could gather 250 measurements per film roll, not just four measurements, as we were used to. We weren't trying to measure a peanut with a yardstick anymore."

The old testing method was simply too inferior, according to Bachmann. Before, they could have workers take a physical sample from the film roll only every 1,000 feet. Moreover, the samples were taken from the edges of the material, the scrap area of the film where there was much less quality control in general over such factors as thickness and UV optical density. The new system enabled a measurement every fifteen feet and took that reading from a center point in the material, with no manpower whatsoever.

The production line on which film was made also had an automated production data "historian," which had the capability of monitoring hundreds of process variables on an ongoing basis. Pressures, temperatures, rates, flows, and all kinds of other inputs were logged. This "historian" looked at about 500 inputs every thirty seconds and logged a vector with those numbers. "It was a Six Sigma dream, because we could see how all these variables changed in accordance with optical density changes," says Bachmann.

Bachmann's analysis suggested that there was a disruption in the vacuum levels during each one of its cycles, resulting in a nonuniform delivery of UV dye. This resulted in a substantial cyclical change in the UV optical density in the finished product.

As simple as the final solution would seem, Bachmann went though a tremendous amount of investigation and trouble to find it. There was a period of time in which they had to collect data by hand, because their source-tracing efforts led them to a production location that could not be measured automatically. In the end, the solution was to turn off the vacuum system while making film. With the vacuum off, the variation in UV optical density decreased dramatically.

Turning off the vacuum during film production was not a problem for DuPont, because the line typically runs for just a few days while making the product. Bachmann had ensured that all of the film made as a result of the bonding process would be accepted by Cyrel, which brought DTF $200,000 in soft benefits such as increased efficiency and less waste, as well as another $250,000 in expanded capacity.

## CHAPTER 6

OPERATIONS-LEVEL Q&A WITH MIKEL HARRY AND DON LINSENMANN

1. How can a local implementation cell align its operational needs to the parent deployment platform's goals and objectives?

We cannot overemphasize the importance of properly defining and designating implementation cells, which is critical to the success of Six Sigma. If they're configured incorrectly, it can be devastating to a Six Sigma thrust.

A corporation adopts Six Sigma because it is dissatisfied with its current performance. That means its current strategies, structure, culture, and systems aren't yielding their expected value, and most probably have not for some time. The corporation needs a capability and capacity for breakthrough that it doesn't have. Because of this, Six Sigma is initially snapped onto a corporation's existing structure in a way that enables what was formerly unachievable.

It is vital to correctly designate the necessary cells within a given deployment platform, configure their boundaries, and identify the type and number of projects they will execute. This allows a corporation to extend the integrity of Six Sigma beyond the platform level down into the operational segments that have the leverage to make changes a reality.

Implementation cells, like deployment platforms, are not generally configured according to geography, physical location, horizontal function, or vertical business segments. They are configured in accordance with the Six Sigma aims of the corporation, the specific goals and culture of the platform, and the needs of the implementation cells themselves.

A platform in one corporation, for example, was a matrix organization in which there were thirty-two factories in various countries. Due to the specific goals of the platform (related to capacity, customer satisfaction, cost, etc.), in some cases a factory was also an implementation cell. At DuPont, each business chose its cell structure for deployment. Nylon, for example, looked at the opportunities by line of business, such as apparel, flooring, and industrial, due to the similar market forces in each line, regardless of geography. Other businesses, such as Titanium Technologies, looked at a cell as a function, with manufacturing and sales being the two cells. In other cases, such as when the platform goal was to improve certain aspects of design, an implementation cell was splintered across many plants and locations. In still other cases, a particular product determined the definition and boundaries of a cell, as the problems associated with it were pervasive and important enough to justify such a high priority.

Other platforms in other corporations have segmented their cells according to the extent of need and priority in manufacturing and transactional areas, whether those areas were contained in one location, spread out across many, or concentrated in a few. Still others organize around classes of customer problems, if that is the predominant center of gravity for their Six Sigma goals. The possibilities are nearly endless, though the nature and specifications of the need are what drives the constellation of goals, which determines the configuration of the implementation cells within a platform.

Some sites may house two or three implementation cells, or simply contain parts of others. Other sites are combined with counterparts to form a cell that crosses over many locations. Whatever the case, cells are configured by a flow-down process in which the goals of the platform are disaggregated into their logical blocks for further attention.

Once configured, a Project Champion is selected to lead each cell through the process of project selection, Black Belt selection, and project execution. It then is a process of negotiation between the cell-level Champion and platform deployment Champion, along with any other business or operational leaders that have a stake or say in which projects are selected, how many are selected, how they are prioritized, and how the cell will come up with the required people and resources. The general idea is to achieve alignment between the needs and goals of the platform and the needs and goals of the cell. A good example of this process was in DuPont's Crop Protection business. Each Champion would bring a project for consideration to a decision board. The board would evaluate the relative priority of the project and assign resources accordingly. This helps reconcile any differences between the Champion's outlook and the business needs of the over-all deployment.

Negotiations involve the number of people, primarily Black Belts, and the type of projects that can be absorbed by the various cells in the platform.

It can be challenging to achieve the right alignment between a deployment platform and its various cells. When such alignment becomes too difficult, it's a clear indication that certain cells will have to carry more weight than others, or that the platform should refine and adjust its cell configuration. Maybe a different delineation strategy would work better. Or perhaps the platform leadership needs to revisit some of its cells with a harder line of demand. For example, at DuPont's nonwovens business, the deployment cell did not have aggressive goals relative to other businesses early on because its strategy was focused on growth. Once the Six Sigma tools on methodologies were developed for top-line growth, that business changed Champions and set higher goals. It's not an option for platform leadership to return to corporate leadership with a case for reducing its already negotiated contribution, since this would undermine the integrity of the overall thrust.

Only perfect connectivity and alignment is an acceptable starting point for launching into Six Sigma implementation. This means that all the contributions of the implementation cells within a platform roll together to satisfy the platform's overall goals and financial commitment to Six Sigma. It also means that the local needs of the cells are met while preserving their full autonomy, ownership, and accountability for making the planned gains. In addition, both of these objectives must be achieved while simultaneously meeting all corporate non-negotiable requirements, such as average dollars returned per year per Black Belt.

A good example of this at DuPont is in its Titanium Technologies business. While one of the overall business objectives was to improve output, many projects needed to be linked together to impact the overall metric. Each cell Champion would identify the possible projects that could contribute to overall yield. Each individual project needed to meet the corporate requirement of delivering at least $175,000, but also had to contribute to the business goal of improved yield. The Champion would look at how each project connected to the others to assign resources, as the output on one project might be the input of the next. Managing the entirety of the program for Titanium Technologies was the job of the platform Champion, assisted by the many Black Belts working in this general area.

A strong Six Sigma Champion structure ensures the alignment of operational needs with deployment platform goals and objectives. The case-by-case negotiation and documentation of project selection criteria cements this alignment into place. Beyond this, a platform must tackle the details of implementation before it can truly determine if the DNA of its various cells is compatible with that of the larger organism.

2. How should a local implementation cell go about developing and focusing a Six Sigma implementation plan?

Once an implementation cell has set its financial target, selected its Champion, designated the number of Black Belts it will train, and solidified the criteria it will use to select projects, it must formulate a plan for actually implementing Six Sigma in a way that maximizes the probability of yielding the intended results. It must do this with a sense of urgency, and with an imperative to make decisions and act quickly in the interests of its specifically defined commitment to quantum change.

There is a strong tendency among corporations, platforms, and cells not to pay as much attention to implementation planning as they do to other aspects of Six Sigma, such as the tactical deployment components, which is the "doing" part. This includes setting up training, picking belts, organizing project reviews, and dealing with communications and HR issues. The point is that an organization must also look at the big picture of what Six Sigma is doing to make sure alignment is in place. It's about taking a look at the forest rather than getting more bark in your nose! By the time local cells become actively involved, the need to get projects under way and achieve tangible results overshadows the need to come up with a sound implementation.

But as a corporation looks forward after it commits to Six Sigma, it should consider the generic needs of local cells, such as all of the IT support, HR support, and local leadership support Black Belts will need in planning for successful project implementation. It should view implementation planning as a way to minimize the risk of flawed project implementation. With a robust plan in place, a local implementation cell has the greatest chance of fulfilling its commitments. If a cell is not meeting its commitments, an implementation plan provides a basis for evaluating what might be wrong and why, an important part of keeping local efforts on track and avoiding a cell- or platform-specific Six Sigma reset. For example, examining the number of Black Belts assigned in a local deployment can quickly lead to projecting the output of that group. Armed with the data that a given Black Belt should produce, say, $1 million of benefits per year, the implementation plan can quickly assess the most likely dollar output by examining the number of Black Belts assigned.

While some corporations leave the details of implementation planning to the local cells, we strongly recommend that the deployment platform or even the corporation do the structuring. In this way, the platform or corporation can ensure that certain basic questions are answered, general requirements are fulfilled, implementation guidelines are followed, and principles are visibly embraced. Sample guidelines to be put in place corporately could include minimum dollar benefit per project ($175,000 in DuPont), minimum number of projects a Black Belt should do in a year (three at DuPont), full-time Black Belt roles, and adherence to corporate standards for data reporting.

The best tool is a simple implementation-planning template with a set of questions to answer, blanks to fill in, and criteria to meet. The template might prompt the local cell Champion and his or her implementation team members to document how they have aligned the goals of the cell with the goals of the parent platform. It might ask them to document their criteria for selecting projects for the coming year, along with a list of guidelines and tips for doing so. It might further ask the cell to document its plan for unfreezing the attitudes of its people toward change initiatives, and for locking attitudes back in once a new direction is set and established. DuPont used a concept of the CTQ flow-down to do this. A CTQ is a critical-to-quality element of a plan. It could be sales growth, cash generation, or new-product introductions, for example. Once the objective is laid out, the questions can be asked and projects can be defined to support hierarchical goals of the flow-down.

In addition to this template, the local implementation cell should have access to a package of materials checklists that it can use to work through the process of developing a sound implementation plan and become educated about the general process of implementation.

A local cell also should assemble a cross-functional team of leaders who reflect the overall implementation focus and represent the various areas that will be affected, such as was done in the Crop Protection business. There the business leader used his multifunctional staff as a decision board to align the projects with the resource. So if R&D was the high-priority area, for example, this team could orient resources toward R&D projects. This multidisciplinary approach avoids the trap of suboptimizing resource within a given function. Such a team is a necessary condition for success, as Six Sigma implementation involves much more than Champions and Black Belts. Significant change doesn't happen merely at the behest of a handful of people in an implementation cell; it happens as a result of tangible commitment, broad and deep involvement, and intense coordination among domains of operational and business activity.

This kind of group works through a process of implementation planning that draws on various standard inputs (corporate guidelines, platform goals such as number of projects or number of belts, and project-selection criteria such as Six Sigma goals on cost savings, etc.) and turns out various standard outputs (plan for culture change, training schedule, list of projects, etc.). In this way, top-down meets bottom-up, and a viable plan is born. The local implementation cell has a preloaded view of what it needs to do to be successful, while the parent platform has an insurance policy against poorly executed implementation.

There are sequence-type activities and events that must be planned for the implementation phase, such as the ones related to kicking off the initiative, training Black Belts, scheduling the beginning of selected projects, selecting Black Belt team members, and conducting regular project reviews. There are other logistics and activities to plan, such as acquiring laptops and software and training people in their use, and the recognition and certification of Black Belts and team members. Further, there should be a plan in place for developing internal Master Black Belts who can take over the training and mentoring function after the consultant is gone.

In addition to these items, an effective local implementation plan should contain a localized rationale for why it is implementing Six Sigma, a message that can be leveraged often by the Champions and

Black Belts during implementation. For example, one rationale might be "Our plant has not been producing first-quality product at the rate of our sister plants and we will use Six Sigma to accomplish that." There should be a documented reference to the nature of Black Belt training to ensure that instructors have a consistent basis upon which to set up specific course content. It is essential that a standard curriculum of Six Sigma training be in place, because the local deployment will not invent their own training. Following the corporate training curriculum gives all Black Belts the common language that will allow them to communicate, leverage, and learn from others in different sites. Lastly, there needs to be a rationale for project reviews as well as a set of guidelines so people know what reviews are, why they are important, and how they will occur. Project reviews are the way the Black Belt can present information to the leadership and also get recognized. These reviews will open communications to align everyone on the site, so that all know what is important and what progress is being made.

Even if there is a circumspect and structured process of Six Sigma deployment, unstructured and undisciplined Six Sigma implementation can hurt a project. This would belie the nature of Six Sigma and contaminate the lifeblood of a Six Sigma thrust at the very point when it moves from expectation to actualization. A well-structured and disciplined implementation approach can significantly catapult a cell, a platform, and a corporation toward their respective and interconnected goals.

If an implementation cell is lagging behind in completing projects or delivering its share of dollars, the implementation plan becomes a reference point for intervention. In some cases platform leaders can use the implementation plan to hold local managers to their commitments. In other cases, the plan becomes an archaeological document used to diagnose the nature or even the root of the problem. In either case, the presence of the plan is a critical success factor in ensuring the integrity and effectiveness of Six Sigma implementation.

The alternative is to charge cell Champions and managers to implement Six Sigma in a way that yields the right results—no matter how they might do so within the specifications established by the corporation. While such a keep-your-fingers-crossed approach might seem expedient in the face of pressing urgency, that same urgency is a good reason to ensure first-time precision, since there is precious little time or space for error. Only the machine-like progression of unfettered project implementation across all cells will yield the level of results needed to undo a corporation's dissatisfaction with the past.

3. How should a local implementation cell assess the relative effectiveness of its Six Sigma implementation plan?

By monitoring the aggregate financial impact of its completed and validated projects. The primary output of Six Sigma is cash, even though that cash is generated by focusing on the factors that make it more available, not by focusing on the cash itself. The implementation plan of an implementation cell can be considered effective only if it produces the financial gain for which it was formed.

As a corporation expects substantive return on its Six Sigma investment, and as a deployment platform commits to ambitious goals, an implementation cell garners its legitimacy from the same thrust. Six Sigma is about improving the balance sheet of a corporation through comprehensive and coordinated effort among the people and processes that create value. The implementation cells are the nexus points for this coordination and value creation. They are the entities that directly oversee project definition, selection, prioritization, implementation, validation, and integration. Implementation cells are factories for making successful projects, and they have a preconfigured capability and capacity for doing what they do.

Measuring project yield financially and by activities provides a strong basis upon which to evaluate implementation success. Such metrics might be structured around number of projects completed, annual dollar return per Black Belt, or quarterly net income saved. One of the most powerful aggregate metrics is project dollars validated per year per Black Belt. This metric not only helps to see which deployment cells are effective, but also can be used as a leading indicator of benefits by knowing the number of Black Belts in the cell. Each project gets finally validated by an independent financial manager. The values are the recorded benefit for that project. The body of work of a Black Belt is pooled for the year, and the total is used as an efficacy measure.

Aggregate measures of project output indicate how well a cell is utilizing Six Sigma and achieving its overall financial objective. These measures provide platform leaders and local managers with a big-picture view of how a cell is performing when it comes to Six Sigma. They are typically the first pieces of information platform leaders turn to in order to narrow their vision and see how their cells are performing relative to their peers.

The next aspect of assessing implementation efficacy carries the most assessment leverage but is also the most difficult. A corporation must create a diagnostic-friendly environment in which to quickly and effectively determine the nature and locus of implementation problems. This can be achieved by requiring all implementation cells and platforms to create similar metrics so that problems can be easily pinpointed and understood company-wide.

Anyone who has been involved in a Six Sigma initiative understands that measurement is the most difficult and time-consuming aspect of the Breakthrough Strategy. Different operations and processes are measured in different ways by different cell leaders and managers.

In terms of pure integrity of implementation, it would be sufficient for all the various platforms and cells to ensure that their performance metrics are correlated with those at the next level up, even if they differ within and across vertical silos. The overall performance metric of, say, $1 million per Black Belt per year is a common metric that can be used to evaluate performance across the company. Some vertical organizations may have metrics just on the number of projects a Black

Belt has, and this may be important to them, but not as important to another business that could have larger, more homogeneous product lines.

Just because cells measure different X's—one might measure only yield, while another measures defects per unit, a third process capability, and another waste—doesn't mean they all aren't reducing the cost of poor quality, the Y. In terms of integrity, they have all made valid connections and have upheld the Six Sigma principles of correlated metrics and deterministic reasoning. Looking at the overall cost of poor quality for a company is an effective way to judge the impact of a Six Sigma deployment. The common denominator is the dollars. Each local cell could have a different component that it is looking to improve. One business could be after fixed-cost reduction, another inventory, and still another inefficiencies in purchased material. Each counts and would be rolled up to chip away at the overall corporate cost of poor quality.

What they haven't done is create an environment in which the many implementation cells and platforms of a corporation can compare their performance, internally benchmark with other cells, and establish a standard measurement framework within which to discuss and share knowledge. This can occur only when metrics are not only correlated but also standardized. A standard that all businesses could compare would be something like validated project dollars as a percentage of revenue. This way, a big business and a small business could look at their relative performance. With standardized stratification, a platform can readily isolate statistically significant conditions within and across cells and platforms.

It behooves a corporation to require such standardization so that business leaders and deployment Champions peruse the same type of numbers in the same fields across cells and platforms. Such an approach forces alignment and brings insight that ultimately renders strategic and tactical advancements in future cycles of deployment and implementation.

We highly recommend that a corporation develop a standardized set of implementation CTPs. These CTPs, or activity- and process-based metrics, can be developed at the corporate level based on expert knowledge and then standardized on the basis of experience for subsequent cycles of implementation. Using consultants or industry experience based on benchmarked performance will act as the "expert" knowledge.

A corporation can ensure the use of common metrics throughout all of its platforms and cells by requiring all platforms and cells to display this set of metrics, even if they continue to track others as a function of running their respective businesses. At DuPont, there is a standard dashboard that shows the validated pretax profit benefits as a percent of revenue. This is done for all deployments. Each cell has its own metrics, but this is done company-wide.

4. How can a local implementation cell utilize performance metrics to augment or modify its Six Sigma implementation plan?

DuPont had built a database of thousands of projects after its first year of system-wide Six Sigma implementation. The basic structure of this database was designed by a pilot platform, Specialty Chemicals (now DuPont Chemical Solutions Enterprise), which was the first DuPont business unit to implement Six Sigma. That pilot developed the structure of the database.

The database contains the capability to capture and categorize project data, such as schedule, phase of DMAIC, validation dollars, type of project, people on the project, and reports, in nearly every imaginable way. For example, it would be easy to search on a query such as all top-line revenue growth projects in Europe in the Crop Protection business and their projected earnings impact. For DuPont, or for any corporation, such capability is crucial if it is to learn from the past and incorporate that learning into successive cycles of implementation.

The database is a large repository of information that can be turned into knowledge. Each Black Belt could search the database with a query. So if a Black Belt was assigned a project on steam traps, he or she could look in the database for every other project that did an improvement in steam traps, and can find the Black Belt, the approach, and the data that would allow the new project to be done more effectively and efficiently. In this way, companies can discover leverage and gain wisdom about the Six Sigma process and end products. For example, if a particular implementation cell checks the database and realizes it's lagging far behind its peers in reducing its cost of poor quality, it would have pinpointed a weakness.

This robust, system-wide database also contains average project cycle time per Black Belt, Project Champion, region, platform, cell, type of project, and time of year. It has information on numbers of projects completed per deployment Champion, platform, Project Champion, cell, region, month, quarter, year, and so on. And it can characterize projects by size (small or large plant) or characterize cells by the number of projects in the pipeline. These are just some of the possible data fields around which a corporation can structure postmortem factorial studies after, say, six months of Six Sigma implementation. The overall intention, of course, is to optimize the implementation process, or the way in which projects are selected and executed under different circumstances. Utilizing various tools, a company could generate a battery of interaction plots that would reveal certain points of leverage.

Maybe there is an interaction between project cycle time, financial benefit, and project location. A corporation might discover that it can expect longer cycle times on high-savings projects at large sites, such as a project to evaluate the overall capacity of a site. One project at DuPont Fluoroproducts discovered that the batch cycle time to load autoclaves could be reduced. While this project took a lot of time, it racked up savings of more than $10 million. In another case, a corporation could find that at-the-customer sales projects have a longer cycle time. This is due to the fact that the customer has to agree to the problem and share in the data gathering and the solution. This extra layer of approvals takes time but in the end proves to be a valuable way to build customer loyalty. So increased cycle time might not be a negative, as it may seem. The company might further discover that cycle time is low on projects at small sites, whether savings are small or large. An implementation cell can use this information to prepare for the variable of savings while also improving its ability to forecast project cycle times.

A corporation can determine the ideal combination of fields in its database to give it better forecasting ability with the least possible amount of variation and the strongest signal—for a platform, a region, a cell, a given location, or any other category, resulting in better planning sophistication and better implementation efficiency. For DuPont, dollars validated combined with the number of projects and the cycle time became the strongest predictors of future savings.

Even at the cell level, certain data can be accessed and analyzed to yield valuable implementation knowledge and insight. A cell in a particular business located at a plant in Asia, for instance, might have data that, say, 80 percent of its variation in cycle time is due to the variable of project size. If the data also support the supposition that reducing project size by 10 percent will reduce cycle time variation by 70 percent, then the cell has a pretty good case for altering its project selection criteria. Selecting projects with slightly smaller savings targets, as a rule, will allow the cell to complete more projects while improving the cycle time predictability in the system.

If a cell can make its case in this way, management will listen, especially within the context of a Six Sigma initiative. This is one of the pervasive cultural changes that occurs as a corporation moves beyond initial deployment and well into the first generation of projects. At the process level, Black Belts become empowered with the voice of data as they move their projects and teams through the Breakthrough Strategy. Project Champions become equipped to diagnose problems and identify opportunities within their respective implementation cells. Deployment Champions develop a deep grasp of the myriad of operational contingencies within their respective platforms.

DuPont has tracked the value of its project-leveraging efforts in terms of project cycle time and Black Belt time investment through a network of Master Black Belts, who communicate primarily through a server-based Lotus Notes community. The children of such parent projects at DuPont have been completed in 30 percent less time and have required 40 percent less effort from their respective Black Belts, showing Champions and Black Belts that the learning of the whole organism far outweighs the learning of any one implementation cell.

Common metrics and a common language lead to better project execution at the process level, better implementation efficacy at the cell level, better deployment integrity at the platform level, and better strategic validity at the corporate level. Over time, Six Sigma operates on its own—not automatically but by design. Six Sigma essentially ties all of the pieces of the organization together. The expertise resides at the lowest project level, while the knowledge can be shared all the way to the top of the organization.

Another key way to make an implementation effective is for an implementation cell to institute an upstream checking mechanism for validating the expected financial savings of projects, as well as for confirming that projects are executable. The need for such a mechanism is grounded in the well-established fact that the most difficult and time-consuming aspect of Six Sigma is characterizing the performance of any given process or, more specifically, measuring it.

It sometimes becomes clear during the measurement phase of the Breakthrough Strategy that a certain project or certain family of projects will not yield a result sizable enough to justify its continued execution. It therefore benefits an implementation cell to institute a system whereby projects can be killed or reconfigured before committing more time and resources that in the end would not be justified.

DuPont's way of doing this has been for Black Belts to work with Process Owners and certified finance people to examine project technicals during the measure phase of the Breakthrough Strategy. Based on the expected returns and the measurability of its CTQs, the team determines if it is worth continuing. The overall project on yield and uptime at DuPont Titanium Technologies was such a project where the team actually gave the overall responsibility to Rob Johns, the Champion for Manufacturing. Sometimes a Master Black Belt becomes involved, particularly when the nature and details of the project are challenging.

Once a process is sanctioned as a viable and executable endeavor, an implementation cell is committed to see it through the analysis, improvement, and control phases of the Breakthrough Strategy. The point of no return has been reached. But to make sure that this point of no return leads to the correct path, Black Belts and Champions must establish a mentality and framework within which to challenge the wishes of business leaders when necessary. This means if a Black Belt runs into legitimate problems, he or she should immediately solicit the involvement of the Project Champion to coordinate an appropriate intervention. If a Project Champion is having difficulty in getting the ear and support of business leaders, it should be taken up with the deployment Champion.

The last thing that should happen is for a problematic project to continue under the reasoning that "management wants it done, so we should do it." The Black Belt should exercise leadership by defining the problem and exposing it to the proper authorities. Similarly, if an implementation cell as a whole is experiencing difficulty in any aspect of executing its implementation plan, the onus is on the Champion of that cell to spearhead and coordinate a solution. When the integrity of Six Sigma is at stake, the wheels of implementation must stop turning until a better course of action can be mapped.

5. How does a local implementation cell leverage Six Sigma projects to realize breakthrough performance?

This is a concern that, ideally, comes into play very early in the life path of an implementation cell, when its Six Sigma capability is low and the risk of failure is high. It is much more difficult to leverage projects at the beginning of a Six Sigma thrust than it is after the education that comes with a cycle or two of implementation.

During this pioneering time, an experienced consultant can make the necessary connections between global Six Sigma goals, product-specific market conditions, and local implementation objectives. In a contracting market, it might be viable for an implementation cell to focus projects on improving customer satisfaction, particularly in a price-insensitive industry. For example, at Ford Motor Company, the targets for Six Sigma were all about consumer satisfaction, which was unique in deployments. This is a simplified and straightforward example, and the reality of accurately configuring the various focuses for application projects in various implementation cells is usually more complex and requires great insight and expertise.

It is highly advisable for a corporation to retain support from a competent diagnostician who is intimately familiar with the capability and capacity of Six Sigma. Such a consultant can be tremendously helpful for an implementation cell in its early stages. The diagnostician should be knowledgeable about all aspects of business management across many industries, and particularly about the inner workings of how various processes, functions, and operations roll together to achieve the primary aim of a corporation: to make money.

Ideally, a good consulting resource is heavily involved in the formation of deployment platforms and implementation cells, with a view of how Black Belts and projects should be allocated within the various cells to optimize the overall effort. And within specified platforms and cells, capable outside help can identify the pathway of leverage for installing Six Sigma, establishing goals, and configuring project aims. For every platform and cell, there is an optimal configuration of projects focused on such objectives as overhead reduction, capacity increase, process-capability improvement, customer-satisfaction improvement, cycle-time reduction, defect reduction, and so on.

Without such initial outside help, existing business leaders tend to make judgments and decisions that mirror existing organizational cultures, objectives, structures, and practices. During the executive session for the General Services Business of DuPont, Rich Schroeder suggested a completely different business model for that organization. While the immediate reaction was to stick with the current structure, several approaches were eventually taken that led to a different structure. Even newly appointed platform and cell Six Sigma leaders might tend to select projects that reflect their former expectations and biases.

It is critically important to correctly set Six Sigma in motion and configure the first generation of projects. In doing so, a corporation minimizes the risk of watering down the potential of Six Sigma or compromising the validity and vitality of its initial waves of projects. A consultant can help do this during the initial six-month phase.

After an implementation cell has completed a cycle or two of projects (four to nine months), it begins to identify sources of leverage based on its own internal experience, as well as the experiences of others throughout a corporation. The initiative becomes more scientific in that more project data become available for analysis and for improving the implementation process itself. When it comes to this point, outside help should no longer be necessary, especially if a critical mass of implementation cells have achieved their objectives and, in doing so, have accrued a treasure-house of learning that can be leveraged in the future.

6. How does a local implementation cell ensure that the gains resulting from Six Sigma projects are sustained over time?

By requiring Process Owners to install a control plan after the completion of each and every project. While this is enforced at the cell level through project reviews, it is designed at the corporate level, where senior business leaders recognize the need for control and define its requirements. Just as a corporation designs a mechanism for validating project savings, it must also install a mechanism for ensuring that those gains are sustained over time.

There are certain Six Sigma must-dos that are best written in stone by a corporation. These are the global elements of Six Sigma success that cut across all businesses, platforms, departments, cells, and functions and that provide the basis for the synergistic deployment, implementation, and realization of Six Sigma aims. Such elements also should empower local implementation cells and should foster their autonomy and ability to mold Six Sigma in their own image.

But such molding absolutely must keep the idea and practice of control at its core. This is why companies such as DuPont require Process Owners to participate on project teams, as these owners are those left behind to implement control plans after Black Belts move on to spearhead other projects.

In the beginning stages, Process Owners serve as subject matter experts, along with technical experts and others who possess firsthand knowledge of how various processes and operations work. Process Owners are also heavily involved in the initial efforts to validate expected or forecasted project savings numbers, as well as efforts to define and measure performance problems, the subject matter of those projects. Having been an integral part of the project team, these owners then play a primary role in controlling the performance gains made after the analyze and improve phases of the Breakthrough Strategy have been completed.

At DuPont, recurring hard project benefits must be verified for a period of six months before they are regarded as legitimate. The overriding idea, for DuPont and for others, is that Six Sigma project results should accrue to a corporation on an annual basis, year after year. To ensure this happens with any degree of reliability, a corporation must require and enforce control—especially after substantive process and operational changes have been made.

Anyone who has run a plant or a major process or who has been involved in various operational improvement initiatives understands the half-life phenomenon. Regardless of its source (TQM, operational excellence, lean manufacturing, Six Sigma, etc.), the natural tendency is for change and improvement to gravitate back toward its historical trend line, like a moving average. The more substantive the change, the greater the risk of reversal. This is why it is vital that every Black Belt project must develop and enact a control plan, as Six Sigma performance improvements tend to be quantum rather than incremental in nature.

The most natural and appropriate person to lead the development and enactment of a control plan is the Process Owner for each Black Belt project. By consistently requiring the involvement of Process Owners and by always working projects all the way through the control phase of the Breakthrough Strategy, a corporation embeds into its genetic code the idea and practice of sustaining gains. Nor should we forget that a properly designed Six Sigma initiative makes a portion of variable pay, even at the cell level, contingent on meeting Six Sigma goals. For example, in a finance area of DuPont, the Black Belt was assigned to improve exchange gains and losses. The role of the Process Owner was to take the control plan from the Black Belt and monitor it on an ongoing basis. A Process Owner was named in this case and now owns the improvement plan and control plan for the output and the savings.

DuPont instituted an additional mechanism of control from which many benefited—an audit process that targets high-savings projects in all the different platforms and cells that completed their Six Sigma implementation at least eighteen months earlier. The idea behind the process is to use sampling theory and statistics to accurately predict the ultimate results from Six Sigma in a given platform or cell. If a corporation can verify the gains of a statistically significant sample of projects within a defined territory (corporation, platform, cell), then it can be sure, within a given degree of certainty, that Six Sigma has yielded what it says it has yielded. By looking at this data, DuPont determined that slightly more than the previously validated benefits were still hitting the bottom line two years after validation, due to changing economic conditions. While not every project performed at this rate, the sample size statistically showed it to be valid with 95 percent confidence.

The final aspect of sustaining application gains is to build project savings into the budgeting process, a practice that has begun to take hold in DuPont's major businesses. Savings that have reached final validation status (six months of benefit) are extracted from the budget of the business, which, in turn, reduces its allocation of dollars to its various cost centers according to their respective Six Sigma contributions. For example, Engineering Polymers looks at the project savings from the prior year and hardwires that new level of cost into their outlook for the coming year.

Such a ratcheting down places real pressure on various deployment platforms and implementation cells to maintain their cost-related gains, as many companies subscribe to the DuPont practice of tying a portion of personal bonus dollars to budget adherence. This practice also holds a certain dose of strategic power for a corporation, as it continues to lower its overall cost basis and frees up cash for investing in areas such as R&D, acquisitions, plants, and equipment. In DuPont's case, the need for capital expenditures decreased during this time from approximately $2.4 billion to $1.5 billion annually, though not all due to Six Sigma. It also keeps people honest because they are aware that their future budgets will hold them to their current claims. The practice has certain limitations, such as currency effects and changing costs for raw materials or other purchased goods, but the overall principle of leveraging the budget process to sustain project gains is sound.

7. How can a local implementation cell capture best practices and leverage those practices so that the Six Sigma implementation methodology will evolve?

As with so many other aspects of Six Sigma success, the effective discovery and distribution of best practices at the cell level is derived from a strong corporate imperative that is tempered by respect for local autonomy. DuPont is an exemplar in this regard, as it clearly placed a premium on sharing best practices by forming its deployment (SBU Champion) network at the very outset of its Six Sigma initiative. While the network's initial charter revolved mostly around the logistics involved in deploying Six Sigma, it quickly became a mechanism for identifying and institutionalizing the best practices that emerged from that experience.

The cycle of breakthrough turns at both the business and operations levels of a corporation, specifically, within platforms and implementation cells. There, it is the job of Master Black Belts to seek out best practices in their own cells, as well as in others, to leverage those practices in the interest of improving the productivity of the Six Sigma methodology itself. For this purpose, it is highly advisable for a corporation to establish a formal network of its Master Black Belts, who both formally and informally mine and share best practices.

Master Black Belts seek and share needed data and know-how across platforms and cells, relying heavily on the Project Champions and Black Belts within their local areas, since they are the users of such knowledge—particularly the Project Champions, who are charged with constantly improving their Six Sigma implementation methodologies.

At DuPont, for instance, a particular cell in the finance group became known and respected for its approach in filling and managing its project pipeline. The Champion for that cell presented the approach to a meeting of the Master Black Belt network, which subsequently leveraged the practice across the company. The Master Black Belts adopted it, and it was easy for them to get trained and use the tool.

In some cases, when the identified best practice can be widely applied and possesses great leverage, it should be elevated even further up the Six Sigma ladder. DuPont utilizes its strategic business unit Champions network for this purpose—the group of twenty-three deployment Champions that represents all of DuPont's eighteen deployment platforms, along with several cross-platform functions, such as finance and information technology. It is the job of this group to review promising best practices with an eye toward establishing them as corporate policy for all to do.

Six Sigma implementation policies flow down to cells while preserving their autonomy, and the innovations that grow out of such autonomy also flow back upward to become policies. Without such a mechanism for identifying and standardizing best implementation practices, they tend to remain the sole and separate property of certain cells and platforms, as the attention of those who own that property is mostly focused inward, as it should be. But looking outward for help should also be part of every cell's drive to refine the way it implements Six Sigma.

One business at DuPont, General Services, developed a unique and powerful financial model for forecasting project savings. It was a breakthrough in the business of doing Six Sigma that others adopted. While the actual execution of projects may not have changed as a result of this best practice, the accuracy of project savings targets has. The business of implementation planning in many cells has improved as a result of this innovation, and the opportunity exists for more cells to improve by adopting the model.

In another case, a particular DuPont business, Titanium Technologies, took it upon itself to institute a practice of requiring all corporate promotables in its control to become Champions or Black Belts. DuPont is like many companies in that it has a corporate HR system for identifying and tracking such people. This practice was then moved up to the Champions network, which decided to recommend it as an across-the-board corporate policy. After consideration by the company's senior executives, the practice was written into law at DuPont.

Thereafter, the onus was on local leaders and managers to work with their promotable people to get them trained as Champions or Black Belts over a multiyear period. It was a best practice born of the future view that a corporation run by former Six Sigma leaders is a corporation well positioned for success.

For any corporation, the idea of capturing and leveraging best practices is dependent upon the presence of a capability for validly and reliably determining what is best. What, exactly, makes a particular implementation method best for a given cell, best for a corporation, best in class, best in the world? This is the question a corporation should ask, and if it is serious about leveraging best practices, it should develop a set of criteria for making such determinations, independent of how often certain practices may have been replicated in a given organization or corporation.

One criterion could be the extent to which a candidate for best practice differs from the old way of doing something. Some general guidelines around such criteria, and a panel of experienced Six Sigma practitioners, would be sufficient for evaluating candidates coming out of various implementation cells. In some cases, it is advisable to include on the panel a few outsiders who have a demonstrated history of recognizing and defining best practices in their careers.

For those companies that truly value the power of shared knowledge, it would not be overkill to designate a special program that is dedicated to promoting and disseminating best practices. Such a program could be housed under the Six Sigma umbrella, as it was at DuPont, or it could be rolled into an existing knowledge-management system. To truly instill the value and practice of sharing and collaboration, an executive-level learning officer should own the best practices program, and there should be a systematic and unbiased way to bring to the surface and sanction what a corporation deems to be the best.

One very important element of a viable program should be some form of certification so that when a cell, Champion, or Black Belt comes up with a best practice, they can be recognized and rewarded for doing so. This fosters the value of sharing knowledge, because the corporation has a way of measuring that value and of reinforcing the behavior of those who embody it.

The overall idea behind leveraging best practices is to proliferate them as widely as possible and not hold them as one's personal property.

8. How should a local implementation cell integrate its lessons learned into the training curriculum and project-selection practices?

There is an important distinction between a Six Sigma curriculum and course content. The curriculum exists to instill the unchanging ideas or concepts and priorities of a given Six Sigma thrust on a system-wide basis. Documenting the voice of the customer, understanding variation, separating the signal from the noise, using self-reporting scales to measure the immeasurable, improving yield by reducing defects—these are just some of the ideas that can form the essence of a corporation's Six Sigma DNA, or curriculum.

Course content comprises the specific materials, tools, simulations, and examples that directly support the effective transfer of knowledge and know-how in the classroom.

As far as curriculum is concerned, a cell basically has to live with the universal curriculum that is passed down by its parent corporation at the outset of a Six Sigma drive. As a cell gains implementation experience and insight, however, it begins to morph the universal Six Sigma ideas and principles to fit its unique circumstances and needs. In a certain transactional environment, such as computing inventory or inventory days supply, for example, the idea of measurement may carry with it a different meaning than the same idea in a different type of transactional environment, and its meaning is definitely different than it would be in a manufacturing setting.

Higher-level concepts, such as capturing the voice of the customer, become understood and applied differently in different cells. Each business has a different approach with its customers. Some have distributors and others are more in touch with consumers. Getting the voice of the customer could range from one-on-one interviews to elaborate use of the "house of quality" or quality function deployment (QFD). Once this experience is gained and a cell has the time and opportunity to develop various best practices, they can be molded back into next-generation curricula for Champions, Black Belts, and Green Belts. The best way to do this is for a corporation to designate certain people, such as

Master Black Belts, whose job it is to create various modules that can be snapped onto a corporation's Six Sigma curricula for all roles.

Capturing the voice of the customer (VOC) should be a central aspect of a company's overall curricula. But after a generation or two of implementation and application experience, the corporation should package various VOC modules for use in areas such as R&D, sales, and engineering. While the general idea of VOC is the same for all areas, the exact conceptual and physical application varies according to need, or type of environment.

Early on, most companies rely on consultant-furnished curricula, which will most likely be as fixed and generic as possible, since they must be applicable to a wide range of industries and corporations. This generality tends to water down the learning process, as materials that resonate with people's experience usually educate better than material that doesn't make a strong connection.

Over time, a corporation should combat this limitation by designing these snap-on modules so that the overall concepts remain static across all cells, while the specific tools of those ideas will tend to change from cell to cell. DuPont created several bolt-ons to accelerate the movement to top-line revenue growth. We had a Black Belt module, "Six Sigma for Growth," that incorporated the design for Six Sigma tools and processes.

This means a Black Belt in sales will assimilate and apply the idea of capturing the customer's voice differently than a Black Belt in engineering or in the finance department. Additionally, Champions and Black Belts in the chemical industry will assimilate Six Sigma concepts differently than those in the computer industry.

A corporation can also package its curriculum for use by people in different countries who have specific language and cultural needs and orientations; DuPont did this successfully.

It should be the role of a corporation, not the role of any one platform or cell, to ensure that the leveragable experience of any one part of the system becomes available to other similar parts via curricula. If left entirely under the control of local areas, enhancements to curricula would become ineffective, as the various localities would tend to either live with what they have or reinvent enhancements that may have already been made by others. Such fragmentation must be avoided, since it could undermine the overall integrity of Six Sigma learning.

When a corporation deploys Six Sigma, the only thing that stands between the unsatisfactory performance of the past and the realization of their new aims is knowledge. They have the people, they have the capability and capacity for installing the necessary structures and systems, and in many cases they have most of the tools needed to realize their aims. What they lack is a way of thinking and a methodology for making Six Sigma come alive.

A corporation must safeguard its best ideas and methods by installing a mechanism for mining them. But it should go one step further to integrate these lessons learned into its curricula—again, in the form of snap-on modules.

Such modules would contain much of what is formally considered to be course content (industry-specific examples and tools, for example). But as packaged modules, these knowledge ornaments can be attached to a company's overall Six Sigma curricula in their proper places. The net effect of this approach is that a company can build a high degree of credibility into its formal Six Sigma learning system, ensuring that each new generation of Six Sigma operatives has access to the company's best implementation practices.

There are cases in which only first-generation Champions receive formal training, while all Black Belts receive formal training. As exemplified by DuPont, this approach can be effective only when a corporation installs a strong capability for selecting, educating, and assimilating new Champions to replace those who complete their tours of duty. A major part of this education and assimilation should entail the effective transfer of the project-selection best practices that are best suited for the type of cell to which the new Champion is assigned. The Black Belts will always pick up the learnings from their peers. We have built in best practices of CTQ, flow-down, mapping, and tool use as well.

ONE DUPONT PROJECT: LEGAL

DuPont's corporate legal department, whose clients are people in any DuPont business who are facing litigation, had been running programs for years to cut cost and improve quality. In addition to about 130 staff attorneys in the United States, DuPont uses some forty outside firms to assist in the caseload. Regardless of the cases handled by DuPont and its network of firms, the goal was to deliver the best value at the lowest possible cost.

Tom Sager, a legal vice president and chief of litigation for all of DuPont, felt that the litigation process could be streamlined and improved, no matter how good it was. Sager, who was a Six Sigma Champion, decided to personally take on a Green Belt project focusing on early case assessment, which he saw as the key to wringing inefficiency out of the litigation process to reduce costs. Early case assessment had leverage because the more comprehensive, holistic, and customer-focused it was, the easier it would be to produce a favorable outcome. When cases are assessed well, cycle time is reduced, cost is decreased, customer satisfaction is increased, and when litigation is necessary, the win rate goes up.

Sager enlisted the help of Julie Mazza, an attorney and a Black Belt who reported to him. Mazza set out to define, measure, analyze, improve, and control an early case assessment system for ensuring the best results for clients every time, and to push the project through to completion.

Mazza was advising the Specialty Chemicals business when it piloted Six Sigma, and she volunteered to become a Black Belt because it fit well with her thinking. She felt that litigation is not usually a good way to solve problems. "I saw litigation as waste," says Mazza, a litigator by background.

"Litigation is a defect in the way we conduct business. The more you can avoid it or resolve it early, the better off the business is."

Mazza saw opportunity for streamlining, standardizing, and improving the quality of the legal process, especially early case assessment. And it became her job to get as many lawyers and legal assistants thinking the same way. "We told our in-house and outside lawyers that they were not working cases; they were solving business problems for clients." The division had been working with outside firms for about twelve years, she noted, and they were happy to work from the same template.

"In my experience, 60 to 70 percent of what a lawyer collects during discovery ends up not being useful or pivotal," says Mazza. "This, in my mind, was a clear opportunity to take out the waste."

The legal department had previously constructed a template and process to assess litigation cases, but Mazza knew the process could work better, even if she didn't yet know how. Six Sigma was used to figure that out.

Sager's project team comprised Mazza, another DuPont lawyer, an outside lawyer, and a consultant from a firm that provides expert testimony on economic matters. Together, they selected eighteen case samples that had been closed in the employment and labor area. They picked these files apart, looking for clues that would lead them to productivity breakthroughs.

For each of the cases, a team member analyzed the complaint or allegation and interviewed the business client to see how it thought the case had been handled. They then assigned a rating, such as 3 for extremely well handled, and correlated the original case assessment to the litigation results in terms of cycle time, cost, client satisfaction, and final payout to plaintiffs, if any. The entire process of evaluating the cases took two months.

The team interviewed inside counsel, outside counsel, and numerous business clients, usually DuPont plant managers or HR managers. With the data derived from all these voices, the team discovered some pretty strong correlations. DuPont asked its consulting firm, Deloitte Touche, to create metrics to analyze the data. What they found was that as early case assessment quality went up, cycle time went down, cost went down, payouts went down, and customer satisfaction went up. This was just as Sager and Mazza had suspected, but now it was corroborated by science.

The DMAIC process also helped the team identify gaps in the early case assessment template and process itself. They didn't just confirm that cases turned out more favorably when the quality of early assessment was high; they also brought a much greater level of focus and detail to the early assessment process itself. Engaging in DMAIC enabled the team to uncover hidden operational blemishes, the root causes of early case assessment defects.

One such blemish concerned insufficient communication among inside counsel. For example, one of the considerations in the early case assessment process was to look at similar prior cases. Before the Six Sigma project, it was something that some but not all of the lawyers did. Mazza and her team changed this by making the process part of a check-list that all DuPont attorneys had to complete in each case. The checklist Mazza created is a three-page document that contained several categories, with lists under each for attorneys to complete in areas such as background information, comparative analysis, strengths and weaknesses of the case, the client's perspective, critical case-specific information, an evaluation of the litigation plan, and budget forecasts.

As might be expected, there was some resistance to the entire checklist at first, but the reality was that assistants could routinely fill in much of the form, leaving the more significant areas for the attorneys themselves.

"For every case there is now a case assessment form," says Mazza. "It's the same form across all litigation. At the end of ninety days, the lawyer in charge gets a reminder e-mail to check the form."

Before instituting the system, the legal department lacked budgetary detail and performance metrics. There also was insufficient communication with business clients. The checklist addressed those gaps.

"We had gathered the client's perspective in our old process, but we never really detailed out what this meant," says Mazza. The new process had nine subcategories of the client's perspective, including marketplace and investment community perception, adverse precedent, and protecting and advancing intellectual property, among others.

Underlying the list were the following questions, the dimensions of quality around which a more disciplined, holistic, documented, and client-focused early case assessment system was created:

- How do we know when a client has a symbiotic rather than totally adversarial relationship with the entity they are suing?
- How does the investment community view our docket of cases in the consumer tort area?
- Should we be suing someone who is suing us for copyright infringement?
- Which witnesses, from a list of thirty, are the five who can give us the most leverage to win a case?

Figuring out the answers to these and other questions gave the legal department the leverage to increase decision-making quality. Stemming from the previously mentioned checklist, each component of the assessment process was complete with its own set of instructions, forms, and templates. Thus equipped, legal assistants could usually conduct the early case assessment interviews and collect the necessary information without the direct involvement of an attorney.

Called the dashboard, the new case assessment template was constantly undergoing refinement as more details were added and modifications made. The system started as a checklist, but it became more than that. "This is not a checklist," says Mazza. "It is a road map of how to deal with a particular set of facts today for this particular client in this particular legal environment."

Part of the new road map was an automated e-mail system that reminded the managing lawyer on a case to review with the team the original assessment, checking for any substantive changes that might have occurred or any assessment defects that might have been overlooked. The system forced ongoing dialogue between all relevant parties. Also, review compliance was made part of the performance evaluations of the inside and outside lawyers working on cases.

After several months of data from the new process, Sager and Mazza were able to validate $1 million in annualized, hard cost reduction to DuPont—all derived from an overall reduction in case cycle times. "The potential has only been scratched, and there is much more to be gained by duplicating our efforts in all the other litigation areas besides labor and employment," says Sager. "There is a lot more Six Sigma work to do in legal.

"As lawyers get more comfortable in working more closely with clients, they will make their jobs easier, and they will be more successful," he says. "When this happens, it will change the culture, and this is what Six Sigma is supposed to do."

## CHAPTER 7

THE SCIENCE OF VALUE CREATION

Six Sigma has been through two major transformations since it was created at Motorola. It began as a standardized methodology for reducing defects during the late '80s. In the mid-'90s, AlliedSignal and General Electric led the way in morphing Six Sigma from a relatively project-specific defect-reduction practice into a widespread cost-reduction initiative. Six Sigma has evolved somewhat like new releases of software, in successive generations. By the late '90s and the early part of the new millennium, General Electric began leveraging Six Sigma "at the customer for the customer."

DuPont's Champions pioneered a new focus for Six Sigma on stimulating top-line growth, while still retaining a strong focus on cost reduction. They essentially expanded the envelope—an expansion that is sure to become institutionalized as other companies benchmark with DuPont on applying Six Sigma to generate additional revenue.

These companies and others have set the stage for what we call Generation 3 (G3) Six Sigma, a new paradigm for business breakthrough in which the customer and the provider realize value in every critical aspect of the business relationship. In other words, Six Sigma can not only drive a pervasive and dramatic reduction in defects, reduce costs, and enhance revenue, but can also create value on a broad and deep scale.

Having successfully grown from a quality-improvement initiative into a full-fledged business initiative, Six Sigma needs to be redefined, not only at the macro level but at the cellular level as well.

THE MYTHS OF SIX SIGMA

- There has been considerable difficulty in applying classic Six Sigma to the design function or, more important, to the widespread proliferation of innovation throughout a business enterprise.

  Resulting Myth: Six Sigma is good at driving quantum change in the mechanical aspects of business operations but not as effective in driving the creative aspects of business innovation.

- The knowledge and tools of Six Sigma have been more difficult to transfer and apply in the customer and service areas, due to a lack of customized curricula and other factors.

  Resulting Myth: Six Sigma works better in manufacturing divisions than it does in R&D, procurement, sales, legal, marketing, and other functional areas.

- Much of what a company does is based on the more intangible aspects of leadership and value creation: ideas, models, decisions, and events. While the Breakthrough Strategy has been applied to the measurable aspects of leadership and value creation, it has not been leveraged as effectively to bring new ideas to fruition, improve decision making, and minimize management risk.

  Resulting Myth: Six Sigma is a powerful tool for breakthrough in data-rich environments but not as powerful in the more ethereal, idea-driven realms of business.

- As widely embraced as it is, Six Sigma is still perceived as a powerful management initiative that is led by a small minority of people in large corporations and applied to only stubbornly ingrained business problems.

Resulting Myth: Six Sigma is an elitist strategy, available to only large corporations—and not very usable by medium and small companies, or by the majority of nonmanagement employees in large corporations.

- Too much time is required to properly train Six Sigma Champions, Black Belts, and Green Belts in nonmanufacturing areas because of their limited experience with collecting data, measurement, statistical analyses, and process improvement.

  Resulting Myth: It takes more time to embed Six Sigma in nonmanufacturing arenas, where processes are more fluid, organic, and nonrepeatable in nature.

In other words, as far as Six Sigma has come, many questions remain about it.

- How can companies make Six Sigma and its power to guide change available to the many rather than the few?
- How can companies leverage Six Sigma to drive innovation and the creation of new products and services, to help them cannibalize a company's own successful products and services in order to create something new?
- How can companies adapt Six Sigma to better strengthen it as a tool in data-poor, process-unfriendly, and experience-intensive environments?
- Can Six Sigma reduce the level of risk inherent when a decision is made or an action is taken, from the smallest and most trivial to those with the most far-reaching implications? Can Six Sigma lower the risk of a loss of value for the business? Can Six Sigma be used by everyone at work or at home?

Six Sigma is about finding the best way to create the most possible value per unit of work and is most robust to contextual variation.

Today, corporations of all sizes face new challenges continually. And one of those challenges is not just to use Six Sigma to improve a business, but to use Six Sigma to improve Six Sigma.

As Six Sigma shifts from generation 2 to generation 3, it becomes less focused on defect and more focused on value creation. In the process, the Breakthrough Strategy is integrated into a larger strategy for creating value called ICRA—innovate, configure, realize, and attenuate (see chart below). The practice of Six Sigma can now be broken into a set of twelve Big Ideas or principles.

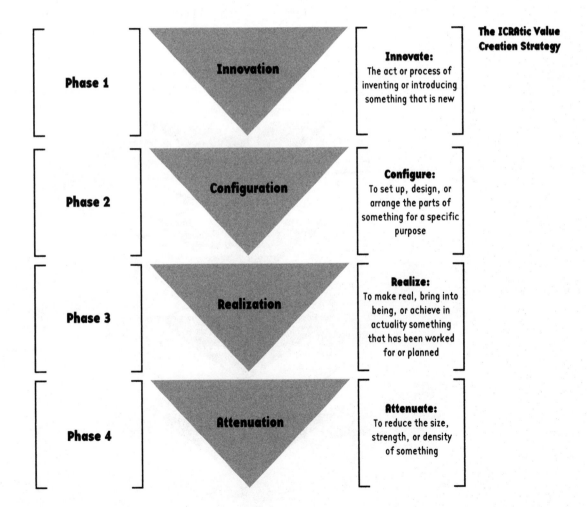

The ICRAtic Value Creation Strategy

Phase 1 — Innovation

Innovate: The act or process of inventing or introducing something that is new

Phase 2 — Configuration

Configure: To set up, design, or arrange the parts of something for a specific purpose

Phase 3 — Realization

Realize: To make real, bring into being, or achieve in actuality something that has been worked for or planned

Phase 4 — Attenuation

Attenuate: To reduce the size, strength, or density of something

The ICRAtic approach to Six Sigma involves creating value—the act or process of inventing or introducing something new (an object or process or event) in such a way that the related elements are purposefully designed, set up, and arranged so that what is being introduced can be brought into being according to plan. Moreover, it does this while concurrently reducing or eliminating deficiencies or defects.

The particulars of value creation involve the chain of events for innovating, configuring, realizing, and attenuating objects and events. This is where the Big Ideas of Six Sigma come into play. They surround the ICRAtic value creation concept. The twelve Big Ideas of Six Sigma form a map of the issues a Six Sigma leader should consider in effectively executing each phase of a Value Creation Strategy (see chart below).

The Value Creation Strategy and the Big Ideas

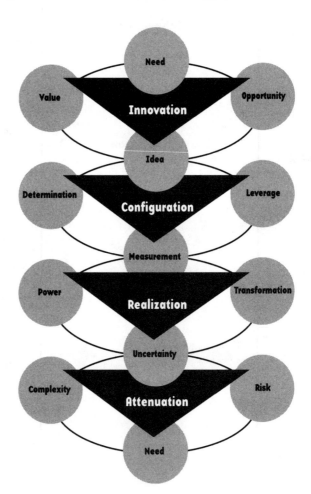

When a business innovates, it begins by attempting to address a need, or a negative gap between what its customers experience and what they expect. The business then turns to Big Ideas of value and opportunity to generate ideas for meeting that need. These ideas are then leveraged and measured as they are tested in an idealized model of value creation.

After a business creates and realizes value (to a greater or lesser extent), it improves its processes by reducing its uncertainty, complexity, and risk. In a full cycle of value creation for a given need, a business comes up with an idea, tests a mental model, realizes some level of success, and then improves it by reducing any undesirable operating conditions. Basically, a business innovates through the science of thinking, configures itself through the science of planning, realizes its potential through the science of doing, and "attenuates" itself through the science of improving.

DEFINING THE IDEAS

Understanding the Big Ideas gives operative meaning to the Value Creation Strategy. The Big Ideas are the portals to better thinking and, therefore, to better application and better value realization.

THE BIG IDEAS EXPANDED

Each Big Idea breaks into a set of two phrases, one a high-level admonishment and the other a more descriptive but still general statement of action. This is how a Six Sigma Black Belt goes about creating ideas before applying the systems, methods, and tools of value creation. Only by stringing the Big Ideas together does a leader begin to see the underlying code of business success. While there is a scientific progression of thought moving through the major phases of the Value Creation Strategy, there is also a progression of thought within each phase as the Big Ideas come into play.

Understanding this, let's run through the Big Ideas to obtain an understanding of how a Six Sigma leader thinks and how an organization creates value. In all businesses, we engage in innovation by identifying a need to be addressed, or a deprived state. Recognizing that business is a "need-do" interaction between a customer and a provider, we then explore the equivalency of value exchange in that interaction.

Next, a business must search for the conditions that are favorable to configuring and realizing the envisioned value proposition. When the conditions are properly identified and aligned, we create the opportunity to realize the mutual exchange of value, which in turn satisfies the need and relieves the deprived state. In theory, this exchange fulfills the customer's need while generating profit for the provider. But this doesn't happen in reality until businesses engage in the phases of configuration, realization, and attenuation.

When we engage in configuration, we refine a conceptual model of how we intend to create and exchange value: We refine our idea, or ideal,

STRATEGY FOR VALUE CREATION				
Phase	**Big Ideas**			
Innovation	Proclaim	To declare	Need	Deprived state
	Prospect	To explore	Value	Equivalent exchange
	Pursue	To search	Opportunity	Favorable conditions
Configuration	Purity	To refine	Idea	Conceptual model
	Pattern	To design	Determinism	Effectual causation
	Parlay	To exploit	Leverage	Mechanistic advantage
Realization	Prescribe	To establish	Measurement	Scaled quantity
	Provide	To supply	Power	Change capability
	Perfect	To improve	Transformation	Change process
Attenuation	Prohibit	To prevent	Uncertainty	Unknown state
	Paralyze	To disable	Complexity	Confounded connections
	Prune	To abate	Risk	Loss exposure

for meeting a need in a profitable way. We then design a system of effectual causation (Y-X chain) for bringing our idea into the real world.

A configuration or design should detail all the utility-, access-, and worth-related critical-to-quality factors of the deliverable product or service at hand. It should take the fuzziness of an idea and document it in the form of a tangible design that can be seen, discussed, and modified by others. Finally, it should align the factors that will help in closing the satisfaction gap—bringing about a deliverable that will satisfy the needs and expectations of the customer while satisfying the goals of the provider.

But before we can realize value, we must establish a measurement by which to gauge progress as we bring our grand plan from its potential to its reality. In the realization phase, we bring our plan into real time.

As we put our plan into operation, we invariably discover that certain conditions are not being optimized. Certain deliverables fall short of their expectation. So we look for ways to grow productively by closing any gaps in quality. In other words, we toggle back and forth between configuration and realization until the bugs have been worked out of the system.

Only then are we ready to move on to the phase of attenuation, which *Webster's* defines as "to make slender or thin, to dilute, to lessen in severity or intensity." We attenuate or lessen the uncertainty, complexity, and risk around the "knobs" that control the most variables in a given value chain. We reduce our distance between any entitlement and a given need or critical-to-quality factors. In fact, we reduce uncertainty, complexity, and risk all the way up and down the chain.

In doing so, corporations can improve and sustain short- and long-term capability. In other words, it gives corporations the ability to produce a high-quality product or service—a deliverable—on a consistent basis over time. As a whole, when a business lessens uncertainty, complexity, and risk, it enhances its ability to realize value for its customers and for itself. Once it accomplishes this, it repeats the entire value-creation cycle, this time using its new knowledge and capability based on its experience.

In summary, the value-creation cycle begins with the innovation of an idea for meeting a need. We then move on to the configuration of an actual design for doing so. After this, we rely on the process of realization to create value. Finally, we lessen complexity, uncertainty, and risk in order to continue the gains we have made. This is the cycle of value creation. We repeat this cycle until all the CTQs, or the gaps between expectation and reality, have been met. Then we find a new need to fulfill—a new opportunity to create and exchange value.

VALUE CREATION AND BREAKTHROUGH

It is interesting to chart the Value Creation Strategy and the Big Ideas against the Breakthrough Strategy. When we do this (as we have below), we can visualize in more detail how the Big Ideas connect the classic mind-set of the Breakthrough Strategy with the more progressive mind-set of the Value Creation Strategy.

During the value-creation phase of innovation, for example, we iden-

Relationship Between Value Creation and Breakthrough

STRATEGY FOR VALUE CREATION				STRATEGY FOR BREAKTHROUGH PERFORMANCE			
Phase	**Big Ideas**			Identification	Characterization	Optimization	Validation
Innovation	Proclaim	To declare	Need	Deprived state	Need	Value	Opportunity	Innovation
	Prospect	To explore	Value	Equivalent exchange				
	Pursue	To search	Opportunity	Favorable conditions				
Configuration	Purity	To refine	Idea	Conceptual model	Idea	Determinism	Leverage	Configuration
	Pattern	To design	Determinism	Effectual causation				
	Parlay	To exploit	Leverage	Mechanistic advantage				
Realization	Prescribe	To establish	Measurement	Scaled quantity	Measurement	Power	Transformation	Realization
	Provide	To supply	Power	Change capability				
	Perfect	To improve	Transformation	Change process				
Attenuation	Prohibit	To prevent	Uncertainty	Unknown state	Uncertainty	Complexity	Risk	Attenuation
	Paralyze	To disable	Complexity	Confounded connections				
	Prune	To abate	Risk	Loss exposure				

tify a need by declaring a deprived state. We characterize value by exploring the equivalency of exchange, and we optimize opportunity by searching for favorable conditions. Finally, we validate or affirm that we have in fact achieved the full intent of innovation. Only when this has been accomplished can we say that we have successfully completed a cycle of innovation, relative to a specific need, in a Six Sigma way.

As a value-creation project leader moves from innovation to configuration, the task becomes one of identifying the ideas, or refining the conceptual model to the point at which it becomes possible to design effectual causation. In turn, when we design effectual causation, we are characterizing the determinism that will bring about the desired change. We are designing, or configuring, a system of effectual causation relative to our value-creation objective. During configuration, we are optimizing and leveraging our design by doing what we can to exploit mechanistic advantage. A project leader then validates that the resulting design or plan has been configured in accordance with the Breakthrough Strategy and the intent of the applicable Big Ideas.

We could continue this train of thought by outlining how the realization and attenuation phases of the Value Creation Strategy interface with the Breakthrough Strategy, but this should be evident from studying the matrix on the previous page. Moreover, there is more to be gained by looking more deeply into the Big Ideas themselves—into the underlying concepts that make them operable. By doing so we can understand what each is made of and how they interact to create a *tsunami of reasoning* in the interest of achieving business breakthrough.

THE PROBLEMATIC IDEAS

The Big Ideas are like the working parts of a mechanical system. While the parts of a mechanical system might help execute the work of, say, drilling or soldering, the Big Ideas help execute the work of thinking. If soldering is the action we wish to perform, then we might pay attention to such problematic variables as temperature and time, and we would have knobs in the process for adjusting those variables.

In an analogous way, as the critical elements in a system of thought, each Big Idea has a set of "knobs" upon which a Six Sigma leader focuses. These are the problematic, or causative, ideas that we adjust in the interest of bringing the Big Ideas to bear on a given business-, operations-, or process-level objective. The chart below breaks each Big Idea down into its component problematic or causative ideas, as well as the relational ideas that define how they will transform thinking for any given big idea.

For example, whenever a business sets out to create value in the interest of meeting a customer need, it introduces the risk of not meeting that need. The simple act of designing a process, product, or service creates risk, inasmuch as it creates opportunity. Any time we take an idea out of its potential realm (design) and transform that idea into its kinetic state (operations), we risk doing so without adhering to the specifications.

The Problematic Ideas of Value Creation

Innovation	Need	=	Experience	−	Entitlement		
	Value	=	Utility	×	Access	×	Worth
	Opportunity	=	Condition	×	Advantage		
Configuration	Idea	=	Reasoning	×	Context		
	Determinism	=	Element	×	Causation		
	Leverage	=	Force	×	Span	×	Advantage
Realization	Measurement	=	Observation	×	Scale		
	Power	=	Force	×	Span	÷	Time
	Transformation	=	Change	×	Induction		
Attenuation	Uncertainty	=	Total	−	Probable		
	Complexity	=	Node	+	Connections		
	Risk	=	Loss	×	Exposure		

But the idea of risk is meaningless in the absence of exposure and loss. Any time we marry a capability with specifications, we create risk or, more accurately, exposure to risk. The portion of the distribution of outcomes falling outside the lower and upper specification limits is the area of exposure. However, this portion is not synonymous with the probability of risk or the probability of loss. The tail ends of a performance distribution (falling outside the specification limits) simply represent the *possibility* of loss. Only when this possibility (exposure) is manifested in the form of a defect (nonconformance to a standard) have we experienced an actual risk consequence, or loss.

While there is risk in the stock market, for instance, we are not exposed to that risk if we are not invested in it. Therefore, we cannot experience loss. If we are invested in the market, however, through index or mutual funds or individual stocks, then we are exposed. But this doesn't mean we will necessarily experience a loss (although exposure always precedes loss).

Here is the key point: A Big Idea is a function of two or more problematic ideas. When you adjust the magnitude of problematic ideas to certain levels, you are able to control the magnitude of the big idea. General Electric's former CEO Jack Welch once said that Six Sigma finally gives us a route to the control function of a corporation. We suggest that a problematic frame of thought allows us to get at the control function of our reasoning.

Let's look at another Big Idea, opportunity. This comprises the problematic ideas of condition and advantage. In other words, these are the causative concepts we consider when looking to produce opportunity. Therefore, an opportunity is a set of conditions configured such that they have an advantage in achieving an envisioned end.

Let us give you one more example. The Big Idea of power is the composite of force, span, and time. We know that in the world of physics, the combination of force and span is called torque; torque is also called work. Therefore, power is the amount of work one can complete in a certain amount of time. For example, if I can install 800 screws in a piece of wood in an eight-hour day, then my power is 100 screws per hour.

**The Philomatics of
Value Creation**

**Strategic
Ideas**

**Relational
Ideas**   f

Innovation	Need	=	Experience	−	Entitlement		
	Value	=	Utility	×	Access	×	Wor
	Opportunity	=	Condition	×	Advantage		
Configuration	Idea	=	Reasoning	×	Context		
	Determinism	=	Element	×	Causation		
	Leverage	=	Force	×	Span	×	Advantage
Realization	Measurement	=	Observation	×	Scale		
	Power	=	Force	×	Span	+	Time
	Transformation	=	Change	×	Induction		
Attenuation	Uncertainty	=	Total	−	Probable		
	Complexity	=	Node	+	Connections		
	Risk	=	Loss	×	Exposure		

Y   **Big
Ideas**

**Problematic
Ideas**   X

Now let's define the Big Idea of *leverage* as a function of force, span, and advantage—or work and advantage. If I use a power drill on my screw heads, I create an advantage, and I expand the amount of work I can do per hour. If I am running a business, by jointly considering the Big Ideas of power and leverage, I open a gateway of thinking relative to customer needs. Driven by virtue of the problematic ideas, and by the ability to integrate these ideas, I am in a much better position to create value.

The chart on the facing page identifies the structure of the Value Creation Strategy and the Big Ideas from a deterministic (Y is a function of X) perspective. Note that the system of thought begins with the strategic ideas of innovation, configuration, realization, and attenuation. It then branches into the Big Ideas, or the Y-related ideas. Finally, it splits into problematic (X-related) and relational (f-related) ideas.

If Y is a function of X, and if thinking can be systematized, we must have a way to relate the problematic ideas—inasmuch as we relate the critical to process factors to optimize the performance of their associated critical-to-quality factors. In relating the problematic ideas, we introduce a new focus that we have called "philomatics," or philosophical mathematics. Developed by Dr. Mikel Harry, philomatics is the practice of applying addition, subtraction, multiplication, and division to various problematic ideas.

The basic rule set is this: If the operator is multiplication, the problematic ideas must occur jointly, even though they are fully independent. If the operator is additive, the problematic ideas cannot occur jointly, as they are mutually exclusive. Either two separate things (thoughts, actions, prayers, ideas, processes, etc.) can occur at the same time and place, or they cannot occur at the same time and place by definition.

Let's consider experience and entitlement, the underlying elements of *need*. While you must have both elements to create a need, the idea of experience (observation) does not interact synergistically with the idea of entitlement (the standards that have been set). They play off each other. In other words, they work in an additive, not multiplicative, way. Therefore, we represent the big idea of need as follows:

Need = Experience − Entitlement

Note that the relational idea is additive by nature, but in its actual operation it is subtractive. We have an experience when we come into contact with a deliverable. We also have a rightful expectation (entitlement). The difference between the two is either positive, negative, or equal to zero. The size of any negative result is synonymous with the size of the need. Any positive value represents the extent to which the need was exceeded. But our main point is that the problematic ideas associated with need do not occur jointly. That is why they are additive rather than multiplicative in nature.

Let's look at the problematic ideas of reasoning and context, which relate synergistically to form an idea. Since we cannot reason outside of a context, the two problematic ideas are multiplicative—they occur jointly (they interact with each other) to generate an outcome or idea. Both reasoning and context must occur at the same time to successfully form an idea.

Earlier we examined the big idea of power. We said that it consists of force, span, and time—the problematic ideas underlying the determination of power. But we didn't mention the way in which these problematic ideas interact, or interrelate, to accomplish power. We didn't address the function as either additive or multiplicative. But the chart on value creation shows that it is the latter.

Let's combine two Big Ideas into a compound Big Idea called "idea power," which consists of certain problematic and relational ideas, as shown below. By manipulating these ideas algebraically, we begin to understand how the Big Ideas can be made philosophically mathematic and, therefore, deterministically operable. We can see, in other words, how idea power is reasoning times context times force times span over time.

$$Idea = Reasoning \times Context$$
$$Power = Force \times Span + Time$$

$$Idea\ Power = \frac{(Reasoning) \times (Context) \times (Force) \times (Span)}{Time}$$

Remember, the multiplicative relation represents the joint occurrence of terms, or problematic ideas. Only when such terms occur simultaneously and synergistically do we have the proper ingredients for creating our idea power. Only by operating on our reasoning, context, force, span, and time can we materially improve our idea power.

Through further algebraic manipulation, we derive the following equation to guide our thinking as to how we can increase our idea power. We see that doing so requires us to either increase our reasoning force, increase our context span, or decrease time.

$$\text{Idea Power} = \frac{(\text{Reasoning Force}) \times (\text{Context Span})}{\text{Time}}$$

Taking this one step further, we might equate the idea of reasoning force with the idea of intellectual capability, or IQ. We further might equate context span with the idea of problem difficulty, as shown below. Therefore, the more difficult the problem, the higher the IQ, and the shorter the time elapsed, the greater the idea power.

$$\text{Idea Power} = \frac{(\text{Intellectual Capability}) \times (\text{Problem Difficulty})}{\text{Time}}$$

From here, we can push our reasoning further, combining the ideas of intellectual capability and problem difficulty into one term that we call applied intelligence per unit of time. As shown below, this can then be broken down into a single metric called intellectual productivity. Given this progression of thought, we now have a framework within which to increase, or at least measure, idea power.

$$\text{Idea Power} = \frac{\text{Applied Intelligence per Unit of Time}}{\text{Intellectual Productivity}}$$

Now let's configure our algebra with a little different spin, namely, the application of idea power to resolving a burning priority. Say the burning issue is safety related, such as the levels of arsenic in city water. Perhaps a large award was just given by a jury to a plaintiff who was exposed to arsenic in the drinking water. As with many cases of litigation, only the potential for injury can be enough to persuade a judge and a jury. Given this, a municipality might implement a highly focused, intense effort to lower arsenic levels in its drinking water.

Guided by the need to generate idea power relative to this burning issue, a Six Sigma Black Belt might configure her thinking as depicted below. Because the issue is hot, she focuses on context force and mentally writes her algebra as reasoning span times context force over time. She then decides that reasoning span is synonymous with intellectual capacity, that context force translates nicely into the idea of issue priority, and that time is best represented by the idea of time to resolution or intervention time.

$$\text{Idea Power} = \frac{(\text{Reasoning}) \times (\text{Context}) \times (\text{Force}) \times (\text{Span})}{\text{Time}}$$

$$= \frac{(\text{Reasoning Span}) \times (\text{Context Force})}{\text{Time}}$$

$$= \frac{(\text{Intellectual Capacity}) \times (\text{Issue Priority})}{\text{Intervention Time}}$$

$$= \text{Knowledge Concentration per Unit of Time}$$

$$= \text{Issue Resolution Efficacy}$$

So what is idea power in the context of potential litigation risk management? It is focusing a team of smart people with different expertise (intellectual capacity) on the issue in a short period of time. Therefore, if I want to increase idea power relative to an issue, then I have to increase intellectual capacity, increase the priority of the issue, or decrease the amount of time it takes to intervene.

If the issue is already fixed as "top priority," then my only options for increasing idea power are to increase intellectual capacity, decrease intervention time, or both. In successfully doing this, I have increased knowledge concentration per unit of time, or issue resolution efficacy. Having reasoned in this fashion, a Six Sigma Black Belt can devise and roll out a system of metrics for reporting the power of ideas generated by an organization when under pressure.

Big Ideas are like critical-to-quality factors, and the problematic ideas are like critical-to-process factors. When we think, we are deterministically arranging ideas in our heads, just as a business adjusts procedures in an office. Just as some people's thoughts are more organized than others, some offices are more systematized than others. The point is, the better a business is designed and operated, the more valuable its output. Likewise, the better we design and direct our thinking, the more valuable our ideas.

The philomatic thinker is a Six Sigma thinker. Why? Because key thoughts are identified, characterized, optimized, and validated. Then they are organized and rolled together to create a tsunami of reasoning—the mental equivalent of performance breakthrough. The problematic ideas roll up through the relational ideas into the Big Ideas, which then roll together to fuel the strategic ideas (innovation, configuration, realization, attenuation).

INFINITE IDEA PERMUTATIONS

How can a philomatic approach open the portals and pathways of logical thought? One Big Idea links with another and melds into the next in a nearly infinite number of possible permutations. Even when just two Big Ideas overlap, they never overlap in the same way twice. Each separate context, each nuance—no matter how simple or complex—makes each idea unique.

Let's say we wanted to improve transformational power in the airline maintenance industry, or in an electrical substation, or in 100 yoga studios. There are countless ways in which we could wield, and think about, transformational power. The same is true in improving measurement power or measurement complexity. We might be compelled to examine our value risk.

What if we wanted to relate the Big Ideas further into three-way combinations, such as deterministic transformational power? What if we needed to understand how such power could compel a constituency toward a certain political objective? The fact is, there are countless situations in which the deterministic transformational power might apply.

The point is, the way of the third-generation Black Belt is to navigate the portals and pathways of value creation. The portals are the Big Ideas and the pathways are the problematic ideas. This is the world in which Black Belts live and make themselves valuable to a corporation. They collect, arrange, devise, think, and create a tsunami of reasoning in the interest of meeting a specific value-creation objective. Only after many years of adjusting the "control functions" of their own reasoning can Black Belts masterfully change the control function of a business, operation, process, activity, or event.

To help the transition from "just doing things" to "thinking things through," let us point out that there are eighty possible pairs of Big Idea combinations. We can think of these as the eighty ways to create value. The last two are luck and fate. To learn to use them all with facility is a worthy goal indeed.

INDEX